Digital Materialities

Digital Materialities

Design and Anthropology

EDITED BY SARAH PINK, ELISENDA ARDÈVOL AND DÉBORA LANZENI

Bloomsbury Academic
An imprint of Bloomsbury Publishing Plc

BLOOMSBURY
LONDON · OXFORD · NEW YORK · NEW DELHI · SYDNEY

Bloomsbury Academic

An imprint of Bloomsbury Publishing Plc

50 Bedford Square	1385 Broadway
London	New York
WC1B 3DP	NY 10018
UK	USA

www.bloomsbury.com

BLOOMSBURY and the Diana logo are trademarks of Bloomsbury Publishing Plc

First published 2016

British Library Cataloguing-in-Publication Data
A catalogue record for this book is available from the British Library.

ISBN:	PB:	978-1-4725-9256-9
	HB:	978-1-4725-9257-6
	ePDF:	978-1-4725-9258-3
	ePub:	978-1-4725-9259-0

Library of Congress Cataloging-in-Publication Data
A catalog record for this book is available from the Library of Congress.

Typeset by Fakenham Prepress Solutions, Fakenham, Norfolk NR21 8NN
Printed and bound in Great Britain

Contents

List of Figures

Acknowledgements

This book has been a pleasure to edit. We have worked with excellent and committed contributors as well as fantastic support and enthusiasm from Bloomsbury's anthropology editors. We would also like to acknowledge the funding sources for the meetings and discussions that made this book possible, working across long distances and with contributors from different continents. Some of the chapters of this book were first presented as part of the *Digital Interventions* seminar series (2013–14) that spanned Melbourne, Barcelona and Perth and was funded generously by the Australian Research Council Centre of Excellence for Creative Industries and Innovation, the Design Research Institute, RMIT University, Australia and the IN3, Universitat Oberta de Catalunya, Spain. Part of our work on this book was also completed during an RMIT EU Centre Visiting Fellowship awarded to Sarah Pink and Elisenda Ardèvol in 2014.

List of contributors

Elisenda Ardèvol is Associate Professor in Social Anthropology at the Department of Arts and Humanities at the Universitat Oberta de Catalunya and director of *mediaccions* Digital Culture Research Group at the Internet Interdisciplinary Institute in Barcelona. She participates in different Master and PhD programmes in media, digital and visual anthropology and has been Visiting Scholar at the Visual Anthropology Centre of the University of Southern California and EU Centre Visiting Fellow at the Digital Ethnography Centre at RMIT University, Melbourne. She is also an active member of international research networks such as the Media Anthropology Network and the Future Anthropology Network of the EASA (European Association of Social Anthropologists) and the Section of Digital Culture and Communication ECREA (European Communication Research and Education Association). Her main research lines are related to digital culture, visuality and media in everyday life. Currently, she is exploring design, creativity and collaborative practices in digital technologies. Her publications include 'Digital Ethnography and Media Practices' in Darling Wolf, *Research Methods in Media Studies* (2014); 'Virtual/Visual Ethnography: Methodological Crossroads at the Intersection of Visual and Internet Research' in Pink, *Advances in Visual Methodology* (2012); 'Playful Practices: Theorising New Media Cultural Production' in Brauchler and Postill, *Theorising Media and Practice* (2010); editor of *Researching Media through Practices* (2009) and the books (in Spanish) *Key Debates* (2014); *A Gaze's Quest* (2006) and *Representation and Audiovisual Culture in Contemporary Societies* (2004).

Tracy Bhamra is Pro Vice Chancellor (Enterprise) and Professor of Sustainable Design at Loughborough University, until 2015 she was Dean of Loughborough Design School. In 2003 she established the Sustainable Design Research Group at Loughborough University that undertakes world-leading research in areas such as Design for Sustainable Behaviour, Methods and Tools for Sustainable Design and Sustainable Design Education. Tracy has over 150 publications associated with her research including the coauthored book *Design for Sustainability: A Practical Approach (2007)*. She has been awarded over £2.5m of research funding from the UK government and research councils and a number of large industrial organizations. Her recent research is focused on approaches to enable designers to integrate sustain- ability into their work, how to move towards designing sustainable services rather than products, and also understanding how design can be used to create more sustainable user behaviour.

David Carlin is a writer, Associate Professor and Co-Director of the nonfictionLab Research Group in the School of Media and Communication at RMIT University, Melbourne, Australia. He led the interdisciplinary Circus Oz Living Archive research project, and co-edited (with Laurene Vaughan) the book *Performing Digital: Multiple Perspectives on a Living Archive* (Ashgate, 2015). He conceived and curated (with Paper Giant) the mixed media exhibition, *Vault: the Nonstop Performing History of Circus Oz*, commissioned by the 2014 Melbourne Festival. David's narrative nonfiction investigates questions of cultural memory, identity, narration and uncertainty; his books include the memoir/biography *The Abyssinian Contortionist* (UWAP, 2015) and the memoir *Our Father Who Wasn't There* (Scribe, 2010), and his creative essays and articles have appeared in *Griffith Review, Overland, TEXT, Newswrite, Victorian Writer, Continuum* and other journals. His research interests extend across memory studies and nonfiction creative practices from the essay and memoir genres to digital media and archives. He has directed *Circus Oz* on New York's 42nd St, and has written and directed award-winning films, documentaries and plays. David is co-director of RMIT's WrICE (Writers Immersion and Cultural Exchange) research program and a co-chair of the international NonfictioNOW Conference.

Paul Dourish is a Professor of Informatics in the Donald Bren School of Information and Computer Sciences at UC Irvine, California, with courtesy appointments in Computer Science and Anthropology, and co-directs the Intel Science and Technology Center for Social Computing. His research focuses primarily on understanding information technology as a site of social and cultural production; his work combines topics in human–computer interaction, ubiquitous computing, and science and technology studies. He has published over 100 scholarly articles, and was elected to the CHI Academy in 2008 in recognition of his contributions to human–computer interaction. He is the author of two books: *Where the Action Is: The Foundations of Embodied Interaction* (MIT Press, 2001), which explores how phenomenological accounts of action can provide an alternative to traditional cognitive analysis for understanding the embodied experience of interactive and computational systems; and, with Genevieve Bell, *Divining a Digital Future: Mess and Mythology in Ubiquitous Computing* (MIT Press, 2011), which examines the social and cultural aspects of the ubiquitous computing research program. Before his arrival at UCI, he was a Senior Member of Research Staff in the

Computer Science Laboratory of Xerox PARC; he has also held research positions at Apple Computer and at Rank Xerox EuroPARC. He holds a PhD in Computer Science from University College, London, and a BSc (Hons) in Artificial Intelligence and Computer Science from the University of Edinburgh.

Jaume Ferrer is Lecturer at the School of Art and Design EDRA and also teaches Interaction Design and Mixed Reality at the Universitat Oberta de Catalunya. Graduated in Fine Arts at the University of Barcelona, he has recently finished his PhD in the International Interdisciplinary Program in Knowledge and Information Society at the Universitat Oberta de Catalunya. He has worked for several years as an illustrator and visual artist and explored net.art as co-founder with David Gomez of the Intangibles Workshop (TAG), carrying out several artistic interventions, workshops and creative projects focused on arts network. He has also collaborated with the Experimentation on Interactive Communication Research Group (CIS) of the Audiovisual Institute of Pompeu Fabra University. He is interested in ethnography as a tool to understand the social construction of technology and as a means of creating the technology itself. He considers himself a 'maker' and situates his current activity at the intersection of arts, interactive digital technology and the social sciences.

Heather Horst is Director, Research Partnerships in the College of Design and Social Context and a Founding Director of the Digital Ethnography Research Centre at RMIT University, Australia. Her research focuses upon understanding how digital media, technology and other forms of material culture mediate relationships, communication, learning, mobility and our sense of being human. Her books examining these themes include *The Cell Phone: An Anthropology of Communication* (Horst and Miller, Berg, 2006), *Hanging Out, Messing Around and Geeking Out: Kids Living and Learning with Digital Media* (Ito, et al. 2010, MIT Press), *Digital Anthropology* (Horst and Miller, Eds., 2012, Berg) and *Digital Ethnography: Principles and Practice* (Pink, Horst, et al. 2016, Sage). Heather's current research, supported by the Australian Research Council and an EU Horizon 20/20 grant, explores transformations in the telecommunications industry and the emergence of new mobile media practices across the Asia-Pacific region.

Débora Lanzeni is a PhD candidate in the Knowledge and Information Society Programme at the IN3 (Internet Interdisciplinary Institute) at the Universitat Oberta de Catalunya. Her training has been in anthropology and filmmaking and incorporates visual and digital anthropology. Her research focuses upon understanding how digital technology and its processes of creation, imagination and production are being made in the context of Urban Labs. She is currently focusing on developments at interface of Smart City and Internet of Things, the study of materiality and moral order.

Kerstin Leder Mackley is a Research Associate at the Loughborough Design School, UK, where she currently explores futures of domestic hot water consumption on the interdisciplinary HotHouse project. HotHouse draws on ethnographic research developed during LEEDR (Low Effort Energy Demand Reduction, 2010–14). Kerstin has a background in qualitative audience research from a broad media and cultural studies perspective. Her research interests include domestic energy consumption, material culture, interdisciplinary methodologies, and the wider study of media and emerging technologies in everyday life. She has published in a variety of journals, including *Media, Culture and Society*, *TOCHI*, *Participations*, and *Sociological Research Online*.

Ian McShane is a Senior Research Fellow at RMIT University's Centre for Urban Research. His research focuses on informal and formal education systems (especially museums, libraries and schools), local infrastructure and community services, and digital technologies. Current research projects are on shared use community infrastructure and service coordination, the development of publicly accessible wireless networks in Australia and internationally, and the representational politics of cultural diversity in Australian museums. Ian has had a long involvement with the Australian museum sector, working as a senior curator at the National Museum of Australia and consulting to other levels of government on museums and culture. In 2013 Ian was appointed to UNESCO's Creative Cities Network external evaluation panel.

Denise Meredyth has worked for some time on projects that explore links between political aspiration and the difficulties of decision-making on civic infrastructure, choice and civic capacity. She has explored this theme in relation to public education, libraries and museums, communications, local planning and community policing. Her most recent work has focused on youth media and social enterprise, on community uses of the digital and physical resources of schools and on digital literacy and information poverty. She has recently moved from positions at RMIT and the Australian Research Council to the role of Pro Vice Chancellor, Division of Education, Arts and Social Sciences at the University of South Australia.

Mike Michael is a sociologist of science and technology, and Professor of Sociology and Social Policy at the University of Sydney, Australia. His research interests include the relation of everyday life to technoscience, biotechnological and biomedical innovation and culture, and process methodology. Current research projects include the interdisciplinary use of sociological and speculative design techniques to explore energy demand reduction. Among his most recent publications are (with Marsha Rosengarten) the co-authored volume *Innovation and Biomedicine: Ethics, Evidence and Expectation in HIV* (Palgrave, 2013), and (with Jennifer Gabrys and Gay Hawkins) the co-edited volume *Accumulation: The Material Politics of Plastic* (Routledge, 2013).

Val Mitchell is Lecturer in the Design School at Loughborough University, UK. Val has over fifteen years' multidisciplinary research experience specializing in the development of User Centred Design (UCD) methodologies for eliciting user requirements for future technologies and services, in particular understanding user needs and requirements for mobile communication and other interactive products. She is particularly interested in the communication of user needs and requirements to designers using scenarios and personas and the design of creative Participatory Design and Co-design methods for eliciting needs from users. Current research interests focus on the use of ICT to promote sustainability within both the transport and domestic sectors. She was the lead human factors researcher in the Services Aggregation Trials for the DTI under The Application Homes Initiative (TAHI). She is currently a senior researcher on the EPSRC/E.On-funded CALEBRE project which is investigating user behaviours and comfort relating to the implementation of energy-saving technologies within the home. She is also a senior researcher on the EPSRC/DoT/TSB-funded User Innovation project which is investigating how user-driven innovation can be used to inform the design of sustainable transport and travel products and services. She is Co I on the EPSRC LEEDR project which is seeking to reduce energy demand in homes through the innovative application of ICT.

Dr Florian 'Floyd' Mueller directs the Exertion Games Lab at RMIT, Melbourne, Australia. Floyd's research has spanned four continents, including research posts at the University of Melbourne (Australia), MIT Media Lab (USA), Media Lab Europe (Ireland), Fuji-Xerox Palo Alto Laboratories (USA) and Xerox PARC (USA). Floyd was also leading a team of twelve researchers at the Commonwealth and Scientific Industrial Research Organisation (CSIRO) on the future of 'Connecting People'. He has been a Fulbright Visiting Scholar at Stanford University (USA). Floyd has also been a Microsoft Research Asia Fellow and has worked at Microsoft Beijing (China) with the research teams developing Xbox's Kinect. Floyd's research work was presented at the top conferences in the field of interaction design and computer games, including several best paper nominations. Floyd's Exertion Games work has been shortlisted for the European Innovation Games Award (next to Nintendo's Wii Fit), received honorary mentions from the Nokia Ubimedia Award, was commissioned by Wired's Nextfest, exhibited worldwide and attracted substantial international research funding, including numerous grants from the US, Australian, UK and German governments. His team's Exertion Games were played by over 20,000 players across three continents and were featured on the BBC, ABC, Discovery Science Channel and *Wired* magazine.

Narcís Parés is Tenure Associate Professor of the ICT Department of Universitat Pompeu Fabra, Barcelona. He has a PhD in Audiovisual Communication, specializing in Virtual Reality (UPF), MSc in Image Processing and Artificial Intelligence (UAB) and BSc in Computer Engineering (UPC). He is co-creator and coordinator of the Master in Cognitive Systems and Interactive Media (UPF). He has an interest in the possibilities of full-body interaction based on current embodied cognition theories in areas such as learning, play and special needs. This research is undertaken from an interdisciplinary standpoint including interaction design and interactive communication, focusing attention mainly on interaction for children and using non-invasive technologies. He is member of the Steering Committee of the ACM SIGCHI and IFIP International Conference on Interaction Design and Children, member of the IFIP TC13 – Human–Computer Interaction, WG 13.9 – Interaction Design and Children, and member of the Editorial Board of the *International Journal of Child-Computer Interaction*, Elsevier.

Sarah Pink is Director of the Digital Ethnography Research Centre, and Professor of Design and Media Ethnography at RMIT University, Australia, Visiting Professor in Applied Social and Cultural Analysis at Halmstad University, Sweden, Visiting Professor in Social Sciences across the Design and Civil and Building Engineering Schools at Loughborough University, UK and Guest Professor at the Free University, Berlin. Her work is usually interdisciplinary and international and brings academic scholarship to applied research problems. Her projects connect anthropological ethnography to design, engineering, documentary and arts practice. Her current focus is on the relationship between design, ethnography and futures research, working through projects that challenge conventional ethnographic temporalities. Sarah's recent books include the co-authored *Digital Ethnography: Principles and Practice* (2016) and her single-authored books *Doing Sensory Ethnography* (2nd edn, 2015), *Doing Visual Ethnography* (3rd edn, 2013) and *Situating Everyday Life* (2012).

Yolande Strengers is a Vice Chancellor's Research Fellow in the Centre for Urban Research, School of Global Urban and Social Studies at RMIT

University, Melbourne, Australia, where she co-leads the Beyond Behaviour Change research program (http://www.rmit.edu.au/cfd/beyondbehaviour). Yolande's research is currently clustered around a series of applied projects which draw on theories of social practice to understand the dynamics of social and environmental change, and possibilities for intervening in the trajectories of practices. Theories of materiality and technological change are a key feature of her research across a number of sustainability domains including energy demand, water consumption, waste management, air travel and telecommunications.

Chris K. Wilson is a Research Fellow at RMIT University's Centre for Urban Research and an Associate Member of the RMIT Centre for Communication, Politics and Culture. His expertise is in examining the historical and contemporary nature of communication infrastructure provision, its underlying social, technological, economic and governmental determinants, and downstream impact on cultural production and innovation. In 2015 he completed the doctoral project *Frequently Modulating: Australian radio's relationship with youth.* He is currently engaged in two substantial programs of research: *Public Wi-Fi as Urban Infrastructure* examines the development of publicly accessible wireless networks in Australia and internationally; *Governing for Innovation* examines the impact that the liberalisation of access to radio broadcast spectrum in Australia in the 1990s had on local cultural innovation within and beyond broadcasting.

Dr Garrath T. Wilson is a Lecturer in Industrial Design and is part of the Sustainable Design Research Group at Loughborough Design School, UK. His research interests include the psychology of energy consumption and behaviour change strategies; the ethics and design considerations of behavioural interventions; design for sustainable and resilient futures; and more recently, emotionally durable design and product-service systems. Drawing upon an industrial design consultancy background, design has always been central to Garrath's research approach, generating design concepts and physical prototypes as speculative and disruptive probes or as behavioural change agents. Garrath has written and talked internationally on the topic of Design for Sustainable Behaviour and is enthusiastic about both industry and public engagement.

1

Digital materiality

Sarah Pink, Elisenda Ardèvol and Débora Lanzeni

Digital Materialities: design and anthropology is a book about research/
knowing, making/doing and intervention/designing in a world where the
digital and the material are not separate but entangled elements of the same
processes, activities and intentionalities. This is also a world that is shared
by researchers, makers and designers – that is, by those of us who seek to
learn about other people's experiences of the world and make new ways of
knowing about them; by those of us who are everyday makers – all of us,
that is, who make the world as we go along and as we inhabit it; and by
those of us who intentionally intervene in the world to try to make change
happen in particular ways, or, put differently, to make making go in a particular
direction. Sometimes those three sets of activities are part of the life and
work of just one person, sometimes they are more dispersed across groups
of people. Whatever the case – and we will see different variations across the
chapters that follow in this book – we are interested in unpacking how they
are co-implicated in processes and activities which involve what we will here
call *digital materiality*. Collectively the contributors to this volume explore how
this is happening, through interrogations of digital materialities in progress, as
they grow, are made, and are activated for specific purposes.

This book is for social, cultural and technological researchers, designers,
and anyone who is interested in the implications of how digital–material
configurations or entanglements are emerging as part of the world that we
share. It refers to, draws on and advances discussions relevant to the ways
that scholars and practitioners from anthropology, design, human geography,
media studies, sociology and other cognate disciplines and interdisciplinary
fields are seeking to engage with change and future-making processes

in environments where the digital–material is part of everyday life. *Digital Materialities* is written in the context of and in a spirit of commentary on an environment for academic scholarship where the increasing need for researchers to do work that has impact in the world is coupled with a growing engagement of designers with the social sciences and humanities. It presents a series of examples of how these intersections have been navigated by the contributors to this book. However, it also engages with this context, and drives towards impact, applied, public and engaged scholarship and design, at a moment where it is becoming impossible to ignore the ways in which digital media, infrastructures, technologies and content are part of our working and living environments. This, together with the demand for us to engage with the digital – as part of the materiality of the world – creates a powerful need for new understandings of the implications and outcomes of our critical research, making and interventions.

In this first chapter we open up this field of research, making and intervention to scrutiny. We also outline how the contributors to this book advance the discussion and definition and point to where we think its future lies. This book was inspired by our shared interest in what we are calling the *digital materiality* of the worlds we inhabit. Through our respective research agendas that sought to understand different elements of digital 'cultures' such as the free culture movement, smart city visions and digital design interventions for homes, we each began to understand practical everyday processes as involving the entanglement of the digital and material. Each of our research agendas in common focused on people who were engaged in processes and activities that sought to make change in the world – whether as ways of living out and improvising in their everyday lives at home or at work, as activists, as makers, or as designers deliberately making interventions to disrupt what was already happening. Our work, we realized, involved witnessing digital materiality in the *making*.

Contributors to existing literatures and practice have begun to work through the digital–material in a range of different ways, and from different disciplinary and practical perspectives. We discuss the advances they have made below. Here we take up this discussion to bring together digital, design and anthropological scholarship and practice and to argue that it can offer a convincing agenda through which to research and intervene in a digital material world. It is this capacity that we believe is needed for an engaged, applied or design anthropology to be able to flourish in a world where digital–material configurations are an almost inevitable element of everyday life experiences, activities and environments. The contributors to this book are precisely working at this intersection and are therefore through their own theory and practice driving towards such an agenda. Here we initiate the task of mapping out this field of interdisciplinary theory and practice, which puts digital materiality at the centre. Yet, as a disclaimer, as for any field of study or emphasis, we do not mean digital materiality in isolation, or digital materiality as the only way to look at the world. But rather we examine and show the benefits of using it as a prism through which to engage (with) wider ecologies of ideas and practices in research, design and intervention.

In this chapter we first focus in on the foundations of this approach as they have developed in the subdisciplines of design anthropology and digital anthropology and through the relationship that both might have with the older tradition of the study of human–computer interaction (HCI). Critically evaluating the trajectories of these subdisciplines, where they have focused, where they have touched on each other, and, perhaps more significantly, where they have not, we propose a formulation of digital materiality that brings together some of their key interests in the digital and material on the one hand, and in ethnography and design on the other. We argue for an approach that evades existing tendencies to both separate the digital and material as things that can then be united and to debate the relationship between anthropology and design in terms of what each discipline can extract from the relationship. It should not be a matter of using design to do better anthropology or vice versa, or a matter of understanding the digital as material, or the material in relation to how it has become digital. Instead we argue for understandings of all these rather different levels of concept and process as relational elements of a possible digital material design anthropology. To do this we explore three key themes that have emerged from our own thinking and which unite the chapters in this book: mess, engaged practice, and methodologies for knowing and intervening.

We finally suggest how the chapters of this book, which we argue are part of an embryonic version of what could be a wider commitment to the digital–material as it emerges in digital design anthropology practice, demonstrate how such an agenda might play out. This book therefore does not claim to be a resolution of this field, but a starting point or an opening out – and it is to this we turn our attention in the next section.

Opening out: Design anthropology, HCI and digital anthropology

One of the inspirations for this book was the perception that there is a gap created and left open by recent advances in the fields of digital and design anthropology. This is not a gap that can simply be filled by a new book. Rather it is a space that calls for further exploration, further opening and ways of engaging with the questions that it poses. Putting it another way, this book has two close relatives: *Digital Anthropology* (Horst and Miller 2012) and *Design Anthropology* (Gunn, Otto and Smith 2013).

These two books respectively begin to map out a field where anthropology intersects with the digital, and with design, yet in both volumes the digital and design largely (with some notable exceptions discussed below) remain separately theorized and part of two distinct worlds of scholarship or *subdisciplines*. This is ironic given how, in *Design Anthropology*, Ton Otto and Rachel Charlotte Smith (2012: 5–6) acknowledge the origins of design anthropology that lie in human–computer interaction (HCI) research, through approaches spearheaded by Lucy Suchman and others in the 1980s (2013: 5–6). We do not recount this history as it is more than adequately documented and discussed elsewhere – not least by Adam Drazin's excellent account in his chapter in *Digital Anthropology* (Drazin 2012) and by Otto and Smith, who also note the critical perspectives that emerged from this field (2013: 7), in relation to the need for design and anthropology to work in such fields on an equal footing, and towards collaborative models.

Drazin (2012) charts a trajectory of entanglement between anthropology, digital media and design, beginning with the emergence of HCI research in the previous century. His account brings to the fore a history of applied design anthropology that has been little accounted for in the emergence of media anthropology (e.g. Ginsburg et al. 2002; Brauchler and Postill 2010), although it has had a higher profile in applied anthropology literatures (e.g. Pink 2005, 2007). Drazin emphasizes the multi-dimensionality of relationships between anthropological scholarship, applied and design research, collaborations with industry, and with research/design participants and digital media – as HCI research and design flourished over the last forty or so years. As he argues, it is important to understand this relationship as being beyond the idea that anthropology might inform design. Instead he maps out a set of future questions which would set out to ask not what anthropology could do for digital design, but 'what can this engagement do for us as anthropologists in the work of producing socio-cultural interpretations, and how has design anthropology work operated within the political field of digital technologies?' through a focus on 'digital knowledge artefacts' (2012: 260). Indeed, as we see in particular in Lanzeni's chapter (this volume), digital working provides distinctive perspectives for design anthropology, one of which is the need to resituate the 'user' or the 'consumer' as a responsible citizen and craftsperson.

Drazin's analysis represents one strand in the history of the relationship between the digital, anthropology and design, and points to a future where digital design anthropologists have a role to navigate that politicizes design and works through an anthropological agenda. He invites anthropologists to make gains from this context for the discipline. In the context of discipline building, which involves for anthropology what Strathern has called a 'community of critics' (2006: 204), this is a valid exercise and we would not disagree with Drazin's call in the sense that all disciplines need to continue to work on themselves in this way. Yet in the context of working on the relationship between anthropology and design there are also other ways to bring together design and anthropology/ethnography, for instance through approaches to design that vary from those of traditional HCI, and also vary from (and are sometimes critical of) traditional anthropology (see Pink and Akama 2015). In this sense, it would be problematic to see the history of the relationship between HCI and design anthropology as the only possible way in which a relationship between digital anthropology and design might evolve and emerge. Indeed, one of the tasks of this book is to take up such possibilities by exploring this through examples of recent practice – such as in Chapters 5 to 7 of this volume by Pink et al., Michael, and Ferrer, Ardèvol and Parés respectively.

Design anthropology and digital media in everyday life

The connections made between digital media and design anthropology in Gunn et al.'s (2013) *Design Anthropology* are also different to those guided by the trajectory of HCI discussed above. For example, Smith makes a move towards digital design anthropology in her chapter discussion of 'Designing Heritage for a Digital Culture' (2013: 117). There she points out that 'If museums and cultural heritage institutions wish to engage audiences in new ways using the opportunities digital media and technologies afford, they need to look more carefully at how these media provide meaning to people through their everyday lives' (2013: 132). Christina Wasson and Crysta Metcalfe likewise bring media in everyday life to the fore when they discuss a collaboration between the Motorola company and a design anthropology class in a university. Here the research focus was on everyday uses of media technologies in kitchens (Wasson and Metcalfe 2013). These two chapters discuss digital design anthropology projects to demonstrate very well how anthropological and design practice can be brought together to do design anthropology in ways that have significant implications for our understanding of digital technologies. In several ways they suggest that new relationships between design, digital media and anthropology are developing along lines that have some things in common with the third HCI paradigm (see also Pink et al. 2013) but that are not necessarily simply *emergent from it*.

However, simultaneously for us, as anthropologists whose work is engaged with questions about digital media in everyday life, there is also an opportunity to connect the work of scholars operating at the interface between anthropology, digital media and design, such as Smith (2013) and Wasson and Metcalfe (2013), to the large body of literature about digital media in everyday life. There has been a recent explosion of work which creates a convergence point between anthropology and media studies. In part this encompasses or includes digital anthropology (e.g. Horst and Miller 2012) as well as the wider field of media anthropology where media studies and anthropology converse (e.g. Braucher and Postill 2010; Moores 2012; Pink et al. 2016). One of the next steps then, we argue, is for a media anthropology of digital technologies in everyday life to be brought together more closely with design anthropology. In this volume, some chapters work specifically towards this by taking a more media/digital anthropology approach to everyday activity (Pink et al., Ferrer et al., Horst), while other chapters do something similar by engaging other approaches, such as sociology or science and technology studies (STS), for the study of the everyday with design (e.g. Michaels, Strengers). As we argue in this book, a bringing together of design and digital ethnographies of everyday life needs precisely to engage not only with meanings of digital media in the world, but with the digital materiality of both everyday life and design objects, activities and processes.

Indeed in many ways this attention to the detail of everyday life is distinctively anthropological – or at least ethnographic. For Miller and Horst (2012), the ethnographic examples offered by their contributors and collaborators are instances of what a focus on the everyday ways in which digital media are shaped as they become part of people's lives can tell us. Through the examples of migrant domestic workers (Madianou and Miller 2013) and disability activists (Ginsburg 2012), they point out that the users of digital technologies are not necessarily always those for whom they were designed, showing how we need to attend to use as emergent (Miller and Horst 2012: 9–10). This point is equally relevant for a digital design anthropology, and is advanced throughout the chapters of this book, from Strenger's critique of the ways in which the everyday of this kind is ignored in utopian smart home visions, through McShane et al.'s account of the development of a community wi-fi system, to Horst's ethnographies of everyday uses of mobile phones.

Going beyond: Surpassing the digital/ material dichotomy

As we have insisted above, the digital and material should not be thought of as two separate things that already independently existed in the world and have now become entangled. However there has been a tendency towards such thinking because in academic scholarship they have been developed as two different concepts that different researchers and disciplines have, since the digital has become thought of as 'ubiquitous', put together in a range of different ways. We now, in this and the following sections, interrogate some of the variations through which this relationship has been constructed conceptually, show how this book contributes to the debates they raise, and continue to argue for a relational concept of digital materiality.

The material has long since been a conceptual focus for scholars across the social sciences and humanities – including from its traditional place in archaeology, museum studies and anthropology of material culture across to cultural studies and now internet and HCI research. Material culture approaches have offered researchers an entry point into analysing social worlds through their materiality. Materials have been central to the work of design, and of course have their own discipline in engineering. Indeed the making of digital material futures is inevitably a task that involves multiple disciplines, and a focus on materials offers one way in which to consider how they might come together.

Scholars across a range of disciplines have also acknowledged that digital content and technologies need to be understood in relation to materiality, and in recent years the notion and the terminology of digital materiality has been discussed across architecture, design and media studies as well as in the social sciences. Yet, we propose that further interrogation of the problematic of the digital–material as inseparable is needed. In the literature of practice-based disciplines of architecture and design, for instance, we see examples of how the digital–material relationship is presented in terms of how it becomes part of a disciplinary practice. Yet the problematic of the physicality of matter versus the intangible digital is generally overlooked. For example, in architecture the concept of digital materiality has come to stand for a particular set of practices involving digital design (see Willman et al. 2013). For instance, writing about architecture, Gramazio and Kohler use the term *digital materiality* 'to describe an emergent transformation in the expression of architecture'. This, they write is a process whereby 'Materiality is increasingly being enriched with digital characteristics, which substantially affect architecture's physis' (2008: 7). Thus, for them, 'Digital materiality evolves through the interplay between digital and material processes in design and construction. The synthesis of two seemingly distinct worlds – the digital and the material – generates new, self-evident realities. Data and material, programming and construction are interwoven' (Gramazio and Kohler 2008: 7). For these architects this way of conceptualizing the process also has implications for practice in that it is a new way of dealing with materials which transforms the possibilities and the professional scope of the architect, since 'Digital materiality leads to a new expression and – surprisingly enough, given the technical associations of the term "digital" – to a new sensuality in architecture' (Gramazio and Kohler, 2008: 7). In this discussion, therefore, the work of blending the digital and material, which are objects with different properties, qualities and affordances, becomes the task of the architect – indeed an element of her/his professional skill.

Similarly in the context of digital design, Tone Bratteteig writes from the position of a designer for whom 'Design is "thinking with materials"' (2010: 148). While we note here that the idea that design is only about materials – of any kind – is contested in that it can also be to do with services and processes (see Akama and Prendiville 2013), Bratteteig shows how digital designers have sought to understand the relationship between the digital and material in digital design in a way that recognizes the multiple dimensions of this. Through a review of this field she proposes that 'Seeing digital design as thinking with concrete abstractions of processes, at different levels of concretizations as well as across them, suggests that digital designers should understand their material in a way that enables them to move between levels of concretization and choose the right abstraction for the actual design process as it evolves in time'. Here again, digital materiality, as for architects, seems to be something that needs to become embedded in the practice of the designer, and becomes likewise part of professional skill, in that Bratteteig concludes that 'The many levels of digital design open up for many different competencies being involved in imagining and building possible futures' (2010: 166).

Likewise in media studies, the question of digital materiality has been acknowledged since the first years of the twenty-first century, but neither here has it been systematically interrogated. Indeed it has been approached from different directions, depending on the purpose of the study. For instance, Fuller (2005: 2) acknowledges that 'objects have explicitly become informational as much as physical but without losing any of their fundamental materiality'. Here, the challenge is to unpack how this materiality can be sensed, how it can be made use of, and how in turn it makes other elements or compositions tangible. The focus in Fuller's work on the informational qualities of objects implies taking their materiality as their original state, and asking how the digital has become part of this. In contrast, for other scholars, whose focus is on the informational or communications uses of media, the question of the materiality of digital elements situates the digital as the original state and asks how materiality has developed as part of it. For instance, José van Dijck writes: 'In the case of lifelogs, the digital materiality of the internet engenders a new type of reflection and communication. This shows traces of the former analogue genre but functions substantially differently' (2004). Here the digital is described as the tool or platform where digital materiality is experienced and expected to be found.

In the field of anthropology, the issue of digital materiality has also been broadly discussed in particular in the areas which have a history of research in both material culture studies and design. A key point in the trajectories of the discussions that we advance in this book is the appropriation of material culture as a way to approach the world anthropologically, as developed in the work of Danny Miller from the 1980s onwards. This field of material culture studies has also intersected with design anthropology, for instance through projects led by Alison Clarke (e.g. Clarke 2010). Given this history of a material culture anthropology, it would be easy to see the digital as a new facet of a material culture approach to the world. It is clear that digital anthropology has impacted on this field, and indeed Alison Clarke reflected in her edited volume on design anthropology that 'Digital anthropology and interaction design are poised to move the theorizing and practice around twenty-first-century object culture far beyond the remit of those early corporate design anthropologists and their preoccupation with big, green photocopier buttons' (Clarke 2010: 13). To be fair to the early corporate anthropologists, we would note that it was Lucy Suchman who advanced an anthropology of design that was also an anthropology *for design* by locating design in a broader perspective than design methods to illuminate design's relevance in contemporary societies as a practice of change, and to interrogate what constitutes transformative change and how it happens (2011: 3). However, a notable difference between the approach of Suchman and that developed by Clarke is that in terms of her approach to object culture, Suchman has been more interested in objects-in-action than in defining their 'materiality' (2005: 381). Moreover, as we note below, there has been little conversation in the existing literatures between mainstream media anthropology and HCI-focused anthropology, thus leaving the intersection between digital anthropology and design – at least initially – primarily in the context of material culture studies.

Since the question of how to understand the nature of the digital has been a central debate in Media Anthropology as well as Digital Anthropology, Media Studies and the Social Studies of the Internet, to understand how the digital–material relationship is being constituted in the social sciences now we first take a step back, to consider how early studies emphasized the ontological status of the things that happened in the virtual worlds constituted through digital technologies and their users. As Ardèvol and Gómez Cruz (2014) argue, in Internet Studies these online contexts were thought as a new social space, the cyberspace, where virtual communities were evolving and where disembodied identities interacted, free from the social and cultural constraints of the real world or reproducing them in these virtual realms (Turkle 1995; Baym 2000; Hine 2000; Nakamura 2002). Later on, this distinction between the virtual and the real was challenged and the relationship between online and offline activity was theorized as a continuum (Miller and Slater 2000; Leander and McKim 2003; Hine 2007) with a focus on explaining precisely the worlding of the virtual world (such as in the virtual platform Second Life) as a world apart (Boellstorff 2008). In their prologue to *Digital Anthropology*, Miller and Horst accurately contested 'approaches that imply that becoming digital has either rendered us less human, less authentic or more mediated'. Instead they argue that 'Not only are we just as human within the digital world, the digital also provides many new opportunities for anthropology to help us understand what it means to be human' (2012: 4). One of the key ways in which the online/offline dichotomy has been challenged is through a focus on the question of the relationship between the digital and material. As Miller and Horst assess it, 'Materiality is thus bedrock for digital anthropology, and this is true in several distinct ways, of which three are of prime importance. First, there is the materiality of digital infrastructure and technology. Second, there is the materiality of digital content, and, third, there is the materiality of digital context' (Miller and Horst 2012: 25). In these definitions, importance is given to how the digital is materially produced. This is an important consideration for determining what digital materiality can involve and which indeed figures in the following chapters in this book. Indeed, Miller and Horst insist on the relationship between the digital and the material and treat it as one of the core principles of their approach to digital anthropology, which acknowledges 'the materiality of digital worlds, which are neither more nor less material than the worlds that preceded them' (Miller and Horst, 2012: 4). Their argument is that 'the digital, as all material culture, is more than a substrate; it is becoming a constitutive part of what makes us human' (2012: xx).

We would not disagree with Miller and Horst's proposal. Here, however, we have a different purpose in that our own agenda is to develop the notion of digital materiality as a way to connect digital and design anthropologies. In stating a concept of digital materiality, we are not seeking to produce a new hybrid ontology by referring to an 'empirical object' that exists 'out there', configured by physical and digital properties. Rather than starting with an a priori definition about what is digital and what is material, we prefer to understand digital materiality as a process, and as emergent, not as an end product or finished object. In doing so we break down the boundaries that are assumed when questions are asked about what is digital and what is not. It is moreover not a question of whether the digital is material or not. This is because in the worlds that the contributors to this volume discuss, the digital, the material and design are not specific and separate things, but are rather more porous elements of processes of research, design and intervention. People design children's experiences, make code, build living archives, develop interactive systems, search for more sustainable homes, rig up public wi-fi networks, create sensors for controlling air pollution, desire healthy environments, want to empower citizens, imagine possible futures. Thus, digital materiality does not define 'something' done, but a process of becoming. Digital materiality refers to the making and to what emerges of these entanglements, not to a state or a quality of matter.

It is because we focus on what is happening that we need a processual concept of digital materiality. Current debates about materiality have called for more materialist modes of analysis and attention to matter and processes of materialization (deLanda 2004; Bennett 2009; Ingold 2011; Hodder 2012). In particular, the New Materialism turn and the vitalism led by Jane Bennett argue for an understanding of matter as alive and as an active force in the making of the world, in sum a 'materiality that is itself vibrant or active' (Bennett 2010: 49). These lines of inquiry propose an ontological reorientation that takes into account post-humanist ideas (Haraway, 1991, 1999; Latour, 2005) and the notion of living matter, thus avoiding conceptualizations of humans as being apart from matter and rejecting the idea of 'matter as an inert substance subject to predictable causal force'. This allows other ways to describe the design process by understanding it as a process of materialization 'complex, pluralistic and relatively open' (Coole and Frost 2010: 7) where matter is a vital force.

Media archaeologists also call for a processual understanding of matter. For instance, Parikka suggests speaking of 'not only of objects, but also as much about non-solids and the processual materiality'. For example, this refers to dirty matter at the level of components, voltages and materials in technological media, but 'is not just machines nor is it just solids, and things, or even objects. Materiality leaks in many directions also concretely (i.e. e-waste)' (Parikka 2011: 98). This position resonates with Ingold's point that 'things are alive because they leak' (Ingold 2008: 10), and that things, like people, are processes: 'it is in the opposite of capture and containment, namely discharge and leakage, that we discover the life of things' (2008: 13). Even Parikka suggests that a big challenge for new materialism is 'to develop a media theory of things – and yet not only thing-powers, but process-power' (Parikka 2011: 98). Beyond these claims, different scholars from philosophy, feminist studies, media and anthropology propose new ontologies that highlight processes of formation rather than discrete entities, delimited objects or final products – instead, to define matter for its living process in the world's formation.

We maintain that digital materiality is part of this living process in the world of design. Our proposal is primarily methodological; in order to centre our attention in the process of making in the mess of everyday life, we need a processual approach to digital materiality. This creates a prism through which to examine the complex interfaces at which we engage with technologies, architectures and narratives that constitute the materiality of the everyday and how futures are imagined, forged and made.

Mess and things: Situated ways to look for the unexpected

That the worlds we research are messy is well acknowledged in the existing literature, whether expressed precisely in that idiom (e.g. Law, 2004) or not. This point might not come as much of a surprise to anthropologists for whom their first fieldwork is likely to be a hands-on training in how to deal with research materials of different qualities and affordances. Anthropology is also a discipline for which a critical dialogue between ethnography is ongoing. This means that as anthropologists we would not expect the theoretical model which we had in mind when approaching our ethnographic site to necessarily frame what we eventually thought we found there. Rather we would expect to discover all kinds of things that would lead us to critique the theory for its universal presumptions. The notion of mess can, however, be useful for reinforcing the point that we don't walk into neatly ordered worlds that can be readily converted into equally neat data. This point has been developed further in much excellent research that focuses on digital material worlds, notably by some of the leading scholars included in our book (e.g. Dourish and Bell 2011; Michael, this volume). However, one thing that concerns us about the contemporary enthusiasm for the idea that the world, and the research we do in it, is messy, is when researchers use their findings to demonstrate this point. Instead we would argue that the sooner researchers, designers and policy makers take up the idea that mess is what they are about to engage with at the beginning of research, design and intervention projects, rather than making mess part of their conclusions, the better. Without wanting to fall into the trap of claiming that anthropologists just knew it all along, we would point out that as part of our (always immersed in particular sites and inevitably very personal) training as anthropological ethnographers we have always been confronted with this complicated question of how to bring together series of things, processes and even other inexplicable phenomena of different kinds, types, qualities and affordances, to tell coherent and consistent stories about what is happening while also accounting for people's self-descriptions. In particular the challenge is also to tell such stories in ways that acknowledge that what people do tends often to be inconsistent, because it is always contingent on changing sets of circumstances.

Indeed we can find similar unruliness wherever we look in research, and in particular with reference to another of the rather sticky concepts that we engage with here: 'things'. Existing discussions in anthropology have long since shown us how things have biographies and that their meanings change as they are (re)appropriated in different contexts (Appadurai 1986; Koppitof 1986; Henare, Holbraad and Wastell 2006). Some ANT and STS scholars (Latour 2005; Pinch 2008) also attribute a certain amount of (albeit distributed or displaced) agency to things. Following this perspective, things can be thought of as 'acting' differently as they move through and participate in different environments.

As we have commented above, there has been a shift in the material culture studies inflected field of design anthropology (e.g. Clarke 2010) towards rethinking the object through the digital. Yet if we take this shift further to focus away from the concept of an object towards that of a 'thing', the relationality between the digital and material comes closer into view. It then becomes easier to conceptualize how the mess we have written about in the previous section and the potential unruliness of things that is the concern of STS scholars (see Michael, this volume) is constituted through the relationality of things.

There is an operational distinction between 'object' and 'thing' that responds to a broad discussion regarding the life and agency of things. Ingold refers to this distinction to explain what happens in the interaction between humans and things in the flow of life. Ingold (2008) critically proposes that according to Actor-Network Theory, objects lack life when they are cut off from the network of distributed agency. He argues that 'things' are alive when they are immersed in the entanglement of forces. It is in the flow of life, as an ongoing process, that things and humans exist. In the terms of Appadurai (2013), objects are alive because they are interlinked with other objects and humans. It is through the process of design that mere things become life objects, under the scrutiny of human activity. Then, for both scholars, things and objects are distinguished by life but in a quite different way, the important point being that by things and objects, we mean divisible non-human unities, which are made alive through different relational circumstances with humans and with other things. The implications of this for our discussion of digital materiality is that materiality does not end in things and objects; materiality is – as Ingold and Appadurai suggest – a process, a flow and connections. The digital materiality happens in an ongoing and openness process that escapes delimitations in discrete units with attributes as tangible, physical or in opposition to other kind of attributes such virtual, binary and, primarily, digital.

Throughout this book we find our contributors confronted with mess and with things that are unpredictable, lines of contingencies, stories that unfold in ways that were not necessarily expected. They approach this mess variously and according to disciplinary preferences in the ways that they give theoretical order to it. However there is a collective consensus that what we are dealing with is something complex, messy and uncertain (see Pink and Akama 2015). For our contributors, this has become embodied in discussions of contingency, conflict, unevenness, idiocy, confusions, technologies not doing what people think they are meant to, people not doing what they are meant to with technologies, and more. There is nothing surprising about the fact that these chapters tell us that digital materiality is just as messy as everything else we are likely to encounter in an ongoing world. Yet, as they also show, this raises the question of why there simultaneously seem to be cultural narratives at play that stand for a utopian hope or expectation that digital material futures (or presents) will not be so messy. We expect that they will – mess and unruly things are here to stay; the challenge for us in research, design and intervention is to learn how to work with them. As we propose in the next section, this means getting into the middle of it with them and recognizing that the methods and technologies we use to research will likewise be unpredictable.

Getting into the mess: Engaged practice from within

All of the contributions to this volume suggest the need for researchers to have deep engagements with digital material environments, processes, things and experiences. They do so across a range of contexts and sites that on the surface appear quite different.

For instance, building on her already significant experience of empirical and theoretical research in this field, Strengers carefully reviews existing debates, research and interventions in the field of the smart home. On the basis of what she finds – which reveals a context where there is a big gap between what smart home designers are working towards and the ways people actually live – she calls for more detailed research into 'the entanglements between and beyond' the digital, material and human. Other chapters that do not report on conventional empirical research nevertheless do involve the authors' long-term engagement with and experience of the things being discussed. In some cases, they also take as their examples design interventions and the ways these have been made or activated. For instance, Dourish draws on his personal experiences of using and programming for early computers when discussing how they might be emulated. By bringing us up close to software in this way, he enables an understanding of what people (think they) are doing with it, and of what it is to be in such a world of digital–material things, where the things discussed might not be quite as they would seem from the outside. Likewise David Carlin's work with Circus Oz, with whom he and his colleagues have developed a digital archive, was informed by thirty years of being associated and working with this organization, at one point as a show director. His chapter charts and reflects on this process, from the perspective of someone who was part of it as it happened and who has participated through what he calls 'an ethics of care' – creating an interesting intersection between his own memories and the ambitions of the archive to house digitalized memories. Carlin's chapter is one where he is right 'in the middle of it' in a different way to the conventional ethnographer, narrating through his own personal trajectory of working with a circus to make digital materiality alive as an evolving interface with human memories through which to remember, re-imagine, or imagine possible futures. Other chapters involve varying degrees and different periods of ethnography and describe correspondingly different forms of immersion in their sites of research and intervention. However, in common, they show that to research digital materiality we need to encounter it as it emerges and to follow it, and to recognize that it is an ongoing process and never a finished object.

In Chapter 5 Pink et al. discuss video ethnographies over four years with twenty households, which occurred over several visits to each household involving not only doing research with them in their homes but also showing them video research materials and pre-publication versions of articles, video and still images. This project developed a form of intensive immersion different from that of conventional long-term fieldwork in one site. As discussed elsewhere, the capacity of video to draw viewers along with it, forward into new ways of knowing and experiencing also formed part of the way in which the research team members participated in the project through its digital materiality (see Pink and Leder Mackley 2012). In Chapter 7 Ferrer et al. describe a process of ethnographic immersion of more than five years following the project of an interactive slide across sites of research, design and intervention transformations, but which was also part of this process (as was the work described by Pink et al. in Chapter 5).

As we noted above, the existing discussions of mess in the social sciences have tended to be about the world we research as being messy. Less has been said about the mess involved in making design interventions. Yet as we have outlined above, and as Dourish and Bell note, 'the practice of any technology in the world is never quite as simple, straightforward, or idealized as it is imagined to be' (Dourish and Bell 2011: 4) and, at least for the case of ubicomp (ubiquitous computing), there will always be variations in the ways technologies are used and experienced (Dourish and Bell 2011: 5). As the contributions to this book also show, technologies are always 'used' by people whom we refer to as everyday designers rather than simply 'users' in ways that are relational and contingent. We might think of these activities as everyday interventions that are part of the process of ongoing making and improvisation in the world that Ingold writes of (2013) and that has also influenced the work of design anthropologists (e.g. see Gunn and Donovan 2012). Mess, thus conceptualized, is therefore also a way of thinking about not only the context in which designers make interventions, but also the context of ongoing everyday intervention such as that discussed by Strengers in Chapter 4, Pink et al. in Chapter 5 and McShane et al. in Chapter 11.

In using the term intervention in this way, we concur with the reclaiming of the concept as Green and Pink have expressed it, where the idea of an intervention is intended to 'bring to the fore the idea of intervening as a way of being active in the world; as a scholar, creative practitioner, activist, or as a person living their everyday life in ways that seek to generate forms of change'. This means appropriating the concept of intervention – 'which has in some contexts been maligned as an act of power' – through an emphasis which among other things 'promotes the importance of research and practice that actively and creatively seeks to make change happen within and through creative research processes, and in ways that involve collaboration with participants in research and in change processes' (Green and Pink 2014: 73). It is in this spirit that we also engage with the idea of intervention, to reclaim it from critical discourses about unwanted and politically problematic forms of change-making and to instead locate it with the concept of design co-interventions towards the participatory ways of understanding, engaging with and 'intervening in' the world that the contributors to this volume discuss.

Therefore, following the above argument, *interventions are inevitably emergent from and made in messy worlds, with unruly things and in relation to a series of unknown future contingencies*. Pink and Akama, with their co-contributors, begin to unravel some of these issues in their *Un/Certainty* iBook (2015), which reports on and discusses a two-day event where a group of about twenty ethnographers, designers and creative practitioners were brought together to explore uncertainty in practice. Indeed, Pink and Akama argue for a greater recognition of uncertainty as being fundamental to intervention practices. Whereas conventionally designers have often sought to find ways in which to construct future scenarios to design into, the contributors to this book similarly acknowledge, and indeed show through their examples, that we cannot know what is going to happen next. Indeed, as we outline in the next section, some have used methods that are deliberately experimental in order to seek new ways of finding out things that they might otherwise not have been able to awake. This might be – as in the case of those projects that discuss how design interventions themselves are implicated in processes – a matter of intervening in the world at the moment or place where digital materiality is particularly actively or obviously intertwined. These ways of engaging experimentally and collaboratively with the sites of and participants in research might not be unusual for designers, and they are also increasingly common in the social sciences. Yet they still go beyond the boundaries of those anthropologists who continue to defend an observational non-intrusive approach: for instance, in the case of Ferrer, Ardèvol and Parés, when the observer ethnographer was involved in the making of an experience of an interactive slide; or in the case of Michael in the placing of networked objects in people's homes; or in the case of Pink et al. of asking participants to collaborate in showing their everyday activities (often with technologies) while being digital–video recorded. These digital–material research and design interventions then become part of worlds in progress, are appropriated in unexpected ways by the people who encounter and engage with them, and perhaps come to be different types of 'thing' to what was expected. In these works, then, the ethnographic process becomes one of understanding what design research can do – that is, what it can tell us about what can happen in the world, opening up the realm of the possible by letting it play out, and enabling us to begin to consider on that basis other possibilities, potentialities and affordances.

While the work of the designer is to intervene in other people's worlds, that of the anthropologist has conventionally been to inhabit other people's worlds and create accounts and understandings of these worlds without changing them. Neither of these, we suggest, remain viable propositions as single activities. As we have noted in the first paragraph of this chapter, the current impulse towards research that has impact, as well as the rise of applied and public scholarship, not only in anthropology but across the social science and humanities disciplines discussed in this book, has shifted this emphasis. It also raises the question of the rights and/or responsibilities that social scientists might now have to intervene in the world and the question of how this might best be done. This question goes beyond the controversies attached to and debated around institutionalized impact agendas. Instead it focuses our attention towards how and where those scholars, researchers and designers who are actively seeking to understand and/or design for and intervene in and through the digital materiality of the world might undertake such work. This leads us on to the next section, in which we reflect on the final theme of the methodologies that are being developed for such tasks.

Methodologies for researching and intervening

There is no single methodology or approach for working across the social sciences, humanities and design through a concept of digital materiality. This point is demonstrated through the variety of disciplinary and technological approaches that have been engaged by the contributing researchers and designers. While we do not see this as a methodology volume, we – like most of our contributors – have also felt compelled to reveal and comment on the processes through which the ways of knowing that are required for and involved in research and intervention through digital materiality are being created.

At the core of ethical and participatory ethnographic and design practice is a reflexive stance – both to the ways in which researchers, designers and participants are positioned within projects and to the outcomes of those projects and the possible meanings they can have in the world. Such an approach is also integral to this book, although it is manifested in different ways in different chapters. For example, we have already noted how in Chapters 2 and 10 respectively Dourish and Carlin both show how they have been, both biographically and through their writing, 'in the middle' of the things and processes they discuss. Here personal biographical experience is self-consciously used through the texts to demonstrate the worlds that are described. These two chapters are not ethnographic in the conventional sense, even if they might be said to develop types of auto-ethnographical thinking, yet they carry through forms of reflexivity that also emerge in the chapters that develop a more (although still not conventional) anthropological type of ethnography, such as Ferrer et al. in Chapter 7 and Pink et al. in Chapter 5. Likewise, Michael uses a revelatory moment in his own experience of using digital media in his home as the opening scene in Chapter 6.

Reflexivity is a core methodological principle in the work discussed in this book; it is also a wave that has rolled across disciplines and forms of creative practice in the social sciences, humanities and design for the last thirty or so years. It is always inflected by the disciplines to which its practitioners belong, and the same can be said for most aspects of research practice. This is demonstrated well in this volume when we compare how, for instance, different sociological and anthropological methodologies are played out, including the variations in the ways that sociologists work. For instance, Strengers in Chapter 4 takes one sociological approach to the everyday – social practice theory – which, at the risk of oversimplification, uses practices as its object of enquiry and key unit of research design, analysis and findings. In contrast, in Chapter 6 Michael, also a sociologist, works with what he calls an idiotic methodology to develop a speculative approach. Anthropology likewise is a diverse discipline; in our own cases, all trained in visual anthropological methodologies, we have not taken distinctively different approaches, but have used different methods. Pink et al.'s sensory video ethnographies of the home are rooted in visual, sensory and digital ethnography methodologies (see Pink 2013, 2015; Pink et al. 2015) and Ferrer et al. have used longer-term ethnography and visual methods to follow the making of the slide over time and to analyse how different users play with the slide. Horst draws on longer term fieldwork to discuss examples from a field site that she has been engaged with through successive visits over the last fifteen years.

Working with digital materiality

Putting digital materiality at the centre of our project is only one way in which to view the future of the relationship between the social sciences and humanities and design. There will be others, and it is not our purpose here to propose that this above all others is the *only* way to go. However there are several very good reasons why, alongside other methods of making interventions towards a more just, equal, environmentally sustainable and healthy world, working through a digital materiality approach to design/anthropology offers ways to rethink the world as a site for research, design and intervention. In part this is because this approach highlights the interactive dimensions between things, humans and environments that in other design fields are less evident.

Most of the chapters in this book discuss projects that, through research and design, seek to 'better' the world in some way – that is, increase forms of well-being and health, work towards environmental sustainability, create equality of access to resources, and similar. These are all reasonably well-established, if unequally distributed, shared global aims stated across the domains of many different governmental, corporate and NGO stakeholders, and also lived out in many cases through everyday life forms of activism and change-making. A digital materiality approach, when applied to question such perennial problems that seem to never get fixed, despite the fact that there is often much ink spilt over them, seems to offer ways of thinking productively about where and how a digital–material design anthropology could usefully research, design and intervene. We cannot cover all possibilities here, therefore in this section we comment on two, as examples.

First, there remains an aspect of the open space between design anthropology and digital anthropology which has been under-acknowledged, and that we wish to flag as part of a next stage of work in this field. Such steps could inform how the capacities of design and anthropology come together in the future and which likewise puts the emergence digital materiality at the centre of its work. Although there are some exceptions, design anthropology remains focused on the 'developed' world where designers design, whereas in the parts of the world that interventions tend to be towards 'development' design is often absent. Important exceptions in the design anthropology literature include the groundbreaking work of Dori Tunstall with indigenous design (Tunstall 2013) and Ian Ewart's discussion of building in Borneo (Ewart 2013).

It has been inevitable that *Digital Materialities* has to some extent reproduced something of this divide. In Part One the critiques that contributors advance of the imaginaries of digital futures are all focused on developed nations and their concerns. But this is in part because although in developing countries digital materiality is equally 'felt', these are not the places where those who present us with digital future imaginaries tend to imagine as the first sites where such digital futures would be played out. Appadurai also highlights this point, suggesting that we have to change our understanding of design as 'only partly a specialist activity' and move to a broader view of design as a 'fundamental human capacity and a primary source of social order' (2013: 254). This movement will allow us to focus attention on other than Western societies seeking how people are designing our future digital imaginaries in their ordinary life.

More work needs to be done on indigenous and local imaginaries of digital futures across the world – not only in those modern societies where utopian visions of smart cities and smart homes give us something to critique, but also in emerging economies. Horst's chapter goes some way towards this, with the proposal that we need to attend to such everyday design. But there is a bigger issue here that also encompasses what are called the emerging economies as well as developing countries – including the fieldwork sites of 'traditional' anthropologists or development anthropologists, such as Indonesia or India, where there are vast markets for digital media as well as locally designed uses for them. Asia is also a key site for the manufacture of digital technologies. In the future this might be a key intersection for digital and design anthropology – and raises the question of how the interventional stances of design and development anthropologies will also intersect or critically encounter each other in such a field of scholarship and practice.

Second, one of the areas of digital materiality that has been little acknowledged is the darker side of digital technologies that Maxwell and Miller discuss in their book *Greening the Media* (2012). In light of discussions over the substrate of the materials that compose the digital infrastructures, e-waste and the kind of materiality that is produced in the aforementioned cycles that have been taking place recently in the fields of media studies and human geography (Gabrys 2011; Parikka 2012), Maxwell and Miller examine contemporary demand for ongoing obsolete digital technologies, and the material and e-waste that is generated through the media manufacturing industries, along with the global inequalities related to the global distribution of the resource mining, manufacturing production, distribution and consumption of digital technologies.

Here the materiality of digital media becomes implicated beyond the making of digital material environments that we inhabit as we go about our everyday lives, and calls our attention to the ways in which digital materiality is also implicated in processes of climate change and the 'natural' and human disasters that are part of this. Elsewhere Hjorth, Pink, Sharpe and Williams (2016) have argued that creative digital arts practice interventions could play a role in working through these issues towards a more sustainable future. Here we suggest that digital design anthropology is likewise ideally positioned to be able to produce understandings and interventions towards designing for the recycling of digital technological and e-waste. Design anthropologists have already shown how the subdiscipline can create ethnographies of future 'possible' recycling systems (Halse 2013). We would also argue for an anthropological approach to designing for sustainable use, reuse and ways of living in everyday environments, with things and through processes that we can think of through the concept of digital materiality.

Our call is for an extended dialogue between design, anthropology, HCI and media studies. By putting digital materiality at the centre of our concerns, we argue for a deeper interrogation of where digital and design anthropologies intersect, and the extent to which they can be separated out in future discussions of how futures are imagined, how interventions can be made in the world, and the roles of people as everyday designers.

A brief introduction to the structure of *Digital Materialities*

This book is divided into three parts titled respectively: *Expectations*, *Co-interventions*, and *Insider Design*. Here we introduce the parts, the chapters they comprise, and the work they do towards mapping out a field of research, design and intervention through digital materiality. In doing so, we chart a trajectory through the book; however this is not a closed route that we wish to guide readers to take, but instead would encourage unexpected routes, thoughts and practices of engagement with the text.

The three chapters in Part One – *Expectations* – focus on the ways in which different digital materialities are imagined and come to being, moving through from software and emulation (Dourish) to urban sensors (Lanzeni) and smart homes (Strengers). Although each of these chapters focuses on different subject matter, they all approach the question of digital materiality through critical interrogations of the ways in which it has been imagined and constituted through design. Each chapter in different ways also shows us how the pursuit of utopian or perfect digital designs is itself a flawed goal, because in fact a study of the ways in which digital materiality plays out and is experienced by people is always unfinished, 'messy' in the sense that we have outlined above, inhabited by unruly things, and contingencies.

For example, in Chapter 2 Dourish discusses a series of intriguing examples of how the digital–material is implicated in the emulation of older computer programs within newer technologies. One of these examples discusses the case of how a researcher found some bugs in the program he was developing an emulation of. Dourish tells us how 'he fixed them for the clone machine so that it would behave correctly', but, he goes on, 'when the machine was nearing completion and people began bringing up software that had been developed for original PDP-10s, they found that some of it failed mysteriously. Investigation revealed that some software was failing because it depended on the very bugs that … [the researcher] had corrected' (this volume page 38). If we unpack the trajectory through which this scenario (and others in the chapter) developed as described in full by Dourish, then we can see clearly how the contingencies through which digital materiality emerges need to be at the centre of our understanding of how future design should proceed.

The notions of smart cities, citizens and homes imply digital–material and human relations of particular kinds. Débora Lanzeni and Yolande Strengers both offer critical discussions of how smart futures have been envisaged through the assumptions attached to these imaginaries. In Chapter 3 Lanzeni points to how the smart concept has been mobilized for imagining 'future technologically enhanced and potentially automated cities, homes and lives' and argues that, instead, in order to understand digital materiality we need to attend to the meaning of smart for smart technology developers themselves, and to their design processes. Lanzeni calls on us to examine how visions of technological futures are in fact situated in the local and everyday experience of the designers. This, she proposes, invites us to rethink our understanding of the roles people play as citizens, and the implications this has for digital design.

In Chapter 4, Strengers interrogates and problematizes the notion of the smart home – as she puts it, 'the future smart home is an imagined one, and it is constantly being reimagined'. She demonstrates how existing research on how both the history of the idea of the automated home and on how so-called smart technologies are used (or disregarded) by people in everyday life, reveals the flaws in the utopian vision of the smart home and the types of persona who would inhabit it. Instead, as Strengers shows, a rather different digital materiality is likely to play out, and it is to this that we need to look in order to design for the future sustainable home. She argues that 'We cannot only be interested in how people "use" smart technologies, but must also focus on how they are reconfiguring both human and technology, and in doing so how they reconstitute the very fabric of everyday life' (page 00). Thus Strengers ends her chapter with a call for further research into the ways that homes are lived, with which we concur, and which implies a double agenda that we seek to play out in this book. This means developing a critique of existing conceptualizations of the digital material that are already playing out in planning, design and policy, as well as undertaking an in-depth analysis of the ways that lived and experienced digital materialities are emergent from everyday life circumstances and how designers might become engaged with these processes and the persons who are active in them as participants. It is to this question that our attention turns in Part Two.

The common thread that links the four chapters in Part Two – *Co-interventions* – is the question of how to understand existing and ongoing emerging forms of digital materiality, and the processes and activities through which humans engage, improvise and live with them. Significantly all these chapters also engage with this question though possible relationships between researching and understanding, and designing and intervening which involve professional designers and/or design researchers. They therefore also consider how the social science and design disciplines might work together through the digital material.

In Chapter 5, Sarah Pink, Kerstin Leder Mackley, Val Mitchell, Garrath T. Wilson and Tracy Bhamra discuss how ethnography and design teams from anthropology, media studies, design and human–computer interaction (HCI) research worked together in a larger interdisciplinary project, which sought to make digital design interventions for energy demand reduction. They show how, in the course of the four-year project, their work tacked between ethnography and design research, theoretical development, and bringing the ethnographic-theoretical dialogue of anthropology to the design–ethnography collaboration. This collaboration focused precisely on some fields of activity that the chapters in Part One of this book reveal as being important – including the ways in which people were engaged as the makers of the digital materi-ality of their own homes. However, it also further advances our discussion of digital materiality, anthropology and design, by showing how, through a focus on the digital materiality of home encompassing methodologies of ethnographic research, design intervention and project dissemination, we can make the relationality of the digital–material operate across different levels and modes of working in interdisciplinary teams.

In Chapter 6 Mike Michael takes up a similar theme, in that he also reflects in part on a project that crossed the social sciences and design (in this case an STS inflected sociological approach) and that was concerned with energy and digital media. Michael's work, however, engages with speculative designers and in doing so develops a speculative sociological methodology. He asks 'is it possible to imagine a way of designing digital materialities that enact such research events and provoke the possible?' by looking at how research methods can be open and unfolding. He playfully suggests an inter-mingling between design and social science research practices by bringing speculative design a step further through what he calls the figure of the 'idiotic object'. This means developing imaginative ways of designing digital materialities that enact research events and provoke the possible to appear by somehow disrupting what would otherwise be everyday situations. This 'method assemblage' has several implications for how research is conceived and carried out as people engage actively in the research process in affective, aesthetic, ethical and political ways.

Next, in Chapter 7, shifting our focus away from energy, which runs through Chapters 4 to 6, Jaume Ferrer, Elisenda Ardèvol and Narcís Parés discuss the relationship between designers and users in the process of making an interactive slide. They centre their analysis in the different understandings of co-design related to how users' interventions are acknowledged to contribute to the interactive design in multiple ways. The chapter problematizes the concept of user as a non-expert person whose participation in the design project serves only for designing user needs. The authors argue that the common justification in participatory or co-design practice for including users because they are experts on their own experiences, simply reinforces an existing tendency to exclude the human person in HCI design. Through an analysis of the multiple ways of experiencing/knowing the interactive slide – of the designers, the children, the ethnographer and the anthropologist – the authors propose a more open and generative understanding of (co)design. In doing so they interrogate the nature of intervention in design – What is the slide? Is the slide the intervention? Is it the (co)design? Is it ethnography? This leads to further questions about different gazes over the making of the slide, the kind of 'thing' that is being created, the intervention of materials, bodies, rules of play, interactions and experiences, and therefore engages the authors in a conversation about the nature of design.

In Chapter 8, the last in this section, Floyd Mueller brings the human into digital design in a different way, through a focus on the human body as part of the digital material design configuration. Mueller's chapter comes from the perspective of a designer, contrasting well with the social science perspectives represented more strongly in earlier chapters, and shows how such processes are played out in particular within the context of exertion games design. This chapter offering us a series of examples of phenomenologically informed design research where ethnography formed part of, but did not lead the design research process, thus providing what Mueller calls 'a future-oriented perspective on the active human body as digital materiality'. These projects form part of an ongoing process of exploration into design for the active human body in a context where the digital and material are not understood as separate from each other, but each continually involved in the user's experience of the world.

The chapters in Part Three – *Insider Design* – all focus in different ways on how the digital material is made through the everyday design or the informed involvement of people who do not actually work as professional designers. In doing so, it also begins to address the problem of how we understand digital

materiality and design in the global South, as well as different conceptualizations of the South, through a focus on a regional city in Australia (McShane
et al.), an urban Australian circus (Carlin) and everyday materialities and
consumption in the Caribbean (Horst).

The section begins with Heather Horst's fascinating account of the ways
in which the Jamaican and Dominican-Haitian participants in her research
planned and designed their mobile phones and the material cultures in
which they were entangled. She takes a different angle on the point made
by the chapters in Part Two of this book, concerning how people who are
not professional designers are also engaged in the design of their everyday
artefacts and processes. In Chapter 10, David Carlin takes us on a journey
through his own trajectory as well as that of the Melbourne-based Circus
Oz to explain how the digital materiality of an online archive emerges
and evolves. This chapter also makes connections with the work of the
authors in Part Two of this book, since Carlin and the designers involved
in the project worked together to create the Circus Oz archive; Carlin also
worked from within his long association with the circus, and with the circus
members who were also part of the archive-making process. Indeed, while
the design ethnography projects discussed in Part Two involved making
things that would be interventions in the lives of participants in research
projects, Carlin's project involved making something more directly with
the circus community who might use that archive, which he refers to as
a living archive – that is, an ongoing emergent form of digital materiality,
in other ways. For Carlin, the design of the digital archive means working
with a meshwork of materials, digital and otherwise, that opens new understandings about what an archive can do, but also new contingencies, such
as the circus members' annotations in the process of digitalizing the old
video recordings.

Chapter 11, the final chapter of this book, tells the story of the emergence
of new digital materialities in the regional Australian city of Goulburn, which
had been missed off the map of public broadband. Ian McShane, Chris K.
Wilson and Denise Meredyth show us how the digital materiality of urban
wireless and the services and experiences that are related to it emerge at a
messy interface of interests, infrastructures and aspirations. Their account is
of an experience of how digital materiality emerges in worlds that are already
messy, uneven, conflicted, contingent and ongoingly changing. Indeed, if we
want to gain a fuller understanding of how digital materiality is being made,
it is precisely these otherwise unmapped realities that we need to delve
into. Comparing the example revealed in this final chapter with the models
critiqued in Part One of this book takes us full circle. As Strengers and Lanzeni
respectively critique the neat utopias and expectations embedded in future
visions of smart homes and smart cities like Barcelona, we see how an urban

digital materiality unfettered by smart models and expectations could emerge through a 'messy' process in a city that was off the map for mainstream public wi-fi. Here, in order to achieve their goals, design had to become the preoccupation of non-designers, again through a process that shows up a series of twists, turns and contingencies.

PART ONE

Expectations

2

Rematerializing the platform: Emulation and the digital–material

Paul Dourish

Introduction

We live – if any number of breathless accounts are to be believed – in the age of the virtual. The movement of digital technology into many realms of life, at least in the developed world and increasingly beyond, means that our experience is populated by 'virtual' objects of all sorts: virtual books, virtual organizations, virtual realities, virtual memory and more. Even where the moniker of 'virtual' is not attached, there is a sense that virtualization attends other aspects of life, such as communication with friends and loved ones mediated by digital technology, such that even mourning and grieving for loved ones becomes an online pursuit (Brubaker et al. 2013). In this world, online shopping replaces the mall; books, CDs and DVDs are replaced with digital downloads; MOOCs replace traditional classroom teaching; paper bills disappear in favour of online transactions. As a site of design, the virtual is compelling precisely for the ways in which it both reproduces and offers the opportunity to reconfigure aspects of the world that might otherwise be beyond our reach as designers (cf. Smith 1986).

Increasingly, however, scholars have argued that this position neglects the significant and persistent materiality of digital technologies. Arguments for the importance of materiality in the age of the virtual have come from different disciplines. Some, for example, have argued that the infrastructures by which digital systems are maintained are themselves thoroughly material, and so we should understand that the digital economy is still based on such material groundings as real estate (for servers and network connections), power and energy (for digital equipment and server farms), and extractive industries (for the materials from which digital systems are constructed, such as the rare earth metals that play important roles in digital equipment fabrication) – material groundings that also embed the 'new' economy in older systems of political economy.

Others (e.g. Orlikowski 2007; Orlikowski and Scott 2008; Leonardi and Barley 2008) have argued from the perspective of organizational theory that we need to attend to the material aspects of organizational processes and the way that new technologies produce not just 'virtual' sites of work and organizing, but also significant challenges, limits and infrastructures that configure how organizational work proceeds. Arguing for a 'socio-material' approach to thinking about technology in organizations, they use the investigation of material forms to counter both the boundless optimism of progressivist technological determinism and the open-endedness of traditional social constructivist approaches.

Designers of various stripes have participated in these discussions too, although their point of engagement is somewhat different. For designers, the struggle with form – what Schön (1984) calls the 'reflexive conversation with materials' – has always been central. From a design perspective, then, the challenge of digital materialities is the challenge associated with the incorporation of the digital into otherwise inert materials. Here, the challenge is to blend digitality with material forms in a way that is respectful of the uniqueness of each. This is not a counter to arguments of virtuality, then, but rather an approach to virtuality that sees it as always somehow in conversation with physical materials.

Just what does it mean for something to be 'virtual'? The traditional rhetoric suggests a dissolution of the physical and its replacement with an ineffable digital abstraction. The alternative approaches argue that the digital needs to be seen alongside the material. However, these alternatives typically leave the duality between materiality and virtuality intact. That is, while one approach or another argues for the need to think about materiality as well as digitality, or materiality in relation to digitality, they largely presume that there is, on the one hand, digitality, and, on the other, materiality.

These critiques, while varying in their specific approaches, have in common the intent to remind us of the significance of the material contexts in which the virtual arises. Nonetheless, they focus their attention less on the digital or the virtual itself. Focusing on the infrastructures, the processes and the objects that surround the digital still leaves the digital itself underexamined; and most problematically of all, they fail to recognize that the digital is itself material (Dourish and Mazmanian 2012; Blanchette 2011).

How should we think about virtuality, virtualism and virtualization in light of a thoroughgoing materialist stance on the digital? What might be opened up for us by a recognition of the digital as material itself?

In this chapter, I want to explore these questions by focusing in particular on one site at which we see these questions played out – that of computer emulation. By examining a number of questions that arise at this particular site, I hope to be able to cast some light on the broader question of the relationship between the virtual and the material and to reconfigure the notion of the virtual as a site of design practice and analysis. My starting point, though, will be on the materialities of digital representations as a foundation for our later discussions.

The digital–material

The essence of the digital is that it is a representational system. It encodes or denotes something else. What does it mean, then, to argue for this representational system as itself having material properties?

A familiar analogy lies in our use of number systems. The Indo-Arabic number system with which we are familiar uses the position of each numeral to indicate an aspect of its magnitude – so, when we write 123, we know that the '1' means '100', and so is larger magnitude than the '3'. We rely upon this positional system when we do simple arithmetic, such as multi-digit multiplication and division. Compare this to Roman numerals, where the number 123 would be represented as CXXIII. How would we go about multi-plying CXXIII by, say, XLV (45)? Unlike the same calculation performed using Arabic numerals, there is no way to break this down into a series of smaller steps based on number positions. So, the representation of the numbers has important consequences for the way that they can be manipulated and used. The two representational systems might denote the same numbers, but different representations can be put to work in different ways.

'Number' seems like an entirely virtual concept, and yet numbers themselves betray the virtuality of the concept by taking on material forms that shape their use. So too do the representational forms that make up the world of the digital. Digitality is an abstract property, but digital things themselves – and even digits – are not.

Much the same argument can be applied to the notational system of programming languages and other digital forms. Consider the very simple program in Figure 2.1. Written in the Python programming language, it is a program that reads a file from the internet and counts word frequencies. Computer programs are often thought of as painfully detailed sets of instruc-tions for carrying out a procedure, so simple and detailed that a computer

```
import urllib2
from collections import defaultdict
from sys import argv

d = defaultdict(int)

data = urllib2.urlopen(argv[1]).read()
data = data.split()

for word in data:
    d[word] += 1

for word in d:
    print d[word], word;
```

FIGURE 2.1 *A simple Python program*

can implement them. And so it is with this program – every addition, every movement from one step to another, every check for errors, and so on, is specified. The sequence of operations – now do this, now do that – is reduced in the programming system to the absolutely simplest set of operations that the computer can perform. Without a program, as we know, the computer can do nothing at all; everything it does, then, must be given to it in the form of a program.

The program, then, dictates everything that the computer will do. But it does not notate everything that the computer will do. This seems a little odd at first. A programming language is a notation, after all, a way of writing; the program is a notation for a set of operations that the computer is to carry out, and, as we've said, the computer only does what the program says. And yet, while the computer does 'only' what the program says, there is more to what the computer does than what the program directly describes. There are ways of going about carrying out the tasks specified in the program that are not part of the program's text, and there are properties of the computational platform that impact the program's execution but which are also not described here.

It's useful to examine what is *not* notated in the program text. The type and characteristics of the network to which the computer is linked are not notated, although perhaps that is more than we would expect, even if they have an important impact on the operation of the program. But other more detailed questions remain. The speed with which the computer proceeds from one instruction to the next is not notated, for example. Nor are the different speeds at which different instructions might be executed, depending on the particular features of the computer and processor on which the program is running. The size of the computer's memory conditions circumstances under which the program will eventually fail, but this is not notated; similarly, the size of the maximum representable number in the computer is not notated but can also cause the program to fail at some indefinite moment. The size of the program itself is not notated, nor the memory capacity needed to run it, nor the performance characteristics of its interpreter.

The materialities of digital systems lie not least, then, in this gap between what is denoted and what is expressed, or between the specification and the execution. A computer program may be a precise series of instructions, and yet the experience that is the result of the program's execution is radically underspecified by that program.

It is in this radical underspecification, and the slippage between notation and enaction, that we find the lie of virtuality. The denial of materiality that is at the centre of the rhetoric of virtuality could be maintained only if the specification were complete: if a program really were an adequate account of what will happen in execution, if an MP3 file really were a complete explanation of how music will be produced, or if a digital 3D model really specified what you'll see through a display. However, none of these is in fact the case. The mechanics of, if you will, de-virtualization – of the production of actual effects on the basis of digital specifications, be that the running of a program or the rendering of an image file – inherently exceeds the reach of the specification itself.

Elsewhere, I have argued that these properties are inherent in the digital, and examined such cases as database representations (Dourish, 2014) and network protocols (Dourish, 2015). The particular lens through which I want to examine the topic of virtuality and materiality in this paper is that of emulation – the production of a virtual computer, in software, in another computer. From the perspective of the dominant rhetoric, this is a case that is twice virtual; however, in practice, it is a site where the problems of virtuality become particularly visible.

Emulation

In 2003, a collaboration between artist Cory Arcangel, Pittsburgh's Andy Warhol Museum and computer scientists at Carnegie Mellon University made available a series of original artworks by Warhol that had been essentially lost for many years (Heddaya, 2014). These were digital artworks, originally produced by Warhol on early versions of Commodore's Amiga personal computer system. Manufactured between 1985 and 1997, the Amiga was marketed on the basis of its advanced graphics and multimedia functions, and for the product launch, Commodore developed relationships with a number of artists, including Warhol, to produce art that would show off the Amiga's capabilities in these areas. The pieces that Warhol produced were archived on floppy disks held in the collection of the Warhol Museum, but they had not been seen or examined since accession; indeed, it would seem that nobody knew what the disks contained until the 2003 examination. However, by 2003, original Amiga computers were hard to come by, particularly the early variants that Warhol had used; and so, in fact, although the artworks had been produced using a piece of software designed specifically for the Amiga computer, no Amiga computer was involved in the retrieval of the images. Instead, the images were retrieved and reconstituted using an Amiga *emulator* – software running on a modern PC that reproduces the experience of using an Amiga computer so accurately that the Amiga software can be executed without modification.

The notion of emulation runs right to the heart and the origins of computer science as a discipline. One of the foundational papers that made computer science possible is Alan Turing's (1936) paper, 'On Computable Numbers with an Application to the *Entscheidungsproblem*.' In this paper, Turing made significant contributions to an open mathematical question first posed by David Hilbert in 1928, which essentially asked whether a mathematical language could be defined in which a definitive answer could be given to the question of whether any statement in that language was valid. Turing's approach was to imagine two types of machine. These machines are not so much mechanical contrivances, more mathematical formalisms, albeit with distinctly machine-like properties. The first type of machine is one whose configuration is equivalent to a mathematical function, so that when the machine operates, its actions produce mathematical results according to that function – perhaps the digits of pi, or the shortest path through a network, or the fixpoints of a graphical function. The second type of machine that Turing imagined is one that can behave like any of the first class of machines according to a configuration that it processes in the form of a set of rules. This is what Turing called a 'universal machine', now conventionally known as a 'Turing machine', and the mathematical analysis of this sort of machine that Turing provides in his paper laid the foundation for contemporary computing. The set of rules for Turing's universal machine is like the software for a modern computer; it encodes a series of instructions that allow a general-purpose device (a computer) to act like a wide range of more specific devices (a word processor, a game, a music player, and so on). Turing's analysis highlights an oft-overlooked aspect of what it means to 'run software'; it means, in the terms of his paper, to configure one machine to act like another.

In this sense, all software is some form of emulator, but the term 'emulation' has a narrower use in conventional technical discourse. An emulator is a piece of software that specifically uses one computer (often called the 'host') to mimic the operation of another computer (the 'guest'). There are a number of reasons why one might want to do such a thing, but three are the most common, and are distinguished, interestingly, by their different temporal relations. The first is a projection into the past: one might want, as in the Warhol example, to emulate a computer which is no longer available, so as to be able to gain access to functions, information and software that has been lost. The second is marked by a condition of contemporaneous reference: one might want to emulate a different type of computer that one might have but doesn't, perhaps to run some software that is only available for that computer (for example, to emulate a smartphone on a desktop computer in order to test software written for the phone). The third is marked by conditions of anticipation: one might emulate a computer system that does not yet exist. This is most commonly done during the development of new computer systems; emulating a new computer's hardware allows software to be developed before the hardware is entirely debugged and available. While this third mode of emulation is fairly specialized and not particularly widespread, examples of the other two are quite broad. For instance, in 2006, when Apple began a design transition from computers based on the PowerPC processor to the x86 Intel architecture, they also modified their operating system to include a facility called Rosetta, an emulator for the PowerPC processor, so that users with new computers that used Intel processors could nonetheless still run software that they owned which had been designed and compiled for the PowerPC. Or again, emulators are a common way for enthusiasts to carry on playing computer games or running other pieces of software originally created for consoles or hardware platforms that are no longer available. On my Mac laptop, I can run *cbm*, an emulator of the Commodore PET 2001, the first computer I ever used; *beeb*, an emulator of the first computer I ever owned; or *simh*, an emulator of the computer I supported for a research group as my first job. I can run *salto*, an emulator of the Alto (Thacker et al. 1979), Xerox's pioneering workstation, the first device with a modern graphical user interface, a computer I have never used or even seen operating.[1] If I want to reproduce the experience of running an early Macintosh, I can visit a web page with a Mac emulator running in Javascript.[2] The technical enthusiast website Ars Technica recently carried a review of a computer game, Karateka, which had been released before the reviewer was born, recreated for a new generation through emulation (Johnston 2013); and as I was completing this chapter, a posting was distributed online describing the procedure by which an enthusiast had booted Windows 3.1 on a virtual MS-DOS PC emulated in Javascript within a web brower.[3]

Emulation speaks to a broad cultural logic, the logic of the virtual. Invocation of the virtual is the central discursive move of digitality. To the extent that digital phenomena are rhetorically opposed to non-digital equivalents, and that they further are connected through a notion of displacement, virtual objects – virtual books, virtual worlds, virtual organizations, virtual spaces, virtual meetings, virtual communities, and so on – are the stock-in-trade of the digerati. The notion of virtuality marks an absence; the designation of 'virtual' marks something that seems to be there but isn't. A virtual book allows us to read without a real book being present; a virtual musical instrument allows us to produce music in the absence of the instrument itself.

One would imagine that the case of emulation is the perfect demonstration of the power of virtuality. If software is already thoroughly virtual, then what could be more appropriate that to 'run' that computer on 'hardware' that it *itself* constructed from the virtual medium of software – that is, an emulator?[4] This rhetoric of absence, though, draws our attention away from the very specific presence of technologies that manifest the emulator and the emulated device. The emulator, after all, does not simply conjure up a virtual computer – a virtual Commodore Amiga or whatever. Rather, it makes that virtual computer manifest within a host platform – a PC running the UAE emulator, a Mac running the Bochs PC emulator, a Raspberry Pi running MAME, and so on. I want here to use the case of emulators to examine virtualization as *rematerialization* – not as a move away from the material to create a domain of the virtual, but rather a new material foundation for digital experience.

In the next section, I will examine a series of problems that occur in the production of an effective emulation. By doing so, I hope to show how virtuality in practice is perhaps better seen as rematerialization. With that in hand, we can take a step back to consider the notion of the virtual as an aspect of the digital landscape.

Problems of materiality in virtual computers

In what ways do the material manifestations of digital objects challenge the idea of a 'virtual' computer in the world of emulation? I will discuss three considerations here: instructions, timing, and input/output.

Instructions and representations

The essence of emulation is the creation of an environment that can run specific pieces of software. Essentially, it does just what a computer should – it reads a program and then it executes it. To understand the difficulty, we need to think for a moment about what a program actually *is*.

A computer program, as stored on a disk or downloaded from the internet, is a series of instructions. These instructions are simply themselves numbers; each number corresponds to a function that the computer's processor can perform, or a data item to which that function should be applied, or a memory address where data to be processed can be found or where execution should shift. Why then is there any need for emulation in order to make some software run? It is needed because different processors and different processor architectures (such as the x86 processors in many desktop computers and the ARM processors in many mobile phones) execute different instructions. It is not simply that they encode the same instructions with different numerical codes (although that is sometimes true); it is rather that they use different so-called 'instruction sets' – sets of functions that make up the processor's catalogue of operations. These differ because processors might provide different kinds of functions in hardware (e.g. one processor might have an instruction for multiplying two numbers directly, while another might support only addition and require that multiplication be performed through repeated addition or through bit-shifting).

The instructions that make up a program are not simply mathematical functions or descriptions. They can be thought of that way, but they can also be thought of as objects that manipulate how a computational mechanism works. Just as a key, inserted into a lock, will reconfigure the tumblers in the lock (hopefully so as to open the door), so an instruction being executed by a processor activates different parts of the processor in order to produce its effect; the key doesn't simply *represent* the configuration of tumblers, and similarly the instruction doesn't simply represent the sequence of action to be taken. The instruction, then, is something that has meaning only relative to the processor in question. There are two important considerations here for the problem of emulation. The first is that, since kinds of processors have different kinds of capacities, as described above, so an instruction that makes sense on one processor may not make any sense on another. You can't simply follow an instruction to add together the values of two registers if your processor doesn't have two registers. In this way, the problem of emulation is more than simply 'finding the equivalent instruction'; there is no logic of equivalences, and local facilities cannot simply 'stand in for' the facilities being emulated. The emulator makes up for these deficiencies; it explicitly stands between the original software and the new processor, reading each instruction and directing the processor to act in a manner that is somehow equivalent.

A second way that instructions are tied to particular manifestations – and arguably the more complicated one – lies in the fact that processors may have bugs, errors, or limits to their use which are part of their implementation but not part of the mathematical formulation; so, in order to produce an accurate emulation, an emulator needs to pay attention not just to what the instruction *ought* to do, but to what it actually does in the computer being emulated. A sterling example is the case documented in Michael Hiltzig's (1999) account of the history of Xerox PARC, concerning the development of a 'clone' (not quite an emulation) of the DEC PDP-10 mainframe computer. The PARC researchers wanted to purchase a DEC PDP-10 computer, but were forbidden to do so by their management, on the basis that the PDP-10 was a competitor to Xerox's own recent entry into the minicomputer market. In response, the researchers decided to build their own clone of the PDP-10, one that would be sufficiently compatible with the original that they could run software developed for the PDP-10 at other research sites. The tasks of reproducing various elements of the PDP-10 system was divided up among lab members, and researcher Ed Fiala was assigned to building support for floating point mathematical functions. In the course of his work, he discovered some small bugs in the PDP-10 implementation, and so he fixed them for the clone machine so that it would behave correctly. However, when the machine was nearing completion and people began bringing up software that had been developed for original PDP-10s, they found that some of it failed mysteriously. Investigation revealed that some software was failing because it depended on the very bugs that Fiala had corrected. With software compatibility as a key requirement for the new computer, only one solution was possible; Fiala was asked to program the bugs back into his implementation, so that it would be wrong, but in the same way as the PDP-10.

The object of attention in an emulation, then, is not simply the sequence of instructions, which needs therefore to be transformed into some different sequence that suits the host processor; rather, what needs to be reproduced and reenacted is the entire mechanism into which those instructions fit when they are taken not as representations of computational action but as components of the mechanism.

Timing

As we discussed earlier, the conventional wisdom about computer programming is that computers must be given complete and detailed descriptions of what to do, and that these descriptions are what constitute a computer program, with no detail left unspecified. This is quite true as far as it goes, but computer instructions nonetheless leave much unsaid, and it is what is unsaid that nonetheless must be recaptured in emulation. The time taken by computer operations is an important case in point. On a MOS 6502 processor – the type of processor that powered the original Apple II computer, among others – the machine instruction sequence A1 44 00[5] means 'fetch the contents of memory address $4400, add to it the value of the X register to produce a new memory address, and load the value stored at that computer address into the accumulator'. However, it doesn't specify, for example, how long that operation will take. Producing an accurate emulation means not just performing the same or equivalent instructions but doing it so as to produce the same effect. Why does the timing matter? Well, it might matter if the computer program relies on the delay produced by issuing a series of instructions to make sure that on-screen activities happen with appropriate synchronization, or that a value will be read from a disk at the right moment, or that an interrupt will be handled before an operation times out.

There are two problems here. One is a problem of scale, and the other a problem of imbalance.

The problem of scale is most visible when there are drastic mismatches between the host system and the guest system. One of the major uses of emulation is in the retrospective mode highlighted earlier – reproducing the experience of using older, perhaps unavailable computer hardware in software on modern hardware. In any emulation, performing the same operations in software as one might in hardware is a good deal slower, and so when one performs an emulation of contemporary hardware in software, there is a significant performance reduction. Modern hardware is, of course, generally much faster than older computer hardware, which means that the situation is different when emulating older hardware. It is quite possible that a contemporary software emulation will execute more quickly, perhaps much more quickly, than the older hardware that is being emulated. There are times when this is an advantage. For instance, in my first research position, I wrote software on Sun workstations that ran an emulator for the custom 'Wildflower' architecture of prototype research computers developed at the Xerox Palo Alto Research Center in the 1970s; the modern emulation was much faster than the original hardware had ever been, representing a significant performance enhancement. In other cases, though, the mismatch might be significantly problematic. If an emulated game runs one hundred times faster in a modern emulation than on the original hardware, it may be *too* fast to play.

The difference between the performance of contemporary computer systems and that of what is sometimes called 'legacy hardware' may be large, but the issue for emulators is not simply the scale of the difference, but also the fact that different aspects of computer systems develop at different rates. Processors, for instance, have generally over time become faster at a rate higher than that of storage systems – so while contemporary storage systems are generally faster than older storage systems, they are not faster by the same factor that characterizes changes in processor performance. In order to account for this, computer system designers have, over the years, developed new computer architectures, or arrangements of system elements, to compensate for the difference.

Modern computer processors, then, are not simply faster than old ones – they are also more heavily pipelined,[6] and might have multiple cores operating simultaneously, as ways of making more efficient use of their 'excess' capacity relative to the data storage system. Similarly, modern graphics processors do more advanced processing on their own, without involving the central processor of the computer, introducing another source of parallelism and hence another architectural difference with implications for performance.

To further complicate the problems of timing in emulation, we should remember one other important thing: computers consist of more than processors. Those other things – peripheral devices, subsidiary electronics and non-digital components – all have their own timing considerations that software might need to account for.

As an example, remember that, before the days of LCD screens, most computer displays were cathode-ray tubes (CRTs). A CRT operates by sweeping an electron beam rapidly over a phosphor-lined screen, from side to side and top to bottom, switching rapidly on and off, causing spots of phosphor to either glow or not. These spots of glowing phosphor become the pixels that make up the display, and since they rapidly decay in brightness, they must be 'repainted' again and again by the scanning electron beam. This constant need to repaint the screen, and to do it within the timeframe demanded by the electron beam and the phosphor, and to supply the data to drive the display, became a significant demand on the design of early computers – Xerox's original Alto computer spent fully 66 per cent of its time managing the display. (Butler Lampson, one of the designers of the Xerox Alto, recounted in a 2001 talk at the Computer History Museum that one of his most important contributions to the project was to reduce the time taken by the code supplying the display driver with data from seven micro-instruction cycles to six, so that it occupied only 66 per cent of the computer's time and not 80 per cent.)[7]

One especially important aspect of this arrangement for many microcomputers and game systems was the existence of what was called the 'vertical blanking interval', which is the period when the CRT's electron beam would be turned off and would reposition itself from the bottom right to the top left of the screen, to begin a new painting cycle. Many pieces of software – especially programs like graphical games – would pay a lot of attention to the vertical blanking interval, for two reasons. The first is that a period of time when the screen was not being repainted might suddenly be a period when more processing time is available – a good time to do more complicated calculations. The second is that a period of time when the screen is not being repainted is a good time to make updates to on-screen objects so that there wouldn't be any of the flickering that might result if the objects were updated at the same time as being painted onto the screen. As Montford and Bogost (2009) document in their book *Racing the Beam*, programmers on the early Atari VCS game system needed essentially to organize their entire programs around the timing of instructions relative to the horizontal and vertical sweeps of the electron beam.

The timing that needs to be reproduced in an emulator, then, is not simply the timing of the processor, but the timing of analog elements such as the CRT beam, not to mention such features as the characteristic operating speed of disks or the temporal performance of memory. In other words, the production of the virtual 'guest' computer means the reproduction not only of the digital elements of the original machine, but also thoroughly non-digital components – a further intrusion of the obstreperously non-virtual.

Input and output

Perhaps one of the most complicated areas of challenge that emulation throws up is the problem of input and output – recreating and emulating aspects of how graphics and perhaps especially sound work. The problems here reflect and intensify some that we have already discussed. Part of the difficulty is that input and output operations are ones that go beyond the traditional mathematical descriptions that are the foundation of how we reason about computers.

As I have outlined, the mathematical theory upon which computer science is founded – the Church-Turing Theorem – describes a class of computable functions (basically, a class of solvable mathematical problems) and a computational mechanism that can solve them. So-called 'Turing-equivalent machines' are machines or mechanisms that can calculate any of that class of functions.

However, in practice, it turns out that actual computers – the ones we all use – are both *more than* and *less than* Turing-equivalent machines. They are less than Turing-equivalent in that the abstract description of the Turing machine postulates infinite storage. In comparison to the extremely simple operation of a Turing machine, a modern computer might have so much storage that it is *essentially* infinite – but it is (obviously) not *in fact* infinite. In other words, there can be functions that are solvable by a Turing machine but not necessarily solvable by specific actual computers that we might use, not because the problems make unresolvable computational demands but because they make unresolvable storage demands. So in this way, contemporary computers are less than formal mathematical Turing machines. At the same time, though, they are also more than formal mathematical Turing machines in that they have capacities that Turing machines don't have, especially in their connection to the world. For instance, we expect that any computer we buy today will be capable of playing music; and yet, the functions needed to play music – that is, to be able to control the voltage on a connection to speakers or headphones so that music can be heard – are unavailable to the formal mathematical Turing machine. The theory of Turing equivalence is the theory of what can be calculated, but it stops where calculation ends. So we might be able to show how a Turing-equivalent machine can decode a description of music that has been encoded in the MP3 format, but there is no way to describe the actual playing of the music.

The case of input/output – of playing music, for instance – highlights the way that computer systems, as physical objects and as cultural objects, escape the mathematical accounts of computation. A real 'Turing machine' wouldn't sell very well in the marketplace, because those functions that we demands of our computers – the ability to print documents, to communicate on networks, or to video-conference with friends – are entirely outside of its capacities. This means, then, that while we might imagine that Turing's theorem – which, after all, describes a machine that can emulate another machine – should be a guarantee that emulation is straightforward, the truth is rather more complicated. To make things even more difficult for someone writing an emulator, these functions, like network communication and processing audio and video, are generally not performed by the central processing unit of the computer, but rather delegated to dedicated signal processing hardware that can be controlled by the processor. Input/output operations, indeed, are often handled in parallel with the operation of the processor, especially in the case of modern machines whose separate graphical processor units – themselves highly parallel – are often more capable computational devices (within a limited sphere) than the central processor itself.

As in other cases we have seen, then, there is no simple one-to-one equivalence between one context and another. Emulation is not simply a question of looking at each instruction and issuing the local equivalent; rather, the behaviour of the original system must be reproduced, in all its material specificity.

Virtualization and rematerialization

I have focused here on the example of emulation because it provides us with a particularly fruitful perspective on the questions of virtuality. Software is already a thoroughly virtual good, in the terms of the traditional rhetoric; born digital, it lives entirely in digital media, operates entirely within the computer, is transmitted wholesale from place to place, can be duplicated digitally, protected cryptographically, and processed algorithmically. Emulation, then, is doubly virtual; by using one piece of software to produce the actions of another, it seems to constitute an even more radical separation of software from hardware, creating a thoroughly virtual environment for the operation of an already virtual object.

In practice, though, this realm of pure virtuality is hard to find. Emulation seems to be not so much an exercise in virtuality as one in brutal materiality – an engagement with all the specific material constraints of both platforms, those elements that lie outside what is notated by software systems but that are critical to the manifested expression of running software.

Rather than being doubly virtual, then, the case of emulation is instead doubly material. First, the software being executed as the guest system cannot be regarded purely as a virtual expression of desired behaviour, but as a tool for configuring a material arrangement of the delicately entwined digital and analog components that made up the original computer system – complete with flaws, mistakes, problems, undocumented features and unexpected idiosyncracies. Second, the challenge is not to dissolve away these material considerations, but rather to re-enact them in the context of a new materiality – the materiality of the host system. Not only, then, does someone developing emulation software need to pay attention to, for example, the timing arrangements between processor, memory and tertiary storage on the original computer, but these need to be configured so as to operate effectively in light of the timing arrangements among processor, memory and tertiary storage on the current one. It is perhaps, then, less a case of producing a 'virtual' computer to run the original software, but rather of 'rematerializing' that computer in the context of a new one.

This conceptual shift from virtualizing to rematerializing may be an instructive one beyond the domain of emulation. It brings into focus the inevitable processes of rematerialization inherent in any enaction or expression of the virtual. It places the distinction between notation and expression at the heart of any analysis, and illustrates the way that 'virtual' objects of all sorts – representations and encodings – inherently *under*-specify the phenomena that they putatively represent. The gaps between specifications and rematerialized phenomena should not be read here as failures in a process of virtualization, but rather as signals of the unavoidable materiality that underwrites any practice of the virtual. Those objects that traditional technical accounts hold up as virtual are themselves thoroughly material, and indeed to describe them as virtual at all – at least in the transcendent sense of the traditional rhetoric – requires a certain wilful and selective blindness.

Discussions of the materialities of information and their consequences for encounters between social science and design have focused largely on the materialities of information *infrastructures* and the materialites of digital *artefacts*: how the sizes, shapes and physical impositions of iPhones, transoceanic cables and high-rise server farms condition and constrain our encounters with the digital world. The case of emulation helps us to examine

the materialities of digital information itself, and the materialities of representation and representational practices that underwrite our understandings of
the digital. This is not to undermine the digital, of course, but rather to sustain
it by reconnecting it with the world of mechanical effects, economic conditions, scientific practice, cultural appropriation, political debate and social
innovation within which it comes into being.

Acknowledgements

Work on this chapter, and the broader project of which it is a part, has
benefitted immeasurably from the contributions of many colleagues including
Melissa Mazmanian, Geof Bowker, Tom Boellstorff, Sarah Pink, Yoko Akama,
Heather Horst and Danny Miller, as well as support from the Intel Science and
Technology Center for Social Computing.

3

Smart global futures: Designing affordable materialities for a better life

Débora Lanzeni

Introduction

In this chapter I argue for closer attention to the ways in which smart futures are constituted through the relationships between different local and global scales of future visions. To achieve this I propose an understanding of the design of the digital–material environment which builds on two bodies of literature: first, on discussions of 'visions of future' in design and technology research (Dodge and Kitchen 2011; Anderson 2007; Kinsley 2013; Thrift 2005); and second, on the recent call from Design Anthropology to take seriously ethnographic research on imagination (Sneath, Holbraad and Pedersen 2009; Ingold 2013; Halse 2013; Pink 2014; Appadurai 2013). My discussion has an analysis of the future orientations of digital design knowledge and practice at its centre. It examines how the two scales of local and global action and connection are involved in the design of smart technologies, and interrogates the role played by future visions and technological imaginaries within these design processes.

In the following three sections, I develop my analysis through a discussion of the example of low-cost sensor kits. These are seen as affordable technologies made by citizens for citizens. I first unpack the key concepts that inform both how technologies, such as sensors, are thought to be active in the world, and how they are developed: DIY citizenship and its global imaginary, the concept of smart, and the notion of a global future. I then shift the focus to ask how practical knowledge and tangible futures are actually located in the processes through which sensors are designed and developed. To do this I draw on my ethnographic research undertaken with Internet of Things (IoT) designers in urban and companies' labs to provide an in-depth understanding of the processes in which the design of these projects of citizen sensor kits is entangled. I argue for a more specific analysis of how imaginaries and visions of future are implicated in the design processes and in meaning making of smart technologies. Ultimately, I suggest the imaginaries are connected with a broader global future and have less signifi- cance in the design, whereas the visions of future are informed by the local (quotidian) experience of the designers and have a crucial role in the materi- alization of design projects.

In developing this discussion I call for attention to the role of knowledge production as material work. In existing and ongoing debates in the literature about digital materiality (Leonardi 2010) emphasis has usually been put on the double nature of the 'thing': the physicality of the hardware and the intangi- bility of the software. To understand the implications of such digital–material forms more fully, I call for further attention to another aspect of the 'intan- gible' – that is, to focus on the forms of *knowledge* that the design process materializes.

'Sensors for the people'

The case of low-cost sensors is particularly interesting for this task precisely because these sensors have become part of different contexts of production and use, as recently rhetorically reported in *Nature*:

> *How polluted is your home or neighbourhood?* Until recently it was difficult to answer that question because data were available only from networks of expensive sensors in relatively limited locations. The *do-it-yourself movement* has led to the emergence of *low-cost sensors* that can be purchased or build from online instructions. (Kat Austen, *Nature*, 7 January 2015, my italics)

This statement, published in the prestigious *Nature International Weekly Journal of Science*,[1] pointed out a commonly held belief around DIY smart things design, that the new affordable sensors could change the way that we know/experience our environment. Affordable here means low-cost and reachable: people could have access to these sensors and could also fabricate them themselves. These three kinds of particulate sensor nodes have been designed in accordance with the open source hardware[2] initiative

FIGURE 3.1 *Smart Citizen Kit. Photograph courtesy of Smart Citizen.*

and have been catalogued as inexpensive Do-It-Yourself technologies.[3] In the *Nature* article cited above, an explicit connection between the low-cost sensors and both 'the people' and the DIY movement is claimed.[4] Moreover, according to the editorial, the DIY movement has led to both the Air Quality Egg (AQE) and the Smart Citizen Kit (SCK). In the remainder of this section I examine what the concept of the smart citizen stands for and where smart citizens are located.

During my ethnographic fieldwork I followed processes related to DIY, Maker and open source hardware initiatives, as well as some of the stakeholders involved in the sensor projects introduced above. In the set of practices and discourses around DIY the concept of *citizenship/citizen* is a huge concern; it is now at the core of almost all references around the topic. For the people who are involved in activities that they believe are parts of DIY logic and practice, exercising their citizenship is a value that is inherent in making things themselves. Moreover being a *DIY citizen* entails encompassing shared conceptions and goals with other citizens. The DIY citizen is one who expresses himself/herself 'through making, through designing and engineering' (Light 2014: 265). However, the making of things by DIY citizens entails a very specific approach to the use and design of technology.

As critical making scholars Ratto and Boler assert, someone who is involved in DIY – that is, a DIY citizen – has to be critical about his/her practice because practice and processes are integrated in the making. Then, the practices of making things 'are potentially linked to critically infused reflection about aspects of the processes itself' (Ratto and Boler 2014: 3). Likewise, most of the recent academic work on DIY citizenship seeks to understand the practices and processes around the making of things by ordinary people (Ratto and Boler 2014). Yet this invites us to ask three questions: first, how are the notions of People and Citizen related in our (mainly Western) imaginaries?; second, how has citizenship become such a powerful global imaginary?; and finally, how is it linked to digital design? By unpacking these questions we can begin answer the question of how smart futures are constituted, by interrogating the role of the concept of citizen in this process.

DIY citizenship is 'a term intended to highlight the diversity of ways cit zenship is enacted and performed' (Ratto and Boler 2014: 3). One exercises citizenship when one actively and responsibly engages with the world. In the words of Tomás, who is one of the developers of the Smart Citizen Kit (a citizen sensor for measuring air quality), as citizens, 'the end users are being enhanced and amplified, from being just mere consumers of given technologies, to become producers of data, things and knowledge' (Diez 2014).

Predominantly, in the global imaginaries shared by developers engaged in DIY and makers' initiatives, one of the conditions for being a citizen (a DIY citizen, for instance) is to adopt a critical attitude and show some kind of social concern. Thus, the distinction between ordinary people and citizen is enacted as long as citizenship is enacted. However, to be a citizen through technology requires a degree of knowledge and manoeuvre of materials that no trained people have to learn – or at least, it is a practice that must be enhanced. This means that if you are a DIY citizen, you should also care about people and be willing to contribute to develop citizenship, and sometimes to intervene in things that you consider neglected by government (see Ratto and Boler 2014). In the example of sensor technologies, making sensors (technology) for society is a way to spread citizenship and encourage people to become citizens by giving them the means to participate in the production of knowledge, both in the public sphere and through their more intimate concerns about quality of life. Personal involvement in DIY often comes through group efforts and from the position of 'being a citizen' rather than merely a consumer (Mann 2014: 35). This idea of becoming citizens through the making and control of technology is also part of a shared DIY imaginary that was brought to the fore by the participants in my research. For instance, Alex, one of the main developers of SCK, told me that 'People need to know what is happening around them'. At the time he was concerned about new technologies, introduced to measure gas consumed in homes, which had been deployed by energy companies. According to him, these kinds of devices produce a type of radio wave that is not safe for humans. He claimed that the 'energy companies are not providing us with information about this technology and its implication, so we need to work on it'.

As Goanar and Povinelli highlight, democratic social imaginaries and material technologies (of public speaking in their case) energize and innovate new forms of social life and action (2003: 386). One of the other demands of those democratic social imaginaries is a form of citizenship, the notion of common citizens. This form of citizenship is then called on to intervene in the process of knowledge-making through technology, which is a demand endorsed particularly by the DIY movement.

Moreover, this notion of citizenship is part of a 'global imaginary' and the air quality sensors, represented in *Nature* discussed above, are equally global. Although their developers are inevitably based in specific localities in the world, the sensors are not simply local examples or locally specific material manifestations of a global imaginary that might inform us about these global movements, processes and subjectivities. Instead, the people and communities that are locally involved in developing these citizen technologies are simultaneously in the 'transnational, cosmopolitan or global' flow (Ratto and Boler 2014: 18). The sensormakers are as much part of a global movement (like the DIY or open source hardware movements) as the shared imaginaries they do or do not enact (I return to this point later).

A further aspect of this global imaginary concerns the range that these interventions, such as sensors, are expected to reach. In this sense, they embody the liaison of global expectations and local implications set out in the notion of 'Think globally, act locally' (Dourish, 2010: 6). This means the design is intended to intervene in a transnational scene loaded by global meanings, but it is developed in a local frame of action. Yet, as I demonstrate below, the case of the sensors reveals an alternative possible scenario in that while imaginaries act globally, people think locally. In other words, the 'local' for citizen technology developers is not a physical place, but rather it is where their projects and communities are located. In contrast, the global is where they want to intervene, in order to transform the world for the better. They intervene in the world – that is, in a global imaginary – through their daily activity of making things for society. Or, to put it another way, they are enacting a form of citizenship through making a specific kind of technology whereby they see the the 'smart citizen' as leading or working alongside the 'smart city' paradigm.

Imagining smartness

The concept of smart has been part of the way in which future technologically enhanced and potentially automated cities, homes and lives have been imagined. However, to gain an understanding of this concept and how it is mobilized in relation to constituting digital–material worlds, we need to unpack what 'smart' means for people who are involved in the development of smart technologies.

In the 'smart paradigm' (or the 'smart city agenda') there are two shared understandings about where the 'smartness' is coming from. One is that intelligence arises from the information-processing capacity of digital technologies which is done at different levels: embedded (smart devices), fog (in the concentrator devices), or cloud (in a server); the second is that society has to enhance people's skills regarding the understanding and practical uses of these technologies. To advance this agenda, Nam and Pardo, working on smart policies and open government, have developed a strategic principle which would align what they consider to be the three main dimensions (technology, people and institutions) of the smart city paradigm: integration of infrastructures and technology-mediated services; social learning for strengthening human infrastructure; and governance for institutional improvement and citizen engagement (Nam and Pardo 2011). The essence of their idea revolves around the perceived need to coordinate and integrate technologies and people in information processes. The aim is to improve the current social life: cities, homes, cars, factories, schools, clothes, and so on. Indeed, the smart city needs the smart citizen to exist. In addition, other stakeholders in this agenda advocate for 'smartness' to come from the production of digital technology and data by the citizens themselves. According to this proposal, some other developers claim that the citizen must share with others the knowhow and expertise by *opening* the making of digital technologies. This belief is manifested in the ways in which the two projects – Air Quality Egg and Smart Citizen Kit – operate.

Smart Citizen's designers and backers are concerned with air quality. They are also concerned with the absence of governmental voice in the discussions that matter for people. On the night that the project was launched beyond the small circle that gave life to it, the developers gathered everyone who collaborated in Kickstarter in the Fab Lab in Barcelona. The venue was one of the spots where SCK mainly circulated and the building where the Fab Lab and a prestigious architecture institute were located. We were occupying the central salon, a microphone was on the podium and a mountain of sensor kits was spread over a table (I noted that all the kits were wireless). Tomás – who is seen as the face of Smart Citizen by most of the backers because he is always the speaker at the events – opened the night by thanking everyone who had trusted them. The atmosphere was quiet and everyone was attentive to what was happening above the podium. Alex, another member of the SCK core, spoke after Tomás, explaining the next phase of SCK, which was the deployment of the kits by everyone in the room. 'Now', Alex said, 'is the time when we have to trust you.' At the same time Tomás and Guillem (one of the workers at the Fab Lab) were delivering the kits to the backers by calling them by name to come up to the podium. Alex continued: 'You now have the beginning of Smart Citizen in your hands, and it will depend on what you do with the kits. We'll provide you with all the information and support needed to deploy the SCK, but the project is now in your hands.'

Alex insisted on the point that, while they would be engaged with the deployment, the main task would depend on the people who would set up the kits. Tomás and Alex used the word *trust* to express the expectations that they had for the deployment of the sensors. Indeed, the success of SCK would require people's engagement with the deployment: the setting up of the sensors; the maintenance of the hardware; the production, sharing and visualization of data; and the feedback to the community designers about the performance of the sensors. Therefore, the designers trusted people to materialize the projects while the people trusted the designers to bring the kits into existence. Thus smartness became a matter of trust and engagement. This set of relations is far from the notion of the smart as intelligent infrastructure to be deployed in the city, or as technological planning policies coming down from local government. The initiative to separate technology and knowledge on the one hand from urban infrastructure and government initiatives on the other is the starting point, for designers and backers, to understand smartness as being located and actualized in the cycle of actions which are followed in order to materialize sensor kits. The imaginary of the smart is placed in different parts of the development of the projects according to the participants and the stages of the process design. The smart is performed by the relationship between the kits, the designers and backers.

The Smart Citizen Kit was launched as a democratizing device for people to use to monitor their own air environment. The developers and stakeholders understood this as a way of empowering people. Moreover, the people who enthusiastically invested in it believed in that idea. One of the premises that underpinned the SCK and AQE projects was the idea that the production of technological knowledge about our intimate environments will no longer remain solely the domain of governments, scientific companies and academic researchers. This was a dream – as highlighted in *Nature* – that was shared by the developers of the kit, the people that funded it and its potential users.

These different stakeholders shared an underlying idea in their agenda for the smart citizens – that the individual's air quality needs could be determined via measurement information generated by a crowd of concerned citizens and monitored through participatory actions, instead of by a centralized and expert system controlled only by the government. It did not matter if there were some practical problems to solve – one of which is the difficulty in getting a sufficiently high standard of air quality measurements for this to be really useful and comparable to the commercial standards – because they had proven that it was possible and affordable.

To sum up, in the case of the smart city paradigm, the global imaginaries[5] of citizenship are put into play through visions of future *for a better life*. These visions are materialized in the development of the software and hardware of the device (the AQE or the SCK), the webpage that collects the data, etc. Therefore, the visions of future that the SCK or the AQE perform articulate the imaginary of a smart citizen with a practical goal to materialize the citizen sensors projects. In the next section I unpack the visions of future that participate in the making of the digital materialities associated with sensor technologies. Then in the section that follows I turn to my ethnographic materials to show how these were played out.

Visions of (and in) a global future

The anthropologist Henrietta Moore suggests that utopian visions are engaged with the present and the future simultaneously. It is when a society is facing a crucial experience of social and economic change that the utopian visions of a future life emerge. Utopian visions 'depend for their efficacy on the fact that they are written in the present whenever that present might be' (Moore 1990: 16). But these visions are about possible forms of social organization placed in a reachable future. This reachable future is not any specific one and the possible worlds are not infinite; both are linked to the conditions of the present. Hence the visions of future have to be attuned with the present society and with what is possible in order to exert any antici-patory influence on the present society (Elias 1998). Significantly, according to this argument, visions of future articulate present and future through the possible, and its enactment eagerness to social change. The same can be said regarding technological visions of future. These visions of future should not be confused with future imaginaries, although they are related.

Visions imply a 'willed social change' while imaginaries are experienced as an inspiration for creativity. Both are related allies, for example in science fiction narratives, and have a central role in design (Dourish and Bell 2011; Galloway 2013). 'Visions of future' lie in the core of design processes in technologies (Suchman 2012; Anderson 2010; Kinsley 2010; Galloway 2013) as design has a robust future orientation (Gunn, Otto and Smith 2013) and a well-developed set of practices and strategies to go there. One of these sets of practices and strategies – perhaps the most used in technology development – is that of the anticipatory practices (Anderson 2007; Kinsley 2012; Galloway 2013). These are what designers do in the present to anticipate or rehearse possible futures. These practices suggest that there is a state of things that can be advanced through concrete actions which provide and demonstrate whether that possible future is viable and whether it is the best to choose. This notion of anticipation relies on an image of what Dourish and Bell call the 'near future', a very close time at which we could arrive any time soon but that is 'reachable' in the present through anticipatory practices (2011). For example, smart city design relies on an expanding set of interdisciplinary knowledge (geography, economy, biology, chemistry, computing science, social science, etc.). At its core lies a process of foresight around what people could/should do with the data gathered from the sensors. Therefore, here 'visions of future' operate in the design process that brings together the technologies of sensors with the imaginary of a smart city, in a pragmatic manner, connecting global imaginaries and local expectations. This interplay between visions and imaginaries of future might be understood through the distinction made by Appadurai between design (locally) and planning (globally): 'where design can be caught up in an immediate need, trend, or material opportunity, planning aspires to be design with a social conscience and to connect the world of goods to the world of politics, justice and long-term resource constraints' (2013: 266).

The significance of *Future* in the design of low-cost sensors is twofold: on the one hand is the proposition of possible worlds; on the other hand, these possible worlds guide individual and collective future orientations (Nielsen 2011). The sensors are thus designed to produce social change; to quote Charles Lemert, 'social things' as technological solutions are imagined, designed and created to solve social problems (2006). In this respect, the design of 'sensors for the people' does not only want to solve the problem of air pollution. Rather they are designed to push people to take the initiative to intervene in their world by participating in the production and distribution of local knowledge, thus creating their future. 'Sensors for the people' are the point of intersection between visions and imaginaries of future, and between global plans and local designs. In other words, the design of the citizen sensors happens at the crossroad of local and global, imagination and vision.

Locating practical knowledge and tangible futures

In order to understand how 'visions of future' work as practical actions in the design of the sensors over the imaginaries of a global future, I now focus on the notions of *location* and *materiality* in relation to the people involved in the smart sensors projects.

Researchers have long been interested in how projects and developers are located in relation to digital technology. Academics have looked at this mainly from the study of what I call *techies* (developers involved in techno-logical design) or in what most of the authors call *communities* of them. Some examples include Free Software development communities (Kelty 2008), DEBIAN developers and hackers (Coleman 2008), industrial developers (English-Lueck 2002) and in San Francisco Bay Tech scene (Marwick 2010; Zandbergen 2011). The emplacement/location of technology designers in poles/centres of 'technological saturation' (English-Lueck 2002: 11) has been used to explain the assemblages between local and global that allow the emergence of these communities. To put it differently, 'location' works is an accurate term to describe the specificities of this type of localities. However, 'location' remains quite a vague notion and invites a different association between global and local.

In some ways the notion of 'location' repeats the dialectic of local vs global; however, it remains useful to establish the kind of atmospheres where those low-cost smart sensors projects are placed. As Marwick (who studied the use of social media among technological entrepreneurs in San Francisco Bay) says, if you are not located in San Francisco you become technologically irrelevant (2010). The same goes for those not physically placed 'locations', such as one Smart Citizen Kit stakeholder told me: 'if you're not part of "that" community or if you are not one of those within "such" project, you become technically off the point.' Location matters because these atmos-pheres boost the very synergies that are required so that these projects can emerge. Deployed technologies, designers, tools, ideas, things and questions converge in those locations, opening new possibilities of thinking and making digital technologies (Suchman 2011; English-Lueck 2002). It is at this point where visions of future enter the scene.

During my fieldwork, I saw the Air Quality Egg start as an Arduino shield with a cheap case made by 3D printing. The designers never focused on the quality of the sensors per se but on their possibilities as accessible technology for knowledge-making at community level. One of the goals at the beginning of the design stage was to make a difference regarding quality of life in small communities affected by pollution. At that moment the AQE project was mainly circulating in the Internet of Things (IoT) social platforms. As *Nature* journal highlighted, the AQE was circulating essentially among a group of hackers, makers and artists who called themselves the Sensemakers, gathering at meet-ups among IoT communities in Amsterdam and New York.[6] Sensemakers came to IoT London and IoT Barcelona looking for feedback and to engage more people to be part of the project.[7] Further on, one of the initiators of the project was working in Cosm – a beta platform to visualize and share data in the cloud obtained from IoT devices[8] – which was one of the most prominent project backers. The ideas of having a horizontal decision-making procedure as well as the openness to receive insights from any member of the communities linked to the project were main vectors of the Air Quality Egg evolution. Launching this in Kickstarter was a point-of-inflection for AQE because it was the first time that the project had come out of the circle of designers, developers and the IoT community. This was also the big first step taken by any open source project looking for supporters and developers.[9] The prototype had been successfully made during the earlier stages and some solutions and learnings had emerged from the other diverse projects of open source hardware/software groups related at some point with the AQE IoT. For instance, among the events that led up to this was a workshop for the AQE community in the IoT Barcelona group. The meeting was held in the city's Fab Lab because John, one of the organizers of the group, sometimes used its facilities and had become a regular participant who had also joined in with the management of the lab. The attendees were all members of the groups mentioned above, originating in Barcelona and other cities, or were present via Skype. Most of them were involved in the elaboration of code as well as the design of the hardware and the app. Ben, a very active developer of AQE, started the session by sharing the purposes of the workshop, telling us: 'I want all of us to become interconnected sensors producing and sharing knowledge about our local environments.' We spent the evening discussing the accuracy of the shield, the problems that the battery was causing, and arguing around the benefits of keeping a low-range radio.

We also examined a new example made and brought over by a member from Amsterdam, and verified its suitability for fitting with the chip. At this point one of the Fab Lab managers came over to tell us that he and others were working on an IoT project about air measurement. He outlined to Ben a possible scenario where air sensors would be deployed and would gather data across the entire city, but in half of the city the data would show that the air pollution had increased while in the other half it had not. He explained how, with the information gathered by the sensors, we would be able to search for the causes of pollution. He also told us that if the same sensor could also capture other environmental elements, enabling us to crosscut the data, this would possibly bring us closer to understanding what was causing

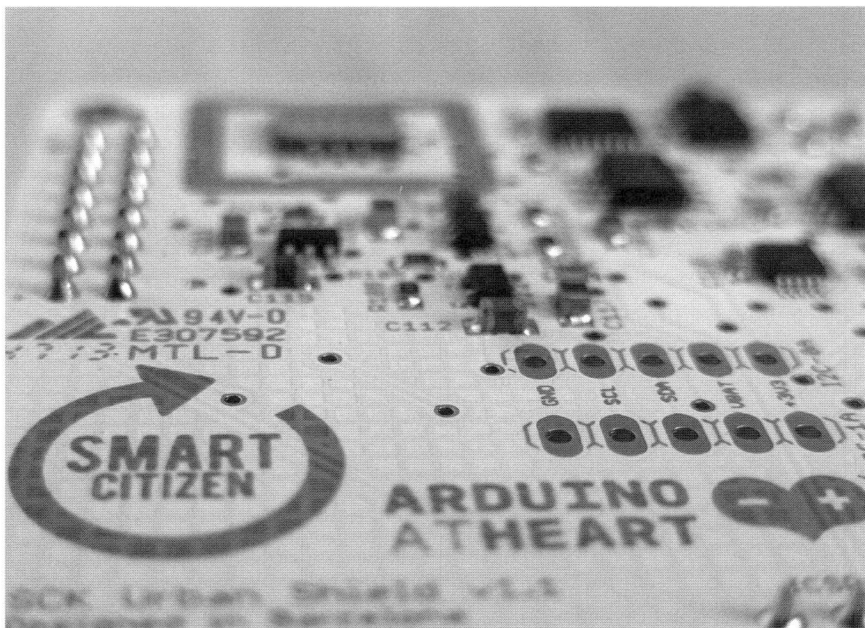

FIGURE 3.2 *Smart Citizen Kit. Photograph courtesy of Smart Citizen.*

the pollution. Most of us immediately became involved in a lively debate about how we could improve AQE, focusing on whether we would have to think about improving the firmware or to move to a different technology. All the discussions were based on the existing possibilities and limitations of the technology that we were making and how we could work on it.

The issue raised by these fieldwork experiences is that the 'visions of future' of what AQE has to be do not distinguish between people and technology or between citizens and governments. Rather these visions are emplaced in the practical knowledge and the possibles of the technology that they are making (Halse 2014; Pink 2014). They imagine continuities and changes for the project as well as possible scenarios where these technologies could become something meaningful for someone other than the developers. AQE might be able to encourage people to participate in the conversation about air quality but first it enabled its designers – sensemakers, as some of them like to call themselves – to imagine and intervene in the sustainable and smart conversation.[10]

For most of the developers working in the field of open source hardware sensors and DIY, Air Quality Egg was a turning point for the sensemakers. The first low-cost air quality sensor generated a huge step in learning that initiated the specific technology design that other projects would continue.

Therefore these projects can be seen as dual sites, as they both produce and are the locus for digital social knowledge. These projects create/crystallize digital interventions on the one hand, as such materializing a way for ordinary people to get involved in knowledge production about important matters in everyday life. On the other hand, they entail the very design of a sensor in a way that makes explicit the relationship between hardware design and the invisible technological knowledge production for most of the people. Thinking in imaginaries as much as visions as something that is making/is being made in the ordinary life of design through concrete actions is a turning point which tends to make visible that 'localized' local and global. Instead of enhancing an invisible ubiquity of sensors, the 'sensors for the people' project developers attempt to make them visible for all.

It is because the sensors became affordable that they brought into existence a 'thing' which is not the hardware or the software of any sensor but a specific way by which knowledge is produced through technology. Citizenship is a matter of how information is gathered and how that could be part of urban ordinary life rather than an entelechy placed in some kind of intangible imaginary. The future becomes something tangible. For the 'sensors for the people' developers, there is a way of materializing the social forms they desire and in which they are involved: by making boards.

Affordable material knowledge

SCK and AQE became realities when they started to be valuable in the circuits of high-technology production. This was due to three movements: first, when the imaginary of citizenship became a commonsensical idea and something that it seemed necessary to play out through techno-logical design; second, through the rise of the Do-It-Yourself and Makers movements as actual actors in the technological scene through 3D printing (Lindtner 2014); and third, with the inclusion of 'people' in the formula of the future technology. I now develop this idea further through a discussion of my fieldwork experience.

My research on the Smart Citizen Kit project began with my first encounter with SCK in March 2012 at an IoT Barcelona meeting. At this point the possi-bility of not depending on government or industry for the city in which we lived to be *smart* was a solid milestone for everyone involved in the devel-opment of the Smart Citizen Kit. There was a strong feeling that governments either did not care about local pollution levels or that there was a lack of ways for local people to take action against pollution. At the last SCK community meeting that I attended at Hangar[11] in November 2014, the idea of opening up science to citizens to produce commitment was also a concern. The big shift during these two-and-a-half years, along with many events and changes in the IoT industry, was that SCK had become a reality for the public and for the industry. In the IoT World Forum edition 2013 which I attended, Smart Citizen Kit was launched in the big leagues sponsored by Cisco.[12] This was the first international event to be devoted exclusively to IoT. People and companies came to Barcelona for this event, which was seen as a hub for information about the cutting edge in sensoring and actuating technology. In the same year, in two different Smart City events hosted in different countries, SCK was present as a novel *people* technology.

However, in the meantime, another important shift was happening with the emergence of the Internet of Everything (IoE). This was a step beyond the Internet of Things. Cisco 'defines the Internet of Everything (IoE) [13] as bringing together people, process, data, and things to make networked connections more relevant and valuable than ever before. Thus turning information into actions that create new capabilities, richer experiences, and unprecedented economic opportunity for businesses, individuals, and countries' (Cisco IoE Homepage 2014). The IoE's ethos aims to connect data, things, people and experience, which is also a goal both for the industry and the open source hardware designers of the IoT. In both Air Quality Egg and Smart Citizen Kit, the visions of future are also connected to the imaginary of what the IoE could give to the world and what people could do with it. The position that SCK took in the IoE scenario allowed the project to extend the possibilities to intervene in other spheres of social knowledge production, from high-tech events to open science discourses. The introduction of *people* as something that matters for the future of this particular technology opens up the possibility for these projects to be considered as part of the cutting edge.

The designers and backers of AQE and SCK are acutely aware of the ways in which they are working and seeking to intervene in society, as well as of the contradictions and cleavages that have been part of the trajectories of these projects. Indeed it is this awareness that enables them to continually resituate their design processes within the smart technologies scenario. Moreover, AQE and SCK projects created *things* that are now part of the world – things that require technical, electronic and digital knowledge to interact with them, thereby producing a new relationship. The things not only encourage 'citizens to participate in a conversation about air quality' (as the SCK designers promoted it) but insist that people are disposed to technological learning. In these projects the hardware matters because it is the intervention in itself. At the same time, the intention of the projects is to create ways for others to intervene through their roles in the production, management and sharing of local knowledge. The *possible* things that people could do with affordable sensors are what endow the projects with their materiality.

At the core of these projects is an 'emergent and relational "process-based"' (Leach and Wilson 2014: 2) way of materializing knowledge. The relationships that the AQE and SCK projects establish with people is what produce knowledge, rather than people producing knowledge as users of sensors. This rethinking of the relationality of people and technologies is akin to Wendy Chun's questioning of the division between software, hardware, the digital and the physical, instead suggesting that both in the code display and the tasks that bring it to life, the material is central (Chun 2004). Here the hardware and protocols have physical attributes, while, as Chun puts it, for common sense 'the human task of making connections, setting switches, and inputting values ("direct programming"), as well as the human and machine task of coordinating the various parts of the computer [...] lacks physicality' (Chun 2004: 28). She also emphasizes that the 'software has become a common abbreviation for culture and hardware, a shortened form of nature' (Chun 2004: 48). These common understandings of digital technologies mask the specific ways that knowledge is produced and the concrete actions that shape a technology and make 'objects' interchangeable. What is at stake here is the role of technology design in making visible the complexities in contemporary public life, through the production of information and by calling for social and political participation in urban everyday life through making and opening up technology (DiSalvo 2009). These intersections are where AQE and SCK are posed for the designers and backers – that is, both for those who focus on building up the IoE and also for the public.

Conclusion

Researching imaginaries is at the core of design anthropology. In this chapter I have proposed that in order to take this seriously we need to understand how imaginaries and visions operate within the design process. In doing so I have also differentiated between two processes: first, the active process of attuning the present and future through envisioning achievable/possible/potential futures in which technologies are designed to participate; and second, the social formation of imaginaries that are vital for conceptualizing designs.

In the case of the low-cost sensor design process addressed here, citizenship, in the form of shared imaginaries, has a distinctive role among other imaginaries. It both plays a role within the process of the development of design projects and is also the goal of the design process. Here, citizenship (as imaginary) is situated through visions of future (of a better life) that guide the design-making processes. Imagination is thus the result of active material practices that bring the sensor kits themselves into social life.

In turn imaginaries are embedded in the realm of the global, which becomes a site of intervention for the designers. Here, the local is not a physical place that constrains and shapes the design experience but rather it is the context where the synergies that nourished the visions of future were generated. Thus global and local connote different things in each specific design processard. They are therefore floating ascriptions, which are contingent on how other dimensions shape the experience of every design process, rather than being explanatory categories that will define the design.

Notions of smart and future are both constituted in processes through which the sensors are made. Smart Futures are updated and made as an outcome of the process through which the technologies are made that they believe are needed in order to attain the *possible worlds* that they aspire to. In short, Smart Futures are both embedded in and materialized through processes of technological making.

The 'ethnographic place' (Pink 2009) is a term that Sarah Pink has used to describe the encounter in which 'different types, qualities and tempora- ralities of things and persons come together as part of the process of the making of ethnographic knowledge' (Pink and Morgan 2013: 354). The people who inhabited the ethnographic place of my fieldwork were aware of the multiplicity of ways and formats that knowledge is produced in design, in technology, and also in the ethnographic encounter. They undertook their own knowledge-based processes in this 'place', shaping in that encounter what *material* means to them, and bringing into existence *possible* technol- ogies that they imagined, based on their experiential knowledge from other projects. What AQE and SCK bring into existence is an affordable way to be part of the making of these possible worlds. They give tangible form to certain processes that other technological forms make invisible for most people. Again affordable means more than low-cost; rather it means that these pieces of open hardware materialize digital–material technological knowledge in accessible and public ways.

4

Envisioning the smart home: Reimagining a smart energy future[1]

Yolande Strengers

The smart home is firmly situated at the nexus between the digital, material and human. Entangled as they are, these ingredients of the smart home are being 'lashed together' (Dourish and Bell 2011) to create new visions and realities for our future. While there is no universal definition, the smart home can be defined as 'a residence equipped with computing and information technology which anticipates and responds to the needs of the occupants' (Aldrich 2003: 17). One key ambition for the smart home, advocated by governments and energy utilities, is to solve national energy demand problems by decarbonizing and 'de-peaking' energy systems by reconfiguring and intervening in the home. With such high stakes being placed on smart homes and their associated technologies, there is a clear need to interrogate the promises they hold, as well as analyse the type of realities that are unfolding now, as people begin to integrate these technologies into their everyday lives. This chapter is dedicated to this task, aiming to demystify, probe and reimagine the visions and alternate realities that the smart home is realizing, and potentially can realize, to achieve a lower energy demand future.

The smart home global appliance market, defined as products with built-in connectivity, is predicted to reach nearly US$25 billion by 2018 (ABIresearch 2013: 1894). A key feature of this luxury market espoused on smart home companies' websites is a commitment to achieving heightened levels of household comfort, cleanliness, convenience, security, entertainment, communication and energy efficiency. This last ambition links to government and energy industry aspirations for a 15 per cent global reduction in green-house gas emissions by 2020 (Climate Group 2008) and a peak electricity demand reduction of between 13 and 24 per cent (IEA 2011: 5) through smart technology. In particular, 'building increased smartness into homes' (DECC 2009: 20), via two-way programmable thermostats and smart appliances, is anticipated to 'unlock the vast potential of the smart grid' (CEA 2011: i), where these technologies will 'empower consumers to monitor, manage and adjust their electricity consumption' (AEMC 2012: 29).

As such, advocates of smart home technologies aim to achieve a somewhat paradoxical interventionist agenda, whereby it is possible to maintain or increase standards of electrically enabled living while simultane-ously reducing electricity consumption and/or shifting it outside peak times.[2] Despite enormous political and marketing investments in these technologies worldwide, there has been very little critical investigation of the effects smart home technologies are likely to have in our everyday lives. Questions remain regarding whether smart homes are able to achieve their intended energy management ambitions in real-life situations. How will they be taken up, contested, rejected and/or modified by householders who incorporate these technologies into their everyday lives? And what does this mean for energy consumption in homes?

More broadly, critics have been quick to point out the unrealistic utopian aspirations of smart technologies (Morozov 2013; Strengers 2013). In his aptly named exposé of all things digital (*To Save Everything Click Here*), Morozov (2013) warns of the dangers of technological 'solutionism' pervading all facets of society, including the smart home, where it manifests as a utopian vision for harmonious, convenient and efficient living. Another obvious reference point (and clear warning sign) comes from the past. Nyborg and Røpke (2011) remind us that the ingredients of the smart home have a long history, with new elements and trends added along the way. Analyses of the 'homes of tomorrow' from the early twentieth century (Horrigan 1986), the 'electronic cottage' from the 1980s (Toffler 1980) and the more recent 'smart house' (Berg 1994) reveal that utopian visions for our future have unfolded very differ-ently from the ways they were imagined.

Current smart homes are similarly characterized by utopian aspirations alongside a disturbing absence of social research conducted with people who actually live in them. Wilson et al.'s (2014: n.p.) review of smart home literature found that only 20 per cent of publications were based in the social sciences (economics, psychology and energy). Over half (61 per cent) came from computer science, engineering and mathematics, and the remainder (19 per cent) sat in medicine, health, nursing and biology. The majority of publica-tions only made cursory mention of 'users'. Of those studies that do include people, most have focused on 'user experiences' with discrete technologies, rather than the broader implications of these technologies for how we live. Studies have focused on 'user acceptance' of smart technologies (Zpryme 2011) or how smart homes can best respond to 'user needs' (Gann et al. 1999). Less attention has been paid to ways in which the human, digital and material come together to constitute new ways of being in the world.

Recognizing these limitations, my starting point here is not what people think about energy or how they 'use' smart home technologies, but how they negotiate everyday living – doing the laundry, cooking dinner, running the air-conditioner – and how these dynamics are disrupted or transformed through smart home technologies. Following scholars of consumption and social practice (Shove 2010; Warde 2005), I am interested in moving beyond human-centred analyses or 'user studies' where there is often a stark demarcation between humans and nonhumans. Recent iterations of social practice theory draw on concepts of materiality and agency from science and technology studies to understand technologies and infrastructures as elements in, or active ingredients of, social practices (Reckwitz 2002; Shove et al. 2012). Reckwitz, for example, argues that the material world 'necessarily participate[s] in social practices just as human beings do' (Reckwitz 2002: 208). This blurs the boundaries between the digital, material and human, and encourages us to understand how they come together to enact new forms of everyday practice.

In the discussion that follows I draw loosely on these theoretical ideas to briefly interrogate three intersecting elements of the vision for smart homes emerging from utility providers, governments and their regulators, and smart home manufacturers, designers and advocates. Notably, these do not represent discrete or separate pathways, but often compete with, overlap and complement each other. I continue by outlining three alternate realities for smart homes. Here I demonstrate how digital technologies, material environments and humans are reconstituting everyday practice in new and unpredictable ways. The analysis focuses specifically on home automation devices and appliances, such as smart washing machines or thermostats, rather than looking more broadly at the suite of technologies proposed for the smart home, such as micro-generation or electric vehicles. As such, this is by no means a complete catalogue of the smart home vision or its manifestations in everyday life, but rather a launching pad from which to engage in discussion regarding the smart home as site of and for intervention aimed at achieving lower and less peaky energy futures. I conclude by considering some alternative possibilities for reimagining and redesigning smart home technologies in ways that support everyday life and the energy demand reductions intended for them.

Envisioning the smart home

The quantified home

Smart home advocates frequently espouse the virtues of capturing and counting numbers to quantify and change consumption and behaviour. This approach mirrors the Quantified Self movement, which involves self-tracking and monitoring of any physical, behavioural or environmental information in order to monitor or instigate change. The movement is gaining advocates and critics in the era of Big Data. Morozov (2013: 260–1), for example, describes the field as 'madly devoted to articulating facts' through numbers, which generates narratives or 'numeric imaginations' that 'seek out quantitative and linear casual explanations that have little respect for the complexity of the actual human world'. This resembles Hacking's (1982: 28) critique of the 'fetishistic collection of overt statistical data' and the 'avalanche of printed numbers' which has played a much broader role in the governance of populations.

The smart home can similarly be viewed as a numerical imagination with its own avalanche of data. From the morning cup of tea to overnight water heating, the assumption is that everything can be better managed (or governed) through counting. The dominant numerical logic found in government and industry reports is as follows: data and information made available via smart energy technologies will 'empower consumers' (OSTP 2012) to 'take control' (CEA 2011) of their consumption and make 'informed choices' (AEMC 2011) about how they use energy, thereby unlocking the 'vast potential' (CEA 2011) of these smart technologies. The ideal energy consumer is thus also imagined to have a numeric imagination, whereby data about energy inform rational and linear decisions to curb or shift energy consumption in the home.

Of course, how householders respond to and integrate energy feedback into their household practices is considerably more complicated than this. As others have warned, quantified energy consumption, displayed through feedback devices such as smartphone apps and in-home displays, can serve to justify or mask existing everyday practices which use energy in the home rather than reconfigure or transform them (Hargreaves et al. 2010, 2013; Marres 2012; Pierce et al. 2010; Strengers 2013). Similarly, increasing information from thermostats can be confusing, misunderstood or ignored, resulting in other potential realities and possibilities as discussed later in this chapter (Meier et al. 2010).

Interestingly, the quantified home does not only require humans to develop numerical imaginations; material appliances, too, are expected to respond to and act on this digital information. In many smart home visions, appliances communicate with dynamic pricing tariffs, enabling what is referred to as 'prices-to-devices', whereby appliances '"listen" to the price of electricity and operate accordingly' (Hledik 2009: 31) to reduce electricity during periods of peak demand or in response to other market signals. Similarly, some automated devices operate by quantifying and then replicating numerically measurable forms of 'user behaviour'. For example, the Nest thermostat develops a 'schedule' of thermostat settings based on occupant usage and input, in addition to providing a graphical interface featuring energy data and information (Yang et al. 2014). This device collects and analyses data to imagine what householders want and provides accordingly. Such manifestations blur the line between who, or what, is in control, and disrupt traditional human–material boundaries through the emergence of new digital relationships. This entanglement is continued in realizing a second element of the smart home vision as a site of automation.

The automated home

While there is nothing inherently new in the idea of replacing human labour with technology, the notion of automating appliances, and by extension everyday practices, changes and reverses some of the human–material roles expected to be performed in the smart home. For example, former *SmartGridNews* editor Jesse Berst (2012) argues that 'we're wasting our time trying to make people smart about energy. We should be making our devices smart about energy.' According to Berst, consumers prefer 'cruise control' when it comes to their energy demand. They should not have to monitor their own energy performance through energy feedback as advocated in the vision for the quantified home; rather, 'they should tell the system (once) how they want it to respond and then let the system do the watching' (Berst 2012). The key idea here is that appliances such as washing machines, dishwashers and air conditioners should do the 'energy work' (and other domestic labour) otherwise assigned to humans. This might mean anticipating washing, dishwashing and comfort 'needs' or habits, or only turning appliances on when energy prices are low.

Smart thermostats readily embody this vision of automated control; they generally involve the automation of cooling and heating appliances, particularly air conditioning. Smart thermostats, also known as two-way thermostats, can communicate with and be controlled by utility providers or demand response systems. They are an extension of programmable thermostats, which have been around for over sixty years, the critical difference being that smart thermostats can be controlled remotely (Hamilton et al. 2012). Smart thermostats can also notify customers (and their air conditioners) of price events and emergencies, and can be programmed by householders (and electricity providers) to automatically lower or raise the temperature during price events (Meier et al. 2010) – a strategy referred to as 'set-and-forget' (Harper-Slaboszewicz et al. 2012).

Oksanen-Sarela and Pantzar (2001: 212) describe these ideas as a form of 'cultural determinism', whereby it is 'natural' to view technologies as replacing people in everyday life contexts. Digital ethnographers have also critiqued the assumptions embedded in this vision of automation, arguing that it requires an 'a priori specificity and rigidity that conflict[s] with a large body of ethnographic research on the organic, opportunistic, and improvisational ways that families construct, maintain, and modify their routines and plans' (Davidoff et al. 2006: 19). Other researchers studying the use of digital technology in the home note that the functional and goal-centred ideals of some technologies such as home automation reflect a masculine image of domestic life (Livingstone 1992: 119) and exclude women, who are more interested in the significance of domestic technology in their lives for minimizing domestic chaos (Livingstone 1992; Logan et al. 1995; Rode et al. 2004).

These studies also remind us of the silencing of domestic labour in this vision of automated practice. Two forms of silencing can be identified here. First, automation is premised on an extremely functional and utilitarian understanding of everyday life where we can identify and separate discrete activities. Wyche et al.'s (2007) study of 'pottering' reminds us that 'pleasure is taken in mundane, seemingly unessential activities' which often have no identifiable boundaries or clear intentions: 'pottering-time is dead, unplanned, unstructured, or [...] insignificant' (Wych et al. 2007: 1896). In other words, much of the activity performed in the home cannot be reduced to a singular identifiable practice (e.g. doing the laundry) but rather represents an unplanned or continuous fluidity best represented by concepts such as 'flow' (Pink and Leder Mackley 2014). In family life, for example, laundry is more likely to be done in opportunistic 'time gaps' rather than when energy is cheaper (Nicholls and Strengers 2015).

A second form of silencing takes place because, unlike other home appliances, automated technologies aim to operate in the background of everyday life. They are not always discrete technologies in their own right, but attach to existing household technologies, such as washing machines, lights, televisions, windows or air conditioners. Indeed, part of the appeal of the smart home is this seamless integration, or what Berry et al. (2007: 240) describe as 'controlled ambience [...] in which technologies recede, blending seamlessly with walls, ceilings and doors, furniture, decorative features and outdoor spaces'. Berry et al. (2007) refer to the first issue of *Australian Smart Home Ideas* (published 2005), which celebrates this fact. The magazine carried advertisements for a sound system which has been made invisible, and presented readers with the challenge of finding its elements: 'There are 42 speakers in this room. Can you find them?' (*Australian Smart Home Ideas*, cited in Berry et al. 2007: 240). In another magazine feature article on smart homes cited by Berry et al. (2007: 240), readers are invited 'to imagine a future freed of the "barrage of switches on every wall"'. Here the digital enables the receding of the material, while seeking to free occupants from the encumbrances of either. Through this promise of freedom from material and digital concerns, such language also points to a third element of the smart home vision – one which seeks to enhance and improve everyday lifestyles.

The enhanced home

The Association of Home Appliance Manufacturers (AHAM) adopts a deceptively neutral definition of a smart appliance, describing it as 'a modernisation of the electricity usage system of a home appliance so that it monitors, protects, and automatically adjusts its operation *to the needs of its owner*' (in Hamilton et al. 2012: 409–10, emphasis added). The central idea embodied in this statement is that automated appliances support, enable and provide predetermined occupant 'needs'. In the last part of the definition, the AHAM avoids any recognition of, or responsibility for, the role that appliance manufacturers may play in establishing what these needs are. This sits at odds with history, which demonstrates how energy utilities and appliance manufacturers have consistently and successfully played a central role in establishing and transforming new 'needs' for comfort, convenience and cleanliness (Forty 1986; Shove 2003).

More explicitly, the vision depicted here reinvents an old idea, where electricity provided 'the modern housewife with a perfect servant – clean, silent and economical' (Forty 1986: 207). Smart technology is again being positioned as a modern servant, meeting and taking care of the needs of home occupants. Close to a century after this vision was first promoted to households, home automation company Control4 (2013) rekindles these ideas and adds new ones by inviting its customers to 'imagine a house that remembers to lock itself at 10pm. Shades that close as the sun hits. A home theatre that takes care of lights, sound and picture in one touch.' The company's tagline – 'life is just better with a little more control' – references the desire to assign housework to someone or something else, featuring automation as the way to be 'in control' of domestic activity (Control4 2013). These ideals are further expanded to encompass not only the control of household labour, but of home security, comfort and entertainment. The outcome or 'selling point' for householders is 'unprecedented levels of convenience', with energy bill savings and increased home security listed as important side benefits (Harper-Slaboszewicz et al. 2012: 393).

Implicit in these sentiments is an underlying commitment to continual lifestyle improvement, where more (convenience, comfort, entertainment, security) is better than less, and in which these expectations depend and thrive on new devices and technologies that use energy. In this way, the smart home also promises to enhance everyday practice by promoting utopian ideals of seamlessly integrated, harmonious and labour-free home life, which is efficiently run, silently managed, and enables new forms of (electrically enabled) pleasure and luxury (Berg 1994; Dourish and Bell 2011).

Taken together, these three elements of the smart home vision – the quantified, automated and enhanced home – remind us that the agenda intended for this digital technology is far from neutral. The smart home seeks to intervene in everyday life to manage energy in very specific and numerical ways, and intends to carry out the labour and enhance the leisure performed and experienced in the home. While by no means a definite list, these elements exist simultaneously to constitute the smart home vision. They embody both an active and passive role for humans, who are expected to take control of their energy consumption through monitoring and management, while concurrently assigning some of this control to digital devices. Putting this vision to one side, I now turn to examples where smart home technologies have entered everyday life, to consider what realities are beginning to unfold as a result.

Alternate realities for the smart home

Coordinating practices

One of the ways in which automation technologies, particularly smart appliances, are entering the home is as a form of coordination, mediation, disruption or intersection across a variety of everyday routines. Davidoff et al. (2006: 19) argue that coordinating technologies are becoming a necessity in a world increasingly characterized by the feeling of being 'out of control due to the complex and rapidly changing logistics that result from integrating and prioritizing work, school, family, and enrichment activities'.

In contrast to the vision of automating what are seen to be largely fixed and immovable practices, Davidoff et al. (2006) refer to smart technology's role in creating increasing degrees of flexibility around different sites of activity. These researchers conclude that 'to give families a sense of control over their lives, a smart home system will have to both support the concept of routine, but not bind families to that notion. Such a system will need to allow plans and routines to evolve organically' (Davidoff et al. 2006: 28). This system, they argue, will need to allow for 'battles' over the thermostat, substantial innovation, 'constantly shifting targets', failed routines, and many time-intensive tasks that are nonetheless 'vital to our identities as Mums, Dads and Families' (Davidoff et al. 2006: 29–31). Automation and control are positioned here as something that is fluid and dynamic, embedded in daily routine, and not explicitly focused on the consumption of energy in and around the home.

Similarly, Leshed and Sengers' (2011: 912) research reveals the cultural complexities associated with being 'busy', which they describe as a social norm that cuts across many lines of domestic activity. They argue that productivity tools have a broader role than the generation of goal-oriented 'to-do' lists. Rather, they are also used by householders to 'renegotiate their goals and priorities, feel socially committed, manage ever-changing real-life interactions, feel in control, and organize not only what they do, but also who they are' (Leshed and Sengers 2011: 912). Similarly, automation technologies might be thought to generate 'downtime', 'slowness' or 'cold spots' of activity (Southerton 2003), not necessarily of the luxurious kind espoused by home automation companies, but more practically experienced as a moment to 'charge the batteries' (Leshed and Sengers 2011: 912). In this example, control does not feature as the technological management or surveillance of the home, but as the ability to dynamically schedule time when no management is required, and where everyday life can be freed from the demands of people and technology. This opens the possibility for smart home technologies to disrupt and reschedule time in ways that might facilitate different peaks in energy.

However, this coordinating role of home automation technologies, while enabling practices to shift to off-peak times of the day, can also increase energy demand overall. For example, Røpke and Christensen (2012: 359) point out that 'ICT contributes to both the increasing complexity of everyday life and to the handling of this complexity – making possible the management of more practices'. Home automation technologies can be thought of in this way, where they feature as devices intended to manage – and do more – increasingly complex tasks. A busy parent can be making plans to pick up a child by SMS while cooking dinner. At the same time, automation may be enabling another domestic activity, such as laundering, to be performed in the background. Røpke and Christensen (2012) note that this ability to perform multiple practices at the same time presents new opportunities for energy to be consumed. The concept of multi-tasking and making use of 'dead time' leads these researchers to suggest that 'more energy can be spent per unit of time' (Røpke and Christensen 2012: 359), presenting opportunities for smart technologies to both increase and decrease household energy consumption.

Delegating practices

A more complicated suite of realities for home automation technologies can be found in fully automated smart homes. One area of past empirical investigation is with communities of Orthodox Jews, who have been using home automation technology for decades to coordinate the religious practice of resting on the Sabbath, and to maintain the modern interpretation, which is that it is forbidden to turn electrical devices on or off on this day (Woodruff et al. 2007). In their qualitative study of home automation technologies in Orthodox Jewish families, Woodruff et al (2007: 529) explain how the Sabbath is experienced 'as a time of peace, relaxation, and reflection', which resonates with the increasing desire to generate downtime or cold spots of activity discussed above.

The concealment of everyday activities is one of the attractions of automation for this community: 'more technology provide[s] the illusion of less technology' (Woodruff et al. 2007: 531). However, this technology also reveals and enhances subtle sensory experiences, adding ambience and atmosphere on the Sabbath through the automation of lighting, water fountains and the scheduled production of meals, thereby reinforcing and establishing new meanings (of aesthetics) and routines (of meal time). Appliances and lighting that might have otherwise remained on (or off) for the entirety of the Sabbath are pre-scheduled to operate in specific rooms at specific times, both saving and using electricity associated with the Sabbath's activities of 'going to synagogue, spending time with family and friends, studying religious materials, reflecting, taking naps, and going for walks' (Woodruff et al. 2007: 529). As well as enabling or enhancing many practices, this has the unanticipated effect of making new demands on practice. This reminds us that home automation technologies are not passive slaves: they act back, taking on human-like characteristics and embodying agency by guiding, facilitating and even recommending action.

For example, in Woodruff et al.'s (2007) study, an automated light turning off in a recreation room sent a 'message' to the children within it to go to bed, thereby performing the role of the parent or carer. Similarly, lights turning off or dimming after the Sabbath meal were an indication that it was time for guests to leave, performing the role of a polite host. These human-like roles enabled by the digital intervention were not viewed negatively or in reference to a judgemental 'Big Brother'. Rather, householders associated automation with 'caretaking, anticipation, and guidance – roles such as servant (sometimes quite a wise servant), mother, and wife' and 'occasional allusions to more godlike or omniscient characteristics' (Woodruff et al. 2007: 533). Such findings raise interesting questions about the human-like characteristics conveyed through different digital–material configurations in the home.

Similarly, Mozer (2005) describes his experience of living in a self-learning smart home as being like living with a housemate. The environment Mozer refers to is one where the smart home learns and predicts its occupants' behaviours, operating seamlessly and invisibly in the background. However, it is precisely its invisible workings that make the automated home so visible to Mozer. He describes how he 'found it disconcerting when ACHE [Adaptive Control of Home Environments] would incorrectly predict my passage into another room and lights would turn on or off in an unoccupied area of the house', and notes that 'when ACHE is disabled, the home seems cold and uninviting' (Mozer 2005: 291). In contrast to the idea that this automated system can and should learn to fit in with and support his routines, Mozer (2005: 292) describes how he found himself trying to fit in with the routines 'learnt' by the system: 'For instance, if I were at work at 8 p.m., I would realize that under ordinary circumstances, I might have left several hours earlier; consequently, ACHE would be expecting me, and I felt compelled to return home. I regularized my schedule in order to accommodate ACHE and its actions.' Koskela et al. (2004: 239) report similar findings in their study of home automation technologies, where the invisibility of automation simultaneous gives the house a 'life of its own'.

These examples remind us that automated technologies do not operate on the basis of some pre-designed or in-built 'scripts' (Akrich, 1992) or morality (Jelsma 2006), nor are they merely appropriated or domesticated into the home (Silverstone et al. 1992). Automation technology's role in practice is more subtle and dynamic than that. In the examples discussed above, they make demands on everyday practice that potentially reconfigure its existing constellation. This is not a unidirectional imposition or reassignment of control; it is a cyclic process in which agency is circulated and redistributed between humans, the digital and the material, through practice.

Absence and DIY

There are two other notable realities for home automation technologies as they encounter everyday life, where they appear as complicated, unworkable, uncontrollable, irrelevant and/or fallible. The first occurs when these technologies are experienced as overly complex, or when they break down or do things that annoy and frustrate householders. In these situations technologies are switched off and regulated to the back of the cupboard; in short, they do not perform anything at all. In some instances smart technologies never even make it out of the box – doomed to be irrelevant from their very entrance into the home (Pierce et al. 2010). In other instances, automation technologies come to constitute a do-it-yourself (DIY) practice of repair and innovation.

In the first of these scenarios householders may lack the skills to use and fix automated functions when they break down or 'play up', or they may not be clear on why they would want to use them in the first place. For example, Meier et al. (2010: 9) find that 'occupants find thermostats cryptic and baffling to operate because manufacturers often rely on obscure, and sometimes even contradictory, terms, symbols, procedures, and icons'. In their review of programmable thermostat usability studies, these researchers cite an impressive list of thermostat (and energy) misconceptions and complaints that illustrate how householders are not always (or often) expert operators of systems, and often use complex thermostats as an on/off switch. In this situation, a smart thermostat is no different from a 'dumb' thermostat, being so complicated that its features are considered unusable.

A second scenario is that the complicated and/or failure-prone system of automation can constitute its own DIY practice, requiring constant interference and attention and rendering the system highly visible and demanding. Rather than rejecting or ignoring this technology, this may lead some householders to participate in practices of maintenance and repair located specifically around this suite of technologies. For example, Woodruff et al.'s (2007: 530) participants note that the automation system X10 is 'notoriously unreliable' and depends on the competence of 'tech-savvy "do-it-yourself-ers"' who have impressive stories of both success and failure.

Like other DIY home improvement practices, the 'project' of home automation involves 'sweat, sawdust, frustrations and satisfactions generated through the active combination of bodies, tools, materials and existing structures, all of which are implicated in repairing, maintaining or improving the home' (Shove et al. 2007: 49). Such projects are emergent in the sense that they never go exactly to plan, and because they always involve complexity, exploration and uncertainty. Importantly, DIY automation necessarily intersects with a range of other practices that it seeks to automate. This arrangement is inherently unstable, perhaps more than practices usually are, because DIY automation is deliberately 'experimental' and does not always 'work', or at least not always as planned. In the case of a DIY automated washing machine, the implication is that the washing might not always 'work' either, or at least not in the ways intended. These realities generate a fluid field of possibilities for automation's role in everyday practice, ranging from having no role whatsoever, through to radical improvisation and intervention.

Digital intervention possibilities

Home automation's stealthy and silent approach positions it as an 'immaterial material' (Pierce and Paulos 2010) in the practices it seeks to automate, making its role as a digital intervention sometimes difficult to pin down. By attaching itself to or merging itself with existing material appliances in the home in order to schedule, anticipate, automate or otherwise enable practice, automation aims, sometimes unsuccessfully, to maintain a passive role in everyday life. In other instances automation can manifest itself in a highly active role, or make very active demands on householders, by requiring constant attention and responses to numerical information, subtly proposing or attempting to enhance existing lifestyles, or by needing constant attention and maintenance.

This analysis thus demonstrates the sometimes surprising and contra-dictory ways in which the smart home is being imagined and enacted in everyday life, where smart technologies can engender multiple realities and intervention possibilities, often simultaneously. A smart thermostat can embody ideals of rational and efficient control of energy demand as well as a more comfortable life. It is also means for householders to take control of managing and controlling home comfort by responding to constant data. Alternatively, or additionally, householders can delegate control of doing this thermal work to the thermostat. The thermostat can also take control, by recommending when it should be used, on what settings, and for how long, thereby bringing new meanings and expectations to the practices of heating and cooling. The smart thermostat can also be completely ignored – its automation functions deemed uncontrollable or irrelevant. Finally, a smart thermostat's complicated and seemingly erratic workings may constitute it as a DIY project – an activity to be continually 'worked on' (or only used by a tech-savvy person). Most importantly, automation can mean all or some of these things at once.

For those seeking to understand the smart home as a potential mode of intervention into everyday life, this analysis presents both significant challenges and opportunities. On the one hand, it is difficult to think beyond visions for passive and utilitarian control, when these understandings continue to pervade industry, policy and design circles, and attract significant funding and investment. On the other, studies of home automation in everyday life, alongside other ethnographic and social research on the home, provide alter-native conceptualizations for redesigning the smart home to support energy demand reductions or other ambitions.

On this more positive note, one possibility might include taking seriously Dourish and Bell's (2011) invitation to engage productively with the concept of 'mess' in everyday life, including ideas of 'pottering' (Wyche et al. 2007) and unplanned 'flow' (Pink and Leder Mackley 2014). Rather than seeking to remove mess, designers could engage with messiness as 'inspiring, productive, generative, and engaging'. Mess is not something to be fixed, tamed or removed; indeed this is an impossible goal. Rather, messiness is 'dynamic, adaptive, fluid, and open' (Dourish and Bell 2011: 93); it is the stuff upon which innovation, improvisation and adaptation is founded. In this way, 'mess' and everyday environments have their own intelligence or smartness which is 'organic, opportunistic and improvisational' (Davidoff et al. 2006: 19). Taking this idea seriously would involve conceptualizing and theorizing mess as something other than mess – a term which tends to provoke negative and chaotic connotations. Mess could be reconceptualized as fine-grained networks of routines, or the outcome of different householders' intersecting practices. It is has dynamics, rhythms and patterns. It is observable and knowable. It could be supported by and through design that seeks to shift domestic activity in new directions (Strengers 2014).

Another suggestion is to broaden our understanding of for whom, or what, we are designing smart homes. This might mean doing away with the gender-less and utilitarian concept of the 'user', by engaging with the eclectic composition of households and their human and nonhuman occupants. Pets and pests, for example, while not often captured in the generalist notion of a 'user', can play a significant role in how practices are performed in the home (Strengers et al. 2014). Similarly, babies and young children often do not directly 'use' technologies, but may be significant for how and why they are used the way they are.

There is also an opportunity here to think about how we might design for different types of time. If part of the aim of the smart home agenda is to shift energy demand to different times of the day, then this translates to a need to shift routines and practices outside their normal peaks. Thinking about how technologies could generate new 'hot spots' or 'cold spots' of activity (Southerton 2003), or designing for different understandings of productivity and busyness (Leshed and Sengers 2011) could be possibilities.

These ideas point towards an imperative for smart home designers and advocates to 'assume new assumptions', and to reimagine the sort of low-energy life we want or could have (Strengers 2014). Following design fiction practitioners and scholars, and research informed by theories of social practice, there is a clear need to speculate on what life might look like with a lower energy footprint and less peaky electricity demand. As Wilson et al. (2014: n.p.) argue, this means seeing smart 'as emerging within users' everyday lives and in the ways technologies are used in the home, not as something that resides in technologies themselves'. There is scope not only to imagine future possibilities, but to draw insights from the past, and from the billions of people who currently have no or extremely limited access to electricity, and who are remarkably and disturbingly absent from smart home visions.

Importantly, this reimagination may not involve anything digital. Instead, questions we might ask include: How could we cool and heat our homes (or bodies) without any or very minimal electricity? How might our practices change around increasing incidences of extreme hot and cold weather? What might bathing look like without the energy- and water-intensive shower that has dominated personal grooming in the twentieth and twenty-first centuries? Indeed, such questions are already the concern of design scholars working with notions of practice and everyday life (Clear et al. 2014; Kuijer et al. 2013). With new imaginaries in mind, there is scope for designing for different possible lower energy and less peaky futures both with, and without, smart technologies.

Reimagining the smart home

Berry et al.'s (2007: 242) observation that the smart home is a 'fluid and unstable field of possibilities' reminds us that the energy demand outcomes for the smart home are far from a confirmed reality. Despite this, policy and energy industry predictions for the smart home assume that the development and proliferation of smart home technologies 'will empower consumers to take control over their energy consumption' (CEA 2011: i) in a way that will enable the 'efficient use of electricity and water without compromising modern lifestyle' (Ausgrid 2012: 1). What follows is a series of predictions and percentages, such as those referenced in the introduction to this chapter, which present the smart home vision as a fait accompli. In adopting this position, smart home policies and research effectively avoid engaging with the possibility that these technologies might enable new ways of living which increase energy demand. Instead, they position smart home technologies as 'neutral slaves', which perform tasks on behalf of their occupants or users, without interfering in how those occupants live (Hamilton et al. 2012).

As I have demonstrated in this chapter, this is an extremely dangerous and misleading position to take. Flanked by a long history of failed utopian promises, the continued critical interrogation of the smart home is necessary if we are to realize the vision's energy reduction and demand shifting ambitions. In continuing this task, I have argued for the removal of common demarcations between the digital, material and human, suggesting instead that we carry out research that explores the entanglements between and beyond them. We cannot only be interested in how people 'use' smart technologies, but must also focus on how they are reconfiguring both human and technology, and in doing so how they reconstitute the very fabric of everyday life. Further, I have suggested that we need to refocus our attention on what (and who) we are designing for: the messy and often improvised flow of everyday activity, rather than discrete utilitarian tasks. This involves viewing the home as a collection of human and nonhuman interactions and relationships, rather than discrete uses between human and machine.

Finally, it is important to remember that the future smart home is an imagined one, and it is constantly being reimagined. By shining a critical light on the smart home vision, other emerging realities, and possible alternatives, we open up new ways of understanding and imagining the smart home that bring us closer to achieving its ambitious agenda of a lower energy demand future.

PART TWO

Co-interventions

5

Refiguring digital interventions for energy demand reduction: Designing for life in the digital–material home

Sarah Pink, Kerstin Leder Mackley, Val Mitchell, Garrath T. Wilson and Tracy Bhamra

Introduction

In this chapter, we argue for an approach to design and intervention that builds on the ability of anthropological ethnography to open up new ways of knowing the world, and that attends to digital media as part of this world. Our ethnographic and design research is therefore undertaken in what we understand as a digital–material and sensory environment, and our approach to intervention and change-making is informed by this conceptualization. In what follows, we draw on our experiences of working in an interdisciplinary team – which draws from anthropology, media studies, design and human–computer interaction (HCI) research – with the aim of making digital design interventions in everyday home life that will help people reduce their energy demand. We show how the possibility for such an approach has emerged through interdisciplinary working that brings together the dialogue between ethnographic practice and theory with design practice, in ways that both challenge our existing assumptions and that are generative of new possibilities.

Our work is set in an academic, activist and policy context where, for decades now, global climate change and local resource scarcity have led to calls for more sustainable energy futures, with digital technologies increasingly expected to provide some, if not *the*, key solutions for transforming consumption. Within this fast-growing field, the digital is often appropriated in one of two ways. One scenario sees sensor technologies within ever more interconnected information and communication networks as enabling automated energy-reduction systems that operate 'in the woodwork' (Weiser 1996); the smarter their processing power, the less responsibility lies with the humans who co-inhabit their environments. A second scenario puts agency (and responsibility) back with individuals by finding innovative ways of engaging them through digital services and devices; the aim is to persuade and enable people to actively monitor, control and reduce their energy consumption, in more or less playful or formulaic ways. The first approach renders digital technologies almost invisible, while the second foregrounds, at least in parts, the importance of people's interactions with new material products and digital interfaces.

Social scientists in particular have been critical of both the utopian notion of digital technologies as providing all answers to energy demand reduction questions (cf. Strengers 2013), and of the simplicity of the above human/ technological agency dichotomy. While underpinning much engineering and design work in this area, a focus on the latter arguably fails to account for complexities and interrelations, as well as for important sociocultural, ethical and political implications. As such, scholars have sought alternative ways in which to conceptualize what people do with both energy and digital media. Débora Lanzeni, Yolande Strengers and Mike Michael (see Chapters 3, 4 and 6, this volume) engage with this context through (differently) critical discussions of the notions of smart cities, smart homes and digital energy feedback technologies and speculative design. By taking specific disciplinary approaches and perspectives to this field, these authors highlight the limitations of approaches that depend on either technological or human agency for the success of design initiatives or on interventions that seek to change human behaviour. For instance, Strengers is interested in a sociologically oriented social practice theory approach, which puts the practices of everyday life at the centre of the analysis. Like other social practice theory-oriented approaches (e.g. Shove 2010), this reveals the problems associated with the ways in which neo-liberal regimes place responsibility on individuals to change their (energy consumption) behaviour once sensitized to it through behaviour change campaigns. An emphasis on changing individuals' behaviour, practice theorists argue, clouds the relevance of, and in the process reinforces, other sociotechnical forces and structures. Michael, in contrast, seeks to undermine the idea of the research question that might be successfully answered through conventional sociological processes. His work on energy demand leans towards a more speculative methodology – which is in many ways more akin to the experimental elements of a sensory ethnography approach to doing ethnography and creating research encounters with participants (see Pink 2015). As these discussions show, there are a number of tensions in terms of how to understand energy consumption and create sociotechnological 'solutions' towards demand reduction. Ultimately, new approaches both to researching with participants and to making everyday life interventions are needed. This, for us, has meant developing ethnographically and theoretically informed ways of engaging with digital media as part of new approaches to design and intervention.

In this chapter, we suggest a reconfiguration of the relationship between theory, research and design intervention that draws on phenomenological anthropology and design research approaches. We explore what happens when the apparent dichotomy of digital presence and affordances and human action and improvisation is both disrupted through ethnographic research and utilized by designers. To do this, we reflect on how concepts for digital interventions for energy demand reduction have emerged, between designers and social science researchers, on an interdisciplinary study of domestic energy consumption and digital media use. In doing so, we draw on our research and practice developed on a project that aimed to use digital innovation in energy demand reduction. The LEEDR (Low Effort Energy Demand Reduction (2010–14)) project brought together engineers, designers, social anthropologists and computer scientists to explore energy use and digital media engagements in twenty UK family homes. It combined longitudinal energy monitoring with in-depth ethnographic fieldwork and family-oriented design research and practice. For further context, we invite readers to our website *Energy and Digital Living* where we present and explain our ethnographic findings and design concepts through video clips and writing for a wider audience (www.energyanddigitalliving.com).

We do not present our project as the perfect 'solution' to the problem of energy demand reduction, or indeed to the question of how to engage with the digital materiality of the home. Because the problem itself is wider and implicates not only the everyday energy consumption activities of individuals in their homes but also a series of other infrastructural and governance issues, it could not be 'solved' through a project such as ours alone. Moreover, the role and significance of digital technologies in this process is yet to be determined (see Strengers, Chapter 4, this volume). Rather our work is part of a journey towards developing new ways of working between ethnographers and designers, within and in relation to a digital–material environment and, in the case of this particular project, towards energy demand reduction. It is in that sense a speculative process, in that we did not know what would emerge from our research relationship when we began. In the spirit of the speculative design processes that are described by Mike Michael and Bill Gaver (see Michael, Chapter 6, this volume), as our project came to a conclusion we found ourselves in a position to show what we have learned from this process and to reflect on how it would enable us to craft future design ethnography relationships in new and generative relationships. Understanding the nature and significance of digital–material dimensions can be considered both a research and a design challenge. It is also this inspiration that we invite readers to take with them as the field of intervention in a digital–material world evolves further and through new projects.

Researching through digital materiality: Project and methods

To be able to understand how and where to make digital design interventions towards everyday sustainability, our project aimed to reframe the approaches to energy demand reduction that are driven by the technological, engineering, behavioural and social practice theory agendas we have highlighted above. Instead we sought to refigure what people do with digital media in their everyday lives in their homes, how digital technologies already form part of everyday life, in both their tangible and intangible forms, and how people improvise with digital technologies in everyday life. In doing so, we appreciate the potential of ordinary people as everyday designers who have a certain form of agency, which emerges through their relationships with digital technologies.

We also create something of a false separation between the environment of and activity in the home, in order to distinguish these for the purposes of understanding the ways that both are implicated in design processes. At the end of the section we bring these together to suggest that their mutuality needs to inform the way we understand the home and the ways that interventions might be produced in it. First, we briefly explain the research methods we used, and the research design that informed the ways in which we developed our ethnographic encounters.

Our research design set out to understand how the home was made, experienced and maintained (and the role of digital media in this), and how a set of specific everyday activities, which had been identified as potentially high energy consuming, including laundry, media use, showering/bathing and use of heating, were actually accomplished. We were also concerned with the contingencies and human improvisations that these activities and environments are shaped by. Our ethnography thus had an emphasis on the experience of home, and how the unspoken, mundane, often invisible and otherwise unknown-about elements of everyday routines and lives underpinned the ways in which energy is consumed. To achieve this, our ethnographic research followed a three-stage process. The video tour was designed to understand the 'sensory aesthetic' of home, how it was made, maintained and experienced (Pink and Leder Mackley 2012). The tours pulled in the things, feelings (sensory and affective) and activities through which the home was constituted as our participants led us on a route through it. They enabled us to learn about how the home was known and sensed, where and how activities were distributed throughout it temporally and spatially. As part of the video tour encounter we also invited our participants to demonstrate to us, through reenactments, how they went about their everyday routines of getting up and going out in the morning and going to bed at night. The reenactment studies enabled us to gain an understanding of the ways in which everyday routines were accomplished, the idiosyncrasies and improvisation that they entailed, and the sensory tacit ways of knowing and moving through the home that were part of the often-never-spoken-about ways in which people consume energy as they make their homes and selves 'feel right' at these pivotal moments of the day (Pink and Leder Mackley 2014). We gave copies of all our video materials to participants and invited them to comment on and ask for edits in them, as part of both our research and ethics process. As the next stage of our research, we also worked with a smaller sample of eleven households, with whom we focused on exploring how they performed a series of everyday activities. These studies of everyday activities enabled us to understand better how the tasks of doing the laundry, showering, using media and other activities are interwoven with each other and with the materiality, sensoriality, affect and atmospheres of home. Our research taught us that these cannot easily be separated out as distinct practices that might be redesigned but, rather – and as we show below – we might need to think of other categories that might be identified through ethnography in order to find ways through which to design for energy demand reduction. This, then, became a matter of reframing what it is that we think we are designing for.

The digital–material environment of home: Presence, co-presence and atmosphere

Our approach to analysing our ethnographic findings was developed through a series of theoretical-ethnographic dialogues which are discussed in more depth elsewhere in the articles we refer to below (see also Leder Mackley and Pink, 2013), and which have contributed to debates in media studies, sociology and human geography. Here we summarize these contributions to outline how we developed a focus on the concepts of presence, co-presence and atmosphere, which eventually played a role in the production of the insights the ethnography team offered to the design team. The purpose of the discussion here is also to present this as a framework for considering how we might understand the environments, actions and atmospheres of homes as sites of possibility for digital design interventions.

Our sensory video ethnographies of home set out to develop a new understanding of energy demand in the home. Our study focused on how and why energy was consumed in the homes of our participants, along with a special or dual focus on the place of media in this process. We were not only interested in how digital media consumed energy, but also in the ways in which they were integral to the mundane lives of our participants, given that our objective was to also produce insights into how and where digital design interventions for energy demand reduction might be introduced. Our approach to the home was informed and underpinned by existing research into the sensory, material and mediated qualities and affordances of home. These three themes offered us a rich ethnographic and theoretical background to build on, and we used existing theoretical ideas in dialogue with our own ethnographic findings. Our ethnographic research drew on the existing tradition of material culture studies of home, as developed by Danny Miller (e.g. 1988, 2001), the notion of the sensory home developed by Sarah Pink (2004) and the tradition of non-mediacentric media studies specifically relating to home, as developed by David Morley (e.g. 2000) and followed through in the more phenomenological work of Shaun Moores (e.g. 2012) and Nick Couldry and Tim Markham (e.g. 2008). These existing works offered us a way of understanding the home that was 1) constituted by its materiality in relation to human actors, 2) a sensory and affective domain filled with things and activities that were not necessarily tangible or ever spoken about but sensed and tacitly known, and 3) a mediated site, where media was part of both the materiality of home and embedded and often appropriated into the routines of human activity and feeling that were co-constitutive of home.

Our work built on this existing understanding of home in two ways that we recount here briefly and to which here we also add an additional layer of analysis by accounting more explicitly for the proposal that digital media are part of the atmosphere of home. As such, we define the digital materiality of home in terms of its qualities not only as a material and sensory/affective environment, but as being constituted as an atmosphere (Pink and Leder Mackley forthcoming). This, we argue, offers a way of bringing together and reframing the materiality, sensoriality and mediatedness of home. It means that we are designing therefore not simply into a material, technological or sensory home but into an atmosphere generated through people's embodied relations with a digital–material–sensory environment. This atmosphere will influence how any interventions are experienced and engaged with, and will itself be impacted by interventions. It is therefore also the atmospheres of home that we suggest need to be accounted for when designing for/with homes. Our existing publications have brought to the fore three key points that have formed the basis for this thinking.

First, through an analysis of how participants in our research understood their digital media technologies in relation to the ambiguous states and statuses of on, off and standby modes, we developed the notion of media as 'presence' (Pink and Leder Mackley 2013). In the non-mediacentric media studies work we have cited above, media still tend to be understood specifically in relation to their uses for content and for communications. Our ethnography showed us how digital media were used in the home in a series of ways beyond their value for content or communication. We learned how people put media on at bedtime to help them go to sleep, unbothered by the programme that was on. We also learned how people's perceptions of the different states of on/off-ness of media was part of the way they sensed their homes, knowing that the home 'felt right' if and when media were switched to the 'right' status. This was often achieved through bedtime routines where, depending on the contingencies of the material and social arrangements of home, media would be put on, off or on a timer to go onto standby mode (Pink and Leder Mackley 2013). The other type of media 'on-ness' can be described through the notion of digital co-presence, whereby through mobile and locative media people are often continually online with the potential to access and 'be with', or with an affective sense of the presence of others who are in different and possibly distant physical locations (see Pink et al. 2015 for a discussion of digital relationships). In terms of energy demand, standby mode can be a relatively high consumer of electricity, and therefore something that would have potential for reduction. Yet it is also a mode of being, of material, sensory and social presence in the home for which we need to account through design.

Second, there has recently been a (re)turn of interest to the concept of atmosphere (e.g. Böhme 1993; 2013), particularly in the work of scholars in human geography (Anderson 2009; Bissell 2011; Edensor 2012, 2014), as well as in anthropology (e.g. Bille et al. 2015). In this literature atmosphere is not seen as something separate from people or environments, but as embodied and affective, emerging from bodies rather than enveloping them from elsewhere. Drawing on the work of Ingold, we have gone on to further theorize atmosphere as something that is also emergent from what Ingold calls 'making' – that is, from the everyday forms of improvisory activity that people engage in during their everyday lives. Therefore we have argued that 'we can understand the atmospheres as emergent from processes of making – that is, from the encounters between people, materials and other elements of the environments of which they are part (e.g. air, light, warmth, scents). Atmospheres are not as such *products* but they are *produced* or *emergent* ongoingly as people improvise their ways through the world' (Pink and Leder Mackley forthcoming). We found, when we looked at the ethnographic detail, that our participants could be understood as everyday makers of atmospheres in their home in precisely this way – for instance, as they walked through their homes at bedtime, switching the lights on and off, closing curtains, plugging in things to charge and setting up technologies to 'work' while they were asleep – as such making the material configuration and atmosphere of the bedtime home as they moved through (Pink and Leder Mackley forthcoming).

Bringing this argument together with that outlined above – where we have argued that media presence is also part of the home – invites us to take this further. This has meant generating a definition of the digital materiality of home, which takes the atmosphere of home to be something that goes beyond the relationship between materiality and the embodied/affective (as advanced in the human geography literature cited above), and which instead also encompasses the affordances and qualities of digital technologies – that is, the digital presence and co-presence that is generated by media in ways that go beyond (but of course also include) their functions for content and communication. The implication of this is that to design for change in the home we need to account for these ways in which media feel and participate in the generation of atmospheres of home, both through their technological presence and through the sociality of digital co-presence of being online *with* others.

The third element of this relates to the ways in which improvisory human activity is part of this process, as outlined in the next section.

Human activity in the home: Flows, movement and making

As we have shown in the last section, for us the digital and material are inseparable elements of the environment of home; they become interwoven in its atmosphere. Energy demand, as we have already indicated above, is also part of the way in which the atmospheres of home are constituted. Within this broad way of understanding the home, however, we also need to understand what people are doing as they go about their normal everyday energy-consuming activities. Conventional psychological studies of how people consume energy tend to focus on human 'behaviour' (e.g. Abrahamse et al. 2007; Steg and Vlek 2009), while it is quite standard in sociology to use a unit of 'social practices' to study and divide up the activities through which people consume energy (e.g. Shove 2010; and see Strengers, this volume). Anthropologists have always been interested in what people do, and have used a range of concepts through which to understand this. Here we draw on the particular branch of phenomenological anthropology that is also closely associated with (and underpins much of) the emergent subdiscipline of design anthropology. In this field, ideas that emphasize the ongoingness of improvisation as part of everyday life, and in particular the work of Ingold (2012) in phenomenological anthropology, have been engaged to inform new approaches to co-design that bring together anthropological ethnography and design research (Gunn and Donnovan 2012; Otto and Smith 2013; Pink et al. 2013; Akama and Prendiville 2013).

As discussed elsewhere (Pink and Leder Mackley forthcoming), by bringing together a focus on the atmospheres of home with the ideas of improvisation and agency, and the focus on movement developed in the work of Ingold (e.g. 2000, 2010), we can begin to understand the question of where and how to design into everyday life in the home in new ways. Our focus in this chapter is more practical and concerned specifically with the ways in which we have brought together ethnography and design practice and ways of knowing, therefore we do not go into detail concerning the theoretical developments that this implies (see Pink and Leder Mackley forthcoming for a detailed account). However, to preface the connection between our ethnographic work and digital design interventions discussed below, we outline how the concepts of movement and improvisation connect to that of atmosphere.

The theoretical work that informs the way in which we understand the purpose and affordances of the digital design interventions discussion involves two sets of concepts. Although these might not be in any objective way different types of concepts, here we are engaging them for different purposes. In the last section we wrote about concepts of atmosphere and presence. These are not static states at all, but ongoingly made and part of the dynamic nature of the home as a site for research and investigation. However, for our purposes here we are identifying these as in some way distinct, in that they are concepts that we are using to define the environment of home. In this section, we focus on a set of concepts that we wish to use in relation to those of atmosphere and presence, which we see as action concepts and which, conceptualized as such, help us to translate them through into the design process. We use these to refer to three forms of action-making/ improvisation, movement and flow. However, we would emphasize the action is of course not only human, but rather in part the action (movement and flow) is also of the atmosphere, thus rendering people, things and intangibles all part of the same moving and changing environment and meaning that action and atmosphere are co-constituting of each other.

The above point stated, because we want to design for and with people – that is, with the participants in our projects – it is, however, necessary to address the question of where and how people are active in this theoretical framework. Questions concerning human agency and intentionality, where these are situated and from where they are derived are complex and difficult to resolve theoretically or empirically. For the purposes of our argument here, Ingold's point which has held currency in design anthropology is useful, particularly because it enables us to focus on the concept of improvisation as a way in which to engage both with the question of what people *do* as they go about their everyday lives, more broadly, and with how they might engage with digital design interventions that are made precisely to become part of their everyday improvisory activities and also part of the ways in which they 'feel' the affective atmospheres of home. As Pink and Leder Mackley emphasize elsewhere, Tim Ingold and Elizabeth Hallam (2007) see improvisation as 'a necessary condition because there is no existing template that instructs us in how to deal with the continually changing contingencies of life' (Pink and Leder Mackley 2015: 283). They theorize improvisation further as 'generative', 'relational', 'temporal', 'inseparable from our performative engagements with the materials that surround us' (Ingold and Hallam 2007: 3), and Ingold proposes that designing is a way of imagining the future that is open-ended 'about hopes and dreams rather than plans and predictions' (Ingold 2012: 29). When we put our participants at the centre of the analysis, we also came to conceptualize our participants as 'directors of flow' in the home. For example, we observed how they would continually be working with, initiating or curtailing flows of warm or cold air, smells, sounds, lighting and more as they navigated these intangible yet mobile affordances of homes through open windows, radiators, cooking, extractor fans and more (Pink and Leder Mackley 2014). Such work requires engaging with the contingencies of the home as a site of ongoing change: socially, materially, and in terms of its intangible and digital elements. It is also work that requires improvisation, which might be on-the-spot or might be part of an ongoing process of changing routines over time through forms of adjustment.

We argue that in order to design digital interventions for everyday change, then, we need to precisely engage with this kind of everyday human activity – that is, the improvisory potential of our research participants – as the route through which to move towards sustainable digital energy futures. In the context of the project discussed here, the digital, material, atmospheric qualities and affordances of home, discussed in the previous section, can therefore be conceptualized as constituting sites for digital design interventions. They are inhabited not just by improvisory active people, sensing feeling bodies, but also by the presence of digital technologies, flows of air, sound and light. They are also, crucially, sites of uncertainty, which people however know enough about and can hope enough for, when they make changes in them, to be able to routinely navigate and accomplish mundane routines that are generative of the very homes they are part of.

From research findings to connecting with design

The work that we report on in the previous section focuses on the findings of the ethnographic–theoretical dialogue through which we were able to develop broad understandings of what our participants were doing in their home. In this section we discuss examples of three of the key insights for design that emerged from this: feeling right; ongoing improvisation; and people as directors of flows. Then in the following section we turn to the design process and to the implications of these findings for the introduction of digital design interventions.

The concept of *feeling right* was at the core of our ethnographic research, in that, as explained above, our initial question to participants related to how they made (or sought to make) their homes feel right. As our ethnographic work developed, we learned how making the home feel right involved a range of different materials, intangible elements and activities which would maintain this feeling. We also learned how participants developed sensations of uneasiness or disquiet when they knew that everyday routines related to energy and technology use were not accomplished. For example, as we describe elsewhere (Pink and Leder Mackley 2013), Alan, one participant, told us how his daughter felt uneasy if all of the electricity sources were not switched off at bedtime, and another participant described a situation where he would have all his young children in the car ready to leave for school and then realize that the oldest son had not switched off his Xbox, but that it was now too late to go back to do so. These ways of making the home feel right, or not, can be theorized in relation to the notion of affective atmospheres of home discussed in the previous section.

The idea of *ongoing improvisation* towards making the home feel right also emerged from our ethnographic work. For example, when our participants discussed their night-time routines with us, we learned about how Alan, mentioned above, had developed ways in which to ensure that switching off at bedtime was easy, through the use of a wooden stick to reach switches and an extension lead in one bedroom. Another participant, Lee, showed us how he used his mobile phone as a light and one of his lights as a memory device (cf. Pink and Leder Mackley 2014). These activities were subsequently understood theoretically as part of the process of ongoing everyday improvisation and creativity discussed in the previous section, and also contributing to the making of affective atmospheres of home.

The notion of *people as directors of flows* who are ongoingly working with and navigating the contingencies of everyday lives emerged from our work with participants that showed us they were continually dealing with the sounds of music or TV, smells, flows of warmth or draughts of cold air and other, often invisible, elements that flow through the home. For instance, Barbara described how she controlled flows of heating, cooking smells, music and lighting in the kitchen so she could communicate with her husband who had a hearing impairment (cf. Pink and Leder Mackley 2015). Rhodes described to us how she would control the flows of sound from the washing machine and boiler, create a particular sensory environment in her son's bedroom and deal with the draughts in the colder parts of her house (cf. Pink and Leder Mackley 2012). These examples and others showed us how our participants were continually working with these different flows and contingencies in relation to each other, again to make the home *feel right*, and as such as part of the making of the affective atmosphere of home.

Refiguring the design process

In this section, we turn to the design process to explain how the approach we take both builds on and departs from existing practice within user-centred design and HCI. We then outline how the reconceptualization of the digital–material and experiential environment of home outlined in the previous section impacts on the ways in which we explore and reframe the design space and our approach to intervention design. In the third part of the discussion our focus then moves on to opening up the design space through a deeper engagement with sensory ethnographic concepts and research materials. Here we outline how three of the key concepts that emerged from the design ethnography approach outlined above are used to rethink the world for which we were designing and how and where digital interventions might participate in this world.

Elsewhere (Pink et al. 2013) we have described the theoretical similarities between the sensory ethnography approach and the notion of embodied interaction (Dourish 2001). Core to both is the notion that the meaning of the world – in this case, the home – is revealed through our encounters with it: how we react to it, move through it and engage with it to meet our needs and contingency plan. The sensory ethnography approach has provided the design team with the opportunity to reframe their consideration of the 'domestic energy problem' and to foreground consideration of how people create their desired experience of home. Previous research (e.g. Strengers 2014) has shown that providing householders with feedback on their energy use has limited success and, therefore, the design team prioritized consideration of how our interventions could be embedded into everyday life. The sensory ethnography research has encouraged us to reframe our thinking, to systemically consider how the different everyday routines which make the home and self 'feel right', and the energy consumed as part of these activities, are in real life interwoven and inseparable, culminating in the creation of tacit bespoke atmospheres in which our interventions will become part of the digital materiality of the home.

Defining, framing and iteratively reframing the problem space is a core component of the creative design process and is part of the evolving collaboration between the design and ethnography teams. We have worked closely together to find innovative approaches and methods for bringing the new ways of knowing emerging from the sensory ethnography into our ideation processes. Bridging from ethnography into design can be problematic: the rich and complex representations of reality emerging from ethnographic encounters can conflict with the designer's desire to structure the messiness of everyday life in order to bound (at least temporarily) the problem space and begin generating solutions. We have sought to overcome this by using the ethnographic materials to provide different entry points for design – in other words, to look for alternative ways to frame the problem space that lead us away from providing direct feedback on energy use. Key to this approach has been to generate forward-facing opportunity statements as an interdisciplinary team.

Opportunity statements reframe identified insights, moving from an understanding of the observed, reenacted and reflected upon towards the creation of speculative 'How might we' statements. For example, from the ethnography it was apparent that households with hot water tanks in their homes treated hot water as a limited, tangible resource, the use of which is negotiated between family members using tacit knowledge of different family members' hygiene routines. For households with a combi-boiler where hot water is heated on demand, water had become like electricity – an apparently infinite resource. Longer and more frequent showering was seen within these households and consequentially higher energy use. This insight was reframed as the opportunity statement: 'How might we encourage householders to consider energy as a finite material resource?' The design response to this was the digital intervention concept 'Finite'. Finite evolved from an initial idea of creating a digital well to tangibly represent energy use (gas, electricity and water). The 'well' gradually drains in line with resource consumption targets set by the householders, visually prompting the householder to consider 'How much do I have left?' rather than trying to make meaning of the often intangible answer to the question 'How much have I consumed?' – a continually cited issue with digital energy feedback technologies. The app, therefore, attempts to use digital media to evoke the materiality of the absent water tank while extending this metaphor to gas and electricity use. When we take the developing of this design concept back to the theoretical work that has informed the ethnographic analysis, we might also posit an explanation that supports this intervention: by evoking the materiality of the water as stored in a tank, we might also evoke the sensation, the feeling that water is finite as a resource – that is, the embodied sensation that the water supply is limited and a way of anticipating its end that is not simply cognitive. Returning to the discussion of the affective atmosphere of home, therefore, the continuing question which could be explored through the use of the app would be to ask how this this relationship between the digital intervention, the making digitally tangible of the materiality of water and embodied feelings about water use have emerged. This feeds into a wider question about how we might design interventions that enable new ways in which sustainable uses of water can be encouraged precisely because they 'feel right'.

A further response to the sensory ethnography is the digital intervention concept 'Anima', an app that focuses on the insights that emerged from ethnographic knowledge on how households manage routines and improvise on an ongoing basis to make the home 'feel right'. In response, the design team were led to speculate whether a digital concept could be designed to encourage households to consider and respond to the well-being of the home in a similar manner to the way that they themselves respond to the mood and well-being of other family members, again attempting to use the digital to create a tangible perception of materiality. Responding to 'How might we' statements concerning the dynamics of multigenerational households, family values and perceptions of time, Anima is a proxy for the heartbeat of the home, a dynamic illustration of the home's energy use and activity levels that adapts in relation to predefined targets (set by the householders). As energy

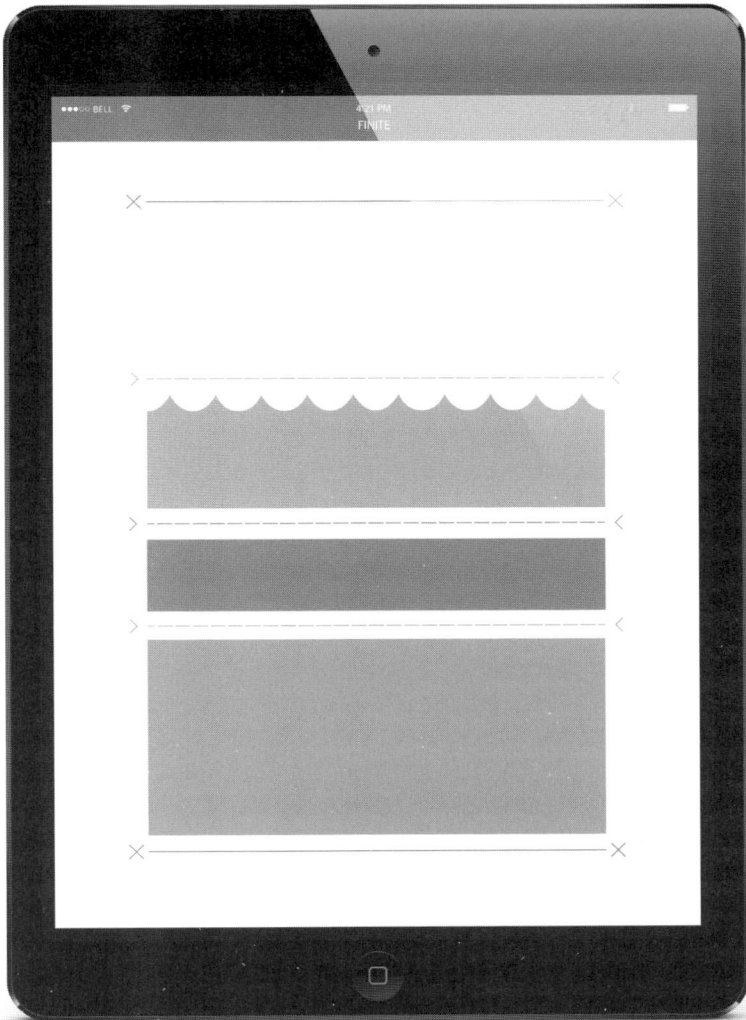

FIGURE 5.1 *Finite – the digital well. (Copyright LEEDR, Loughborough University)*

consumption or activity levels rise above their respective targets, Anima will give the illusion of stress – moving from a calm and regular pulse to an exaggerated, irregular and frenetic pulse. The householder is encouraged to explore, not through (dis)engagement with complex statistical representation, but by pulling, twisting and bouncing the Anima for an active exploration of the invisible consequences of their actions and routines – a critical departure from existing passive feedback 'solutions'. The questions that follow from the possibilities offered by Anima, as for Finite, take us back to the ethnographic analysis. Here Anima connects to the ongoing ways in which our participants were improvising in and modifying their everyday routines and activities, as well as with the ways in which they imagined the longer-term evolution of the materiality of their homes over time. The questions this raises is how Anima will enable its users to engage with these embodied ways of feeling the home, its temporality and its stress as participants seek to make the home 'feel right' via Anima.

Finally, we show how this wider framework shifts emphasis away from what designers increasingly criticize as localized and short-sighted intervention processes to a more integrated approach to media innovation that considers human–technological agency as fluid, multi-sited and contingent.

As the home is increasingly becoming a site of complex systems within systems, permeated by both technocratic and people-led interplay of the networked digital and material, people's perception and the affordances of interrelations is critical to facilitating them as everyday improvisors and directors of flow. Embracing this sensory ethnographic insight, 'Kairos' is a digital intervention concept that allows inhabitants to create ad hoc intelligent profiles for their energy-consuming appliances that are both grounded and situated within their daily lives, potentially solving the problematic dichotomy between human and technological agency. Representing time qualitatively, abandoning traditional approaches to time and activity management, activities

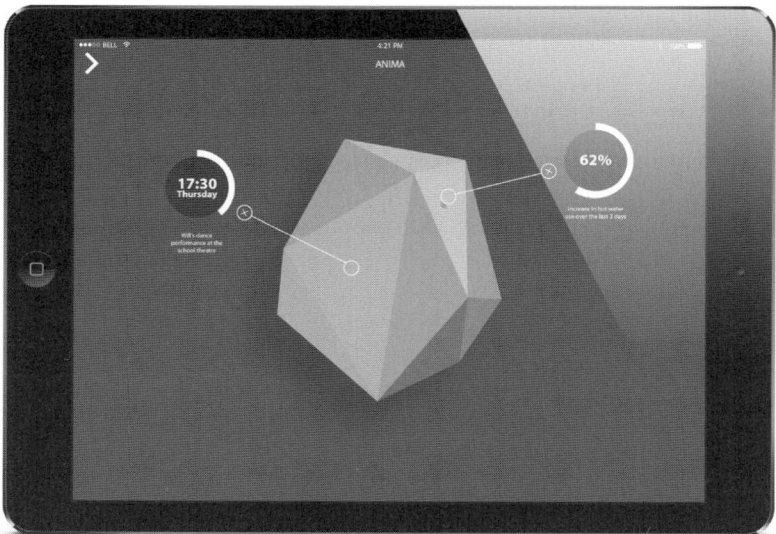

FIGURE 5.2 *Anima – home is where the heart is. (Copyright LEEDR, Loughborough University)*

can be selected to build unique Kairos profiles, as an individual or as a family, with 'user'-created digital flows (using IF/THEN conditional statements) to make new interrelations of activity. For example, the flow of sound by objects (i.e. the sound of the washing machine drum spinning) within the laundry process was identified as a constraint on when laundry activities could be performed; the atmosphere was perceived as unconfigurable and so avoidance measures were implemented. Kairos allows the user to connect a baby's cot (monitored via an inbuilt accelerometer) to the washing machine.

FIGURE 5.3 *Kairos – creating the opportune moment. (Copyright LEEDR, Loughborough University)*

Using the conditional statement 'IF the baby is in light sleep, THEN reduce the washer's spin speed', the new interrelation enables both improvisation (by the user) and optimization (by the technology). Energy is still consumed, but the material and sensory improvisory tendencies of inhabitants are empowered through the design of the digital, enabling the potential for energy reduction. As such, we can interpret Kairos as a technology that will be able to participate in the making of the affective atmospheres of home, in ways that build on inhabitants' existing ways of making their homes 'feel right' in relation to multiple contingencies of everyday life. Kairos in particular connects with our ethnographic insight that people become 'directors of flows' in their own homes, as they improvise in everyday life to make the home feel right. Kairos both acknowledges and has the potential to become a participant in this process, in ways that specifically orient users towards energy demand reduction.

Conclusion

In this chapter, we have drawn together a series of stages and elements of a four-year research project which involved ethnographers and designers learning how to work together, share practices, research materials, ideas and thinking, towards developing digital interventions for energy demand reduction. Just as the analytical trails between the sections of this chapter are not perfect, neither were the connections that run through our collaboration. There are gaps and there are leaps of faith that made these gaps close up. Some of the connections between the digital interventions that have been developed and the research findings did not become apparent until viewed in retrospect. Again, here the connections are not seamless or sure of themselves, but rather, as in the case of the concluding sentence to our presentation of Kairos, they are about the potentiality of these technologies to participate with users in the making of lower energy demand futures.

In the introduction to this chapter, we made reference to critical discourses surrounding the role of digital media in the process of energy demand reduction. Although design concepts for digital interventions constitute key outcomes of our project, we have not been disconnected from these debates but have actively engaged with them through our interdisciplinary collaboration and, particularly, by employing a sensory ethnographic framework that offered new routes towards understanding problems and solutions. As the resultant design concepts exemplify, we have found that explorations of digital–material relations can be instructive as research and (speculative) design challenges in their own right; digital media, with their affordances as both materially and immaterially present – as part and co-constitutive of the home, of its atmosphere and its inhabitants' activities – have lent themselves to the study of energy which itself lacks tangibility but is still, in a variety of ways, linked to material infrastructures. Both can be understood and interrogated through a theoretical framework that attends to the ways in which the home is experienced, known, made and imagined through sensory-embodied sensations and doings.

To conclude, we would reiterate that the relationship between ethnographic practice and digital design is emergent: a work-in-progress, and itself a speculative project. Our own project can be seen as a work in making a set of prototypes that we wish to be successful in their task of enabling energy demand reduction among their users. Yet at the same time we suggest that an equally important outcome of our work concerns what we have been able to learn about how digital technologies, design and human everyday activities and environments of home might come together. This knowledge, we propose, offers a strong basis not only for design in the particular context in which we have worked, but also as a starting point for research design for future work.

6

Speculative design and digital materialities: Idiocy, threat and com-promise

Mike Michael

Introduction

Not so long ago, there was a little incident with my iPhone, my MacBook and my Damson Cisor BT5 Resonating Bluetooth Speaker. I was trying to play music from a playlist on my MacBook's iTunes through a Bluetooth connection to the Damson speaker, but the music coming out of it was wrong. It sounded vaguely familiar, and was certainly very pleasant, but it was not the music that iTunes was saying it was playing. At first I thought I must be picking up music from someone else's system in my apartment building. Quickly I realized this was highly unlikely given what I knew about Bluetooth and its relatively short range. So it must be something else. It was then that I noticed the corner of my iPhone poking out from beneath some papers. Once I had got into the iPhone it became apparent that on switching the Damson speaker on, it had connected 'preferentially' with my iPhone (which, after all, had had a longer 'history' of connectivity with the speaker). I felt slightly idiotic for imagining that my speaker had been hijacked by someone else's music system, but also a little resentful at the apparent autonomy of 'my' devices that had determined their own relations, that had together conspired against my wishes, that had collaboratively misbehaved.

In many ways this is an everyday, more or less trivial, event – barely worth reporting on. And yet something interesting seemed to be going on. That something interesting was not the resort to the anthropomorphic terms in which this episode is couched. Such anthropomorphism is not uncommon and, given the sociotechnical constitution of these technologies, not altogether unjustified (Latour 1992). More immediately relevant is what this apparent 'sociotechnical misbehaviour' signifies. On one level, the software (for playing music, for seeking out Bluetooth devices, for establishing connections, for registering the 'history' of connectivity) and materiality (the physical proximity of the devices, the hiddenness of the phone, the juxtaposition of computer and speaker) together suggested an articulation that, in the setting of my trying to listen to music, made 'no sense'. By 'no sense', I mean I couldn't immediately understand what was going on – I was confused, and my initial attempt at an explanation (my speaker had been hijacked by someone else in the apartment block) was not a little nonsensical. On another level, it is of course possible to make sense of these reactions. The sense of betrayal by the sociotechncial coterie of computer, phone and speaker reflects a feeling that the relation between these devices is structured by a system from which I can be largely excluded, and into which, given my relatively low levels of technical skill, I have only partial and pre-delineated entrée. Here, there might be a critique to be developed around the issue of 'configuring the user' (Woolgar 1991) or the sensitization of users to the digital invasion of their privacy or dilution of their agency (Lupton, 2015).

However – and this is the perspective I want to develop in this chapter – one can also provide a more 'speculative' account of this episode. So the event that includes the 'collaborative misbehaviour' of the devices, and my reaction which sought to lay the blame on others in my apartment block, however, also suggests a more speculative reading. Thus the music I heard was very pleasant, and it might have come from others in my apartment, others who seem to have good taste (according to my preferences, of course). Say, fancifully, I went knocking on the doors of my neighbours, asked them to check their Bluetooth connections, while also commenting on the excellence of the music, is it possible – and I stress 'possible' (see below) – that a new set of conversations begins? Instead of the anonymity that typifies my apartment block, perhaps there will emerge the prospect of a different set of relations? Can we imagine this taking the form of not only a new sociality, but indeed, of a new 'technosociality'? That is to say, do the semi-autonomous communications of digital objects enable the emergence of new social bonds? Here, 'technosociality' can be understood as a movement toward a novel nexus of interrelations and communications among humans, between humans and digital artefacts, and, crucially, amid digital artefacts.

Needless to say, the anecdote presented above is not innocent; it is performative (Michael 2012a) insofar as it entails both the peculiar selection and the ordering of its 'data'. On this score, it is no different from any other means of generating and analysing data (e.g. Law 2004). Arguably, there is an increasing awareness of social scientific method as performative, and, with this, a sense that the epistemological and ontological terrain of social science might be shifting (e.g. Lury and Wakeford 2012). In particular, following such scholars as Isabelle Stengers – as we shall detail below – research events can begin to be treated as open, unfolding, oriented toward the not-as-yet. Is it possible to seek out 'events' that can be narrated with a sort of speculative intent, as in the anecdote above? More provocatively, is it possible to imagine a way of designing digital materialities that enact such research events and provoke the possible?

In response to this last question, this chapter describes a particular tradition in interaction design – let us call it 'speculative design' – that produces devices that can serve within the frame of the speculative social scientific methodology hinted at above. This tradition has long been interested in the design, production and implementation of artefacts, often with digital capacities, that are ambiguous and ludic. As such, these interaction designs playfully interject in, and potentially destabilize, routine social processes and practices, thereby opening up them up to speculative analysis.

In what follows, the chapter begins with an overview of the performativity of method and its implications for doing speculative social scientific research. Drawing on the process philosophical work of Whitehead and Stengers, the chapter suggests that the 'philosophical figure' of the idiot can do useful work in coming to grips with the ways in which we can explore the potential of everyday sociomaterial events, and to ask 'more interesting' questions of them. More specifically, it is proposed that the digital materialities of 'speculative design' are particularly suited for taking on the role of 'proactive idiot' (Michael 2012b). As such, the chapter describes a number of idiotic digital–material designs. However, the chapter also goes on to examine what needs to be in place in order for digital–material 'idiot' to provoke a rethinking of what is stake in the relevant sociomaterial events. The chapter thus ends with a reflection on the affective, aesthetic and ethical qualities of the digital–material idiot, and the 'com-promises' that these might entail.

Research, process, event

In John Law's (2004) *After Method*, a powerful argument is developed and elaborated around the performativity of social scientific method. For Law, methods which aspire to pin down reality and to exercise some form of validity tend to neglect the complexity that, according to Law following Deleuze, characterizes 'reality'. As such, 'reality' is multiple, relational, shifting, emergent. To engage with such complexity is necessarily a process fraught with problems: how does one access that which is shifting, in flux, multiplicitous? In this light, method for Law is better understood as a 'method assemblage', that is to say, an active, halting and uncertain process of engagement that is unavoidably constitutive of the 'reality' it relates to. Key here is the idea that a method assemblage enters into *relations* with this reality marked by flux and multiplicity. Crucially, these relations are not confined to, or exclusively mediated by, the parameters of the social scientific method (e.g. the questionnaire, the focus group, participant observation). Rather, these relations themselves entail flux and multiplicity; for instance, they are sensorially highly complex (e.g. Pink 2012). Even so, the engagements entailed in a method assemblage are always limited; in the end, they comprise the 'crafting of a bundle of ramifying relations that generates presence, manifest absence, and Otherness' (Law 2004: 45). In spite of this chronic boundary work, the advantage of thinking method through the idea of a method assemblage is that we are invited to 'imagine more flexible boundaries, and different forms of presence and absence' (ibid.: 85).

This path-breaking rearticulation of social scientific method nevertheless raises issues. Crucially, in Law's formulation a particular sort of boundary between researcher and researched seems to be enacted: the researcher 'crafts' but does not seem to be 'crafted'; the method assemblage seems by and large unaffected by the assemblages of the world with which it becomes embroiled. Stated so boldly, this does a disservice to Law; I think these issues are implicit in the notion of method assemblage. The rest of the chapter is concerned with following up some of the implications of this dimension of method assemblage, not least by thinking 'method assemblage' in terms of 'research event'.

I take my lead on the notion of the event from the process philosophies of Whitehead, Deleuze and Stengers. In particular, I see events as 'actual occasions' in which a multiplicity of divergent elements – what Whitehead calls prehensions – that span the social/material, the micro/macro, the human/nonhuman, the cognitive/affective come together and merge, or 'concresce' in Whitehead's (1929) terms. However, these 'concrescences' of 'prehensions' can take two broad forms. Thus, the constitutive elements can inter-act and retain their identity or distinctiveness, and cohabit within the event, as it were. Alternatively, they can intra-act (Barad 2007) and mutually change one another, co-becoming in the process of the event's concrescence. For Mariam Fraser (2010), this processual formulation of the event involves a 'becoming with' among its various elements.

As Connolly (2010) remarks, it is not an easy matter to warrant this alternative view of the event with its evocation of 'a world of becoming'. Nevertheless, along with John Law, I follow this view because it opens up new prospects for doing social science research. In the present context, it also allows us to ask whether a method assemblage in the 'research event' of crafting relations with the assemblages with which it engages is itself crafted. Put simply, do the research encounters we enter into simply constitute research events, or can they become something altogether different? Is the researcher who enters an empirical setting mutually changing with the 'objects' of her study, which also becomes something other than a 'study'?

This version of the research event echoes Stengers' (2005) conception of cosmopolitics. In a cosmopolitical event the various actors involved in a political encounter mutually change. In the process, what started out as the issue at stake might itself be transformed. As such, instead of seeking a solution to the original problem which precipitated the cosmopolitical event, the very premises underlying what counts as a problem might shift. Thus, there opens up the possibility of asking better questions; of, as Fraser (2010) phrases it, 'inventive problem-making'. In the case of the research encounter, this translates as follows: rather than look for answers to some pre-existing research question, the researcher is open to the changes wrought by their empirical encounters, changes that enable them to reformulate what the 'research event' is about, and to articulate more inventive problems. In seeking to do this, the researcher is acknowledging the fact that they are embroiled in, and emergent from, the flux and openness of the research event. This implies that the doing of research can no longer be about repre-senting, however modestly, the 'object of research' when it, along with the researcher, are mutually changing, co-becoming. This opens up a more speculative approach which attempts to grapple with the ways in which the 'research event' (though, of course, 'research event' hardly does justice to what might be happening) unfolds, becomes, emerges. Given this openness etc. of the research event, it befits us to resist the temptation to fall back on our usual frames of reference when coming to grips with what is emerging – to rethink what is at stake in the research event. On this score we might follow Stengers (2010: 57), and adopt a strategy that 'affirms the possible […] actively resists the plausible and the probable targeted by approaches that claim to be neutral'.

Idiocy and methodology

How do we access the prospective, the virtual in the research event? At base this is a matter of being open to the emergent. For Connolly (2010), this entails developing what he calls an 'exquisite sensitivity to the world' (a world that is in process, of course). To put it in the terms of Latour (2004), there needs to be cultivated a 'learning to be affected'. However, Connolly is particularly anxious that such sensitivity does not necessarily allow insight into what is potential in the world; there can be a temptation simply to revert to usual framings through which to come to terms with what seems unclear, not-as-yet. Stengers (2005) also attends to this issue, but she does it via the 'conceptual character' of the idiot. In her hands, the idiot 'resists the consensual way in which the situation is presented and in which emergencies mobilize thought or action' (Stengers 2005: 994). By virtue of making little sense within the consensual or standard framing of the event, the idiot 'demands that we slow down, that we don't consider ourselves authorized to believe we possess the meaning of what we know' (ibid.: 995). Our responsibility as, in the present case, social researchers is to 'bestow efficacy upon the murmurings of the idiot, the "there is something more important" that is so easy to forget because it "cannot be taken into account", because the idiot neither objects nor proposes anything that "counts"' (ibid.: 1001). By engaging seriously with the apparent nonsensicalness of the idiot, we become open to a dramatic redefinition of the meaning of the event.

Let us return to the opening example of the 'collective conspiracy' and 'collaborative misbehaviour' of my iPhone, MacBook and Damson Cisor BT5 Resonating Bluetooth Speaker. Here is an idiotic episode; it didn't make much sense in relation to my understanding of the event and my expectations about that event – expectations that ranged from what music I was hoping to hear, to the ways in which such technologies interact and work together. To be sure, I could 'dismiss' this as a simple accident, or more self-deprecatingly as a matter of my own incompetence. However, I could also pay attention to the sense of betrayal and exclusion: these objects had colluded to confuse me. Here, one can recast this in terms of a critical account about the ways in which a user such as myself is heterogeneously constituted, pre- and pro-scribed in particular ways (Latour 1992; Akrich 1992).

But note, this account assumes that there is a preeminent 'I' here under some sort of sociomaterial siege. I do not emerge from this event – as a speculative version of the event would imply – so much as am assailed by it. Of course, this sort of critical analysis is hugely useful and the purpose is not to dismiss critique per se. Rather, the aim here is to add to our analytic arsenal in ways that can further illuminate the immanence of sociomaterial events (for one account of the relation between critique and immanence, see Guess, 1981). It might be suggested that a combination of critique and speculation finds its greatest expression in the work of Donna Haraway (1991, 1997; see also Prins 1995). So, taking a speculative tack, I will focus on my own initial reaction to the playing of unexpected music, namely, that the Bluetooth speaker had been hijacked by someone else's music system somewhere in the apartment building. I suspect that this interpretation draws on the fact that I occasionally notice the presence of other devices under the 'Shared' heading on the sidebar of my Finder file management system. Sometimes I do not recognize these named computers detected by my own. Presumably, I too am a semi-anonymous presence on someone else's computer. And perhaps sometimes (though this is highly unlikely given the limitations of Bluetooth), my music is accidentally played on someone else's music system. Here, there emerges the outline of a different way of engaging with the event of 'the wrong music playing': rather than seeking a practical solution (e.g. clearing up my desk), or political solution (e.g. opening up design to more user input), one aspires to more 'interesting' problems. As such, in this case, one might ask: What is the 'I' that is emergent here? Is it some hybrid combination of computer, music, taste, Bluetooth? Is this hybrid being digitally circulated? Is it potentially encountering others? Does this hint at a sort of 'digital technosociality'? How are we to understand and unpack such a term?

This speculative accounting of the event of 'the wrong music playing' is no doubt stilted, not a little forced, and somewhat simple-minded. The point, however, is not to specify 'a virtuality' or 'the possible' for this particular event, but more modestly to illustrate what 'learning to be affected' (I hesitate to say practising an 'exquisite sensitivity to the world') might look like in doing speculative research and seeking to pose more 'interesting problems'.

Now, being responsive to the idiotic in such events is just one methodological option available. It is also possible to deploy proactively the idiotic as a way of probing the virtual. By introducing something that is idiotic into particular social settings or situations, it is possible that those who must interact with this 'idiotic something' will respond in ways that pose questions about the ways in which that setting or situation is normally understood, enacted and warranted.

More specifically, can we imagine an 'idiotic' digital–material device (or system) that lures the user into expanding their sensibilities – enhancing their sensorium – so that they 'learn to be affected' in new and unexpected ways which in turn enable access to the possibilities and virtualities of the event of which that device and user are a part? This, of course, raises all sorts of further questions: What becomes the 'user' under these sorts of novel configurations of the digital, material, corporeal and ideational? What is the relation of these configurations to matters of affect, aesthetics and ethics, when that which is to be sensed or valued, and which, indeed, does the sensing and the valuing, is redistributed and recirculated? We shall explore some of these questions in the sections that follow. But first, we turn to a discussion of so-called 'speculative design'. It is here, in some versions of 'speculative design', that we can find examples of idiotic digital–material devices. By following the procedures by which these devices are developed, crafted, deployed and engaged, we will begin to see how 'speculative design' might resource a speculative methodology in social science, while also raising 'interesting questions' about the parameters of such a methodology.

'Speculative design'

In the preceding comments on 'speculative design', there has been some circumspection (signalled by the scare quotes) in putting a name to the set of design practices that most resonate with the issues addressed and the arguments developed in this chapter. In part this is because within academic design there seems to be considerable formal and informal debate as to what is to count as 'speculative design', and indeed whether this is an appropriate term in the first place. For the social scientist this complexity is redoubled when one takes into account the collaborative connections between design and social science that are beginning to take shape (e.g. Stormi 2012; Hawkins 2013; Latour 2008).

'Speculative design' can be understood to fall within a lineage that draws in 'participatory design' (where the design process is affected by a direct engagement, indeed collaboration, with potential users – see Ehn 2003) and 'critical design' (where credible technological futures are projected then critiqued through design artefacts that undermine them in some way or other – see Dunne 2005; Dunne and Raby 2001). Latterly, a fascinating combination of these approaches has found expression in 'adversarial design' (DiSalvo 2012). Needless to say, these genres of design blur at certain points – for instance, Dunne and Raby (2013) have, in their recent book *Speculative Everything*, emphasized the speculative dimension of their own and others' design work. Even so, the 'speculative design' practised by Gaver and his colleagues (e.g. Boehner, Gaver and Boucher 2012; Michael and Gaver 2009; Gaver et al. 2008) that I shall be discussing below sits at a tangent to these enterprises in a number of ways, while also displaying a more general family resemblance.

So, the 'speculative design' I am interested in does engage with users, but in a distinctive way. In contrast to participatory design, users are invited through various means such as cultural probes and ethnographic visits to generate material (say, views on the aesthetics of a dwelling's energy use, or idle doodles while talking on the phone, or photographs of a home's spiritual centre) which are combined with other materials (design history, recent media reports, online discussions, and so on). The users are not directly involved in the specification of the design so much as providing materials that inspire the process by which designs are developed. This sort of speculative design thus retains a certain 'mystique' in its design practice. As we shall see, this is because the artefacts that are produced and deployed must be a-functional (in the sense of serving a practical purpose that is unclear), ambiguous, and playful in ways that surprise the user, test their expectations, and enable unforeseen ways of thinking about the issues at stake.

This also differs from critical design where, generally speaking, user engagement plays little or no part. The final product will be a prototype such as the 'Local Barometer' (which displays local advertisements whose geographical source is directed by wind speed and direction) or the 'energy babble' (which 'broadcasts' more or less garbled verbal announcements about energy consumption). These designs are given to users to live with for a relatively extended period of time (as long as a few years). So, while this version of speculative design, like critical design (Dunne and Raby 2013; see also Tonkinwise 2014), contributes its artefacts to design exhibitions in museum and galleries, this is not the primary way in which the public is addressed. Rather the main point of 'contact' between the artefact and the 'public' is through deployment – the installation of the prototype in a setting in which it will be, hopefully, routinely encountered, used, addressed, reflected upon. As such, a crucial part of these designers' practice is regular ethnographic visits, conducted in order to enquire about users' experiences with the prototype, about the sorts of practices that have evolved around the artefact. Whereas critical design is content to generate artefacts that question people's beliefs about the technological future and resource visions of alternatives without necessarily following these up, speculative design is concerned with exploring people's actual practical encounters with these objects. As such, speculative design can be understood as focused on the ways in which people's practical engagements with artefacts that operate in odd, a-functional ways yield unexpected insights and enable the emergence of reformulations of the 'issues at stake'. These empirically derived novel apprehensions of 'what's going on' are themselves reflected upon as part of the design process.

Here, we also see differences across these design genres in the character of the designed object itself. By and large, participatory design's object embodies a utility or functionality that better reflects the requirements of its users (requirements that are not simply practical, but may be social and political). By comparison, critical design's object works in a way that ideally triggers critical reflection of contemporary credible technological futures. In contrast to both, speculative design's object is one that entails a sociomaterial encounter in which users are faced with ambiguity, uncertainty, playfulness that allows for the emergence – through practical engagement – with novel, unexpected insights into the matters that are, or become, relevant to that engagement. Indeed, we might say, critical design tends to operate on a register of 'apprehension', in which understandings, ideation, affect combine to generate a sort of unease that facilitates the emergence critique of current technological and alternative futures. The object of critique and critical object retain their character – this is an event of partial co-becoming. Drawing on the vocabulary of Whitehead, speculative design functions on the register of 'prehension', where practical engagement allows for a co-emergence of object and user, as their interaction encompasses not only ideation and affect but also the physical, the social, and the corporeal (on the differences between apprehension and prehension, and also comprehension, see Michael, 2002). Finally, framing this in terms of the 'idiot', critical design's objects seem to me to be partially idiotic – their idiocy is mediated, and possibly muted, by the context of display (the exhibition). The gallery is a space of critical and speculative reflection, exploration and meditation in which extended practical engagement is lacking, or at best truncated. The idiocy of speculative design's object, and the sorts of responses that idiocy provokes, is interwoven with its deployment and the extent to which its functions and uses are specified. However, as we shall see, the idiocy of objects doesn't always work in this way. We shall examine the notion of the idiot and the role of idiotic in digital–material methodologies in more detail. But before that, I present two cases of speculative design, one in which it was successful, one in which it failed.

Un-successful-ish design

The 'Local Barometer' strikes me as a particularly successful example of speculative design. It was part of a larger design research project that sought to develop a range of 'threshold devices' (Gaver et al. 2008). These were designed to collect information in novel ways from various digital sources related to the home and display this information through ways which were not directly functional, but which nevertheless facilitated new ways of thinking about, for example, the situation of the household – not least its relation to 'larger spatialities', such as the trajectories of an airplane along its flightpath, or socioeconomic distribution and character of neighbourhoods.

In the case of the Local Barometer, this comprised six small devices, each coloured brightly and incorporating a small screen which displayed the images and text of classified advertisements. The Local Barometers themselves were shaped so that they could sit easily within the domestic setting of the household – for instance, attached snugly to a bookshelf. The texts and images themselves were derived from the online site Loot.com which specialized in classified advertisements. The other part of the Local Barometer was a commercially sourced anemometer attached to the roof of the dwelling. This measures wind speed and direction. It was on the basis of these measurements that the advertisements were selected for display. Thus, the stronger the wind was blowing, the further the site of the adver-tised object was located. Similarly, wind direction determined the direction from which the advertisement was digitally 'blown in'. The idea underpinning the design of the Local Barometer addressed how people understood their neighbourhoods; it was thus design to enable people to engage in novel ways with how neighbourhoods were envisioned, say, in terms of their economic, social and cultural characteristics.

The volunteer, R, lived with the Local Barometer for around a month, and during that time members of the design team visited him several times, each visit lasting about half a day, for a total of thirty hours. Field notes (observations, informal interviews) and photographs were collected. From these materials, the following account took shape. R was initially aggravated by the adverts which he saw as yet another commercial intrusion into his home. He started off being resistant to using the barometer, not wanting to be distracted by still more advertising. However, this changed somewhat when he began noticing adverts that were more meaningful to him, for instance those selling vintage guitars. This immediate affective relation also took other forms, for instance negative reactions to sports car advertisements. Through this engagement with the device, he also began to notice that his sense of the neighbourhood, and those surrounding it, was being challenged. While certain objects reinforced his ideas about the area in which they were located, other objects did not seem to 'fit' culturally, socially or economically with their locations. In addition to this – and unexpectedly for the designers – R began to use the location of the advertisements as a way of interpreting the weather (most obviously, one can imagine R might interpret distant advertisements as indicative of windy conditions).

Insofar as the Local Barometer can be said to operate as an idiot (what is the point of sending advertisements into a home on the basis of wind speed and direction?), it becomes apparent that R has co-become with the barometer. Indeed, so too has 'neighbourhood'. R, who was once resistant to the Local Barometer, finds that he is affected by it. The barometer is no longer a conduit of unwanted commercialism, but a digital lens on the surprising character of the surrounding neighbourhoods. And when R begins to read the weather through the advertisements, he is practically posing interesting questions about the idea of neighbourhood: the inventive problem of the neighbourhood now concerns how we conceptualize a neighbourhood. If initially it was comprehended in terms of particular economic, social and cultural features, it came to be apprehended as altogether more surprising in terms of those particular features, and eventually it came to be prehended as something composed of the cultural, the social and the economic but also of the meteorological, the electromagnetic and the digital.

By comparison, the Home Health Monitor (Gaver et al. 2009) was a failure in that it failed to enable any of such speculative prehensions in its users, even though it was meant to 'provide an intriguing reflection on the household's "mood"' (n.p.). The Health Home Monitor was a simplified version of the Home Heath Horoscope (Gaver et al. 2007). The latter entailed a series of sensors around a very large and occasionally hectic household that detected certain physical conditions, frequencies and periods (e.g. whether the door to a particular room was opened or shut for a certain period of time, a sofa was sat on or not, a cleaning cupboard was being used or not). These stood as proxies for particular events such as privacy, social intimacy, cleaning, each of which in turn was indicative (albeit in sometimes ambiguous ways) of well-being, social cohesion, busyness or intimacy. These links between sensors and what was being physically sensed (e.g. door closedness), the activities associated with the physical changes being sensed (e.g. sequestration, privacy), and the meaning of these activities for the household (e.g. intimacy, aggravatingly busy household) were derived from various visits to the household. The data collected through the sensors were sent remotely to a processor that used the frequency and duration of changes, compared these to running totals, and derived the relevant metrics. The two metrics that had changed the most were then used as the basis for drawing on a large collection of statements taken from online horoscopes to generate the final printed output. The system was discussed many times with members of the household, who were less concerned with the accuracy of such statements as 'the household is busy today' as such interpretation of these statements as 'you should slow down'.

As noted above, Home Health Monitor was a simplified version of the Horoscope. This simplification took place for numerous reasons, including the fact that household members focused on the designers' research agenda rather than engaging with the playfulness and ambiguity of output itself. In the transition to the Monitor, the following changes were made: a simpler household was chosen in order to mitigate the Horoscope's over-interpretation of a complex household; as the horoscope genre was not always appropriate, aphorisms were used instead, and later photographs and pie charts of the daily metrics; where the Horoscope sensors were housed in opaque casings which led to some suspicion, the Monitor sensors were rendered more legible by ensuring that their functions were more obvious; whereas the design team were deliberately reticent about their intentions for the Horoscope, for the Monitor they clarified their interest in how to access 'home health'.

Despite all these changes, the Monitor seemed to be an even greater 'failure' than the Horoscope. For instance, the two household members developed a rather critical relation to the Monitor, assessing its outputs in terms of accuracy rather than engaging with their ambiguity as a matter of curiosity and an opportunity for further reflection. At base, they could not see the point of the system; the 'thinness' of the output against the sophistication of the system, the opaqueness of the output statements, the lack of apparent utility for a healthy couple – all of these judgements arose quickly and did not shift over the course of the deployment. This reflected, according to Gaver et al. (2009), a series of disjunctions: the users tolerated rather than engaged with the system, they didn't situate it in relation to other technologies, they didn't domesticate it into household routines, and they didn't greet subsequent changes in and to the system with any interest. Gaver et al. attribute this failure to a number of factors: the system's outputs were too varied and uncontextualized to allow for ready interpretation by the users; the range of inputs was not reflected in the simplicity of the outputs; the Home Health Monitor project was so theoretically oriented that it excluded appropriate considerations of whether the system offered meaningful experiences within a domestic setting.

Let us reconsider the two examples of the Local Barometer and the Home Health Monitor through the conceptual apparatus of the 'idiot'. In the former case, the idiocy of the barometer could be couched in terms of the initial strangeness of having seemingly arbitrary adverts entering into, and being displayed at six different sites around the home. The initial response was one of hostility at what was regarded as commercial invasiveness. However, engagement continued, facilitated by occasional adverts that were seen to be interesting – the idiot was becoming 'useful', and then surprising as advertised objects challenged the user's sense of the socioeconomic character of neighbourhoods, and then productive of a different practical relationship in which the barometer and user co-became something unexpected. By comparison, for the Home Health Monitor, the idiocy of system was never 'penetrated' – the idiot Monitor was rendered, and continued to be rendered, as either incomprehensible or uninteresting.

Toward a conclusion: Idiocy, threat and com-promise

For Stengers, the idiot is a figure that requires a response: we are responsible for paying it heed, for bestowing efficacy upon its murmurings. Yet an idiot that 'murmurs' is a relatively benign or sedate idiot. Idiots also shout, scream and attack. In other words, not making sense takes many forms, including forms that are threatening. Within the relative safety of a philosopher's study, even the more violent expressions of idiocy are food for thought. Yet when the idiot is operationalized as a speculative digital–material device, it can be too 'threatening', leading to incomprehension, disgust, active neglect and a recourse to more conventional ways of thinking (as we glimpsed in the example of the Home Health Monitor).

Now, 'threat' can be taken as a term that in the present case straddles many dimensions: the epistemic, the ethical, the aesthetic, the affective, the social, the political, the economic, and so on (though disambiguating in this way is itself problematic). As noted, the responses to threat take many forms: passivity, avoidance, displaced antagonism, directed aggression, and so on. In addition, threat is relational insofar as what is threatening to one actor is wholly unthreatening to another.

On one level, speculative devices are 'pre-loaded' with a degree of threat in that through their a-functionality and ambiguity they are designed to 'not make sense'. However, the threat of this 'not making sense' can be reinforced in unintended ways: for example, economically (the expense of the design object or project as a whole compared against the apparent triviality of its output); politically or ethically (the issue of home health is pointless for healthy people as opposed to those at risk); the output can be sensorially or aesthetically grating (the invasive noise of Home Health Monitor's printer); epistemically in that the output might not seem to have any value as 'knowledge' (as opposed to inviting reflection on the contingency of knowledge).

According to my online thesaurus at least, the antonym of threat is promise. The sorts of digital–material devices described above can certainly be said to embody promise. Often the speculative devices are highly finished and beautiful (there is a promise of aesthetic pleasure), ambiguous and playful outputs (there is a promise of ludic pleasure), strangely or oddly a-functional (promise of new affects, of self and collective discovery). Further, through initial visit and deployment phases, social relations develop between designers and users (there is a promise of 'sociality'), and in the discussions between users and designers, the design might be framed in terms of wider issues (the promise of a future innovative digital materialities).

In the same way that threat is relational, so too, in the present context, is promise (despite its particular locutionary character – see Austin 1962). As we saw in the case of the Local Barometer, its promise began to overcome its threat: R first became engrossed in some of its content, then practically engaged with aspects of its potentiality. By contrast, its users seemed resolutely to find no promise in the Home Health Monitor. Put simply, whereas R opened himself up to the openness of the Local Barometer, the Monitor's users did not. But then, as Connolly (2011) writes, such openness is perhaps less open to people 'who accede too much to conventional wisdom or power' (2011: 159).

Etymologically, 'promise' can be understood as a 'putting forward'. We might say that the speculative device is designed to 'put itself forward' in a particular way that makes its idiotic 'threat' more approachable, accessible. However, at the same time, the potential users are being read and enacted by the designers as themselves having promise. Users must not 'threaten' the project, they also need to 'put themselves forward' in relation to the idiotic device's 'putting itself forward'. There is, in other words, a putting forward together – a 'com-promise' (where 'com' etymologically signals 'together'). On top of this, as hinted in the foregoing, there is the com-promise that encompasses the designers' engagements with prospective users and their household: a relationship is co-crafted in which there is a tacit exchange of promises about the general nature of the design system, the users' commitments to the project, and so on. We have seen how these com-promises don't always hold fast.

The point of this concluding discussion has been to try and illuminate some of the implicit threats and promises, and their mutual management, in the form of what has here been called 'com-promise'. These com-promises, it has been suggested, undergird speculative research and the digital–material forms it takes. In orienting social scientific research toward the prospective and the virtual of events, com-promises have to be made which favour some prospects over others. These com-promises operate in complex, perhaps even topological, ways across numerous actors, events and relations; we have mentioned only a few here. In the end, the notion of a com-promise is simply a heuristic means of thinking about the virtualities that need to be put in place in order to enable the virtualities of the research event itself.

7

Ethnography and the quest to (co)design a mixed reality interactive slide

Jaume Ferrer, Elisenda Ardèvol and Narcís Parés

Introduction

In recent years, human–computer interaction (HCI) research has increasingly engaged with ethnographic practice as a way to incorporate users into the design process. This has involved exploring ways to account for the user's social context, experience, needs and desires and experimenting with participatory forms of user collaboration, such as co-design, community-oriented or participatory design projects. In this chapter we take these discussions further by rethinking the agency of the user in the creative processes of digital (co)design. To achieve this, we situate the user and designer in a design process, in which their relationship, framed by a context of shared use, embodies experience and digital materiality. In doing so, we carry out an ethnographic exploration of an interactive design process that aims to support children's physical activity and sociality: the Interactive Slide.

The experience, the designers and the embedded ethnographer

The ethnographic experience which is the object of our analysis is based on long-term research which at the time was situated within the field of interactive playgrounds[1] and carried out at the Interactive Systems Lab[2] in Barcelona (hereinafter, the Lab) following different phases of prototyping and development for the Interactive Slide project.

The Interactive Slide is a full-body, multi-user, non-invasive interactive experience composed of a large inflatable slide that is augmented with interactive technology. As it is currently configured, the slide has a sliding surface which also acts as an image projection screen. A computer vision system detects the movements and actions of children to allow them to play with an interactive experience on the sliding surface of the artefact. The idea is therefore to 'augment' the traditional slide structure with a virtual environment. It has been conceived as a *mixed reality* (Rowe 2014) video game platform because the playable structure is defined by the virtuality of the projected images, which, in turn, are dependent on the physical properties of the slide (i.e. gravity, friction, slope, etc.).

When the ethnographer first entered the Lab in 2008, he took on the role of an embedded observer of the design team's daily work. His research was presented as an exploratory study of the relationship between designers and users in a process of digital design that furthered standard practice in its field by exceeding the perspective and concepts of design methodologies. One of the main goals of the research was to produce knowledge based on empirical data on the relationship between the expectations of the designers and the experiences of users, in order to, on the one hand, increase their understanding of the experiences of and meanings of the users, and on the other hand, carry out careful observation of the design process to contribute to improving and evaluating the results of their architecture. But, above all, the apprentice ethnographer (a designer himself) wanted to go beyond using ethnography as a toolkit for evaluating the usability of a design, in order to learn instead about how technology was produced, how a design process worked, and what kinds of relationships existed between the different actors. To this end, he tried to put aside what he knew about design to embrace social sciences, anthropology and the social study of the technology perspective with the (sometimes waning) promise of a broader view of his own ways of doing and understanding his own craft. This text is part of an ongoing dialogue between design and anthropology across his ethnographic fieldwork experience.[3]

As an academic research project, the social problem-solving aim that guided the slide's design was to promote physical activity and face-to-face socialization among children. The project, as with other exertion interface designs (Kjaersgaard 2012; van Delden et al. 2014), aimed to contribute to research in interactive body games as a way of compensating for the increasingly sedentary behaviours and isolated forms of sociality among young generations, usually associated with video games and digital technologies (Cavill et al. 2006). The process of design was planned following the *interaction-driven design* strategy that had been already formalized by the leader of the Lab and applied in previous projects[4]:

> This *interaction-driven design* strategy defines a framework to start designing from *the attitude that we wish the users to have with respect to the application*. In other words, instead of starting the design from a specific content (which would define a content-driven design strategy), we first decide what actions in the users will support the attitude we wish them to adopt, and it is not until later in the process that the content can emerge within the application. (Soler-Adillon, Ferrer and Parés 2009: 134, our italics)

In relation to the interactive design, the 'user' was defined according to: first, the social problem being solved (children's sedentary and social isolation behaviours); second, the cognitive and physical skills associated with a specific age group (children between twelve and sixteen years old); and, third, the *desired attitude* of the users in their interaction with the system. Thus, the desired attitude guided the design of the set of rules for the game, the algorithms of the learning system and the content and aesthetics of the game. The goal was to develop an application that would engage children while at the same time fostering healthy physical activity in a controlled manner. Hence, the system had to detect the amount of physical activity of the users and regulate it by changing the *interaction tempo* of the experience according to specific criteria defined by physical educators or medical experts. Therefore, we can say that the user's behaviour was defined side by side with the interactive system's behaviour, and it would be the correct coordination between both that would bring 'the thing' into its full existence. In the case of the *Robot Factory* application for the slide, it took a musical form:

> With the musical referent of the metronome as a basis, the design process led us to consider actions of the users that could follow clearly mechanical patterns; i.e. it related to a mechanical device so that the tempo could be important in the activation of different mechanisms. One of the references that immediately came up was Charles Chaplin's *Modern Times* movie and his repetitive actions. Robots were another important referent for mechanical actions. An important point for us was to obtain an application

that promoted collaboration among the users. We did not want to allow individualities to succeed in the game and leave the rest of the users aside. We wished to see organization of user tasks emerge as a team that works for the same goal. Therefore, we decided that the system would trigger several actions simultaneously to force different users to act in parallel and they should all work together to, for example, construct something. Finally, since we wanted the users to do some physical activity, we decided that the experience would use as much as possible the whole surface of the slide. This way we would force users to go from top to bottom and from one end to the other. The resulting application was *Robot Factory*. A game inspired by a production line, with a simple goal: to construct a robot. (Soler-Adillon, Ferrer and Parés 2009: 137)

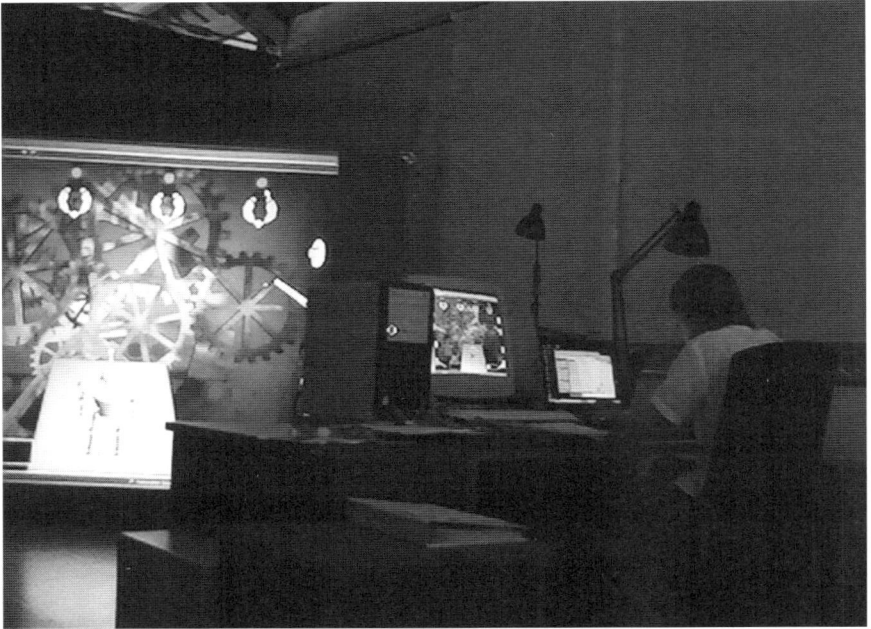

FIGURE 7.1 *Prototype mural screen for* Robot Factory: *the screen is part of the work point where the interactive script's designer works simultaneously as developer and user in order to test the code lines.*

The *desired attitude* was built on the system as a chain of events that entailed ability, speed and team strategy by the users:

They must be well organized to attend the different events that the system is periodically generating. They must be fit to slide down and run back to the top to attend new situations. They must be quick in reflexes to notice the changes in levers or valves to be able to activate or deactivate them within the allotted time. (ibid.: 138)

Although the designers were not trying to design the inner emotional experience of the users, they expected that the physical activity they hoped to achieve in children would be accompanied by a playful experience based on a good balance of cooperation between users and competition with the system, as in many basic game rules. Using these principles, one might say that the designers were following the user experience design model (Kuutti 2001), by which the user is the ultimate consumer of a product or service, and, thus, the person's experience is a key goal of the design.

Finally, the fact that the Interactive Slide experience was developed in a research centre must be taken into account; thus, emphasis was put on the prototyping of a 'new' object/environment that provided new affordances for interactive systems. The development of the slide was part of an academic project, and its development heavily relied on the ability to attract postgraduate students to collaborate as part of their academic training. By way of example, one recruitment call was: 'Student task: develop a game and a brain for the Interactive Slide that detects and understands group behaviours of children playing in it and adapts to their tempo and structure or, on the contrary, challenges them to achieve new goals or configurations.'[5] Thus, following Suchman, the constitution of the Interactive Slide was also a 'strategic resource in the alignment of professional identities and organizational positionings' (Suchman 2005: 4). Within the Lab, the central value that shaped the designers' work was its innovative aim. The slide's value as a scientific object lay in its potential to contribute to the variety of research fields in which the designers were affiliated. As a scientifically affiliated object, the slide (at the time, Spanish patent pending) was part of the daily activity of the researchers in the field of human–computer interaction, artificial intelligence, interactive playgrounds, exertion games, and so on. In the context of the Lab, as we will further explain, the user was theorized, imagined and performed as a critical device together with the digital system, and as the 'other' that the software of the interactive experience had to confront.

The hosts and their guests

In order to avoid ready-made categorizations of what was happening in the Lab and beyond its walls, the ethnographer chose to understand the designer as the 'host' user and the user as the 'guest' user. It was still a binary typology, but symmetrical and complementary, based on the common ground that both designers and end users had an experience when using the slide. The crucial difference between them was not that of expertise, but the fact that they experienced the slide in different ways, at different times, and for different purposes. Grudin (1993) argues that expressions such as 'user' and 'designer' mostly derive from the way computer engineering faced the initial designs for lay people and still influences our understanding of the systems that we analyse. According to Grudin, the term 'user' is commonly understood as a general category of non-experts, but it also implicitly denies the different levels of expertise that any individual can present, both in the use of computers and, more importantly, in the specific fields that are relevant to them for their interaction with computers. On the one hand, we suggest that it also happens with 'designers', as this category is built by covering up the different skills, disciplines and practices that unfold during the design process and erasing the vast amount of know-how that the members of a design team generate. On the other hand, we argue that the 'user' is a necessary figure in computer design, not only because this design is oriented to human inter-action, but also and precisely because of the impossibility of the designers acting as non-experienced users in their own designs, i.e. to experience their creation as a whole and for the purpose it has been created for.

Crabtree et al. (2005) and Stringer et al. (2006) also discuss how, through approaches apparently taking users into account – usually when the user is called to participate in the design process – the user is incorporated without questioning the division between 'user' and 'designer'. Thus, the user is included not as an equal, but as a source of information or, at best, as a guest co-worker who *may* be necessary, as he or she can provide useful infor-mation for optimizing the design or simply knowing what to design, but who is excluded from fundamental decisions in the design process. However, in the case of HCI design, the nub of the issue seems much more complicated; it is also a matter of how the 'thing' that is being created intervenes in their interlocution.

Inspired by Lucy Suchman (2011), our idea was to relocate design production from design methods and theories to the daily experience of use. Thus, we proposed trying to understand users and designers based on what they share, and trying to do it symmetrically. Symmetrically, in Latour's (2005) terms, does not necessarily mean that they must be 'equal' or that there are no power relations, or that they share the same worldviews. Rather, symmetrical here means that the same theoretical framework is applied for everyone on the different sides of a relationship and who shape what that relationship will look like. Thus, we drew upon the idea that there were no ontological differences between host and guest users a priori.

Acknowledging the work of authors like Dourish (2006) and Suchman (2002), we sought an ethnography that went beyond the role of reporting on the habits and practices of a technology's potential end users and instead contributed to the framing of encounters between those seemingly on different sides of a production relationship. Why should we 'separate the technical practices of organization or a set of users from those others with whom they interact, from whom they learn, and with whom they exchange information, artifacts, and people?' (Dourish 2006: 548). One of the virtues of ethnography is exactly that it consists of the possibility of a symmetrical, relational and undivided accounting of persons and things in a given locality (Mackenzie 2003).

For example, examining the user experience design model, McCarthy and Wright (2004) insist that user experience is phenomenological and experiential by nature. User experience, they say, is more than a pattern of behaviour, and a user-oriented design should be sensitive to emotions, expectations, imagination and, moreover, a user's ability to create meaning:

> We don't just use technology; we live with it. Much more deeply than ever before, we are aware that interacting with technology involves us emotionally, intellectually, and sensually. For this reason, those who design, use, and evaluate interactive systems need to be able to understand and analyse people's felt experience with technology. (McCarthy and Wright 2004: preface)

Our question then was: What if we consider designers as 'experiencers' of their own designs? We understand experience from a practice theory approach: as embodied emotions, expectations, desires, and so on, entailed in practical activity (Schatzki et al. 2001). Thus, the experience of the designer includes expectations, emotions and imaginings in relation to the object of design and the future user. Furthermore, when working with the object of design, the designer also gains an experience of the object that modulates his or her further experiences (i.e. learning by experience, having an experience, being an experienced craftsman). Therefore, we might say that designers are users in the sense that they have a direct and very complex experience of using their own technology in the making, and that they also have some (more or less formulated) expectations about what it can do and what they want it to do. In the case of interactive design as we are studying it, these embodied experiences also include the expectations about what the object is able to do in relation to bodily actions, and what meaning these relationships might have for them (and other users). This is the reason that designers invest so much effort in imagining and designing the content and aesthetics of the interactive – they want to create a meaningful experience (for the user and the machine).

From our standpoint, 'users' and 'designers' of an interactive design can be considered 'participants' of a shared user experience that is not fixed once and for all. Nevertheless, the designer is a particular type of participant that, among other things, has a rich embodied experience of the object, while at the same time having expert knowledge of the object's possible behaviours. The designer imagines, from these and other previous experiences, the embodied experience that some other participant might go through in different instances with the thing they are creating.

In designing an experience, the user's body is imagined in its specific relationship with the interactive 'stuff'. Bateson – an anthropologist who has pioneered the concept of cybernetics together with Wiener – refers to the dilemma of who does the thinking: the brain or the machine. He asked this based on the idea that brain and machine are actually an integrated system, just as our body perception does not end where our skin ends. In the same vein, the main process of an interactive system may reside in the machine, but it does not have to. The notion of imagining, understood as an experience of other bodies in relation to our own (Mackenzie 2003: 367), might help us here. For Mackenzie, imagining combines an awareness of relationships between bodies with a certain inadequacy or incompleteness in knowledge:

> This inadequacy or incompleteness need not be seen as a deficit (as it might be in certain accounts of imagination as 'what fills in the gap'). Rather, the incompleteness stems from the fact that bodies in relation are changed by their encounters. Imagining effectively most powerfully connects bodies through the associative mediation of images. But at the same time, it leaves that connection in question. What is imagined may not happen or may not have happened. (Mackenzie 2003: 369)

Imagination in interactive design, as we understand it, is not about hopes and fears, but about bodies and relationships.

Sketches, drawings, diagrams, different kinds of prototypes, graspable models and also gestures are part of the day-to-day work at the Lab. According to Hornecker (2007), these different modulations have different characteristics and suggest or enable different forms of usage, interaction styles and variations in meaning. Creating models and prototypes helps designers to correct and control their ideas and to visualize the interplay of parts. In our Lab meetings, the team leader usually asked the younger designer to sketch some ideas on how to face a particular problem. Imagination was put into play to explore possible relationships between bodies (or the body of the user and its possible interactions with the object). Imagination was also put into play for inquiring into the bodily and material experience of the possible forms or the processes through which it is given articulate yet tentative forms (Halse 2012: 181). This is an excerpt from the field notes:

FIGURE 7.2 *At the Lab, designers exchange views on technical design issues with the help of a notebook on the desk where an application for the Interactive Slide is being developed. To the right of the screen, one can see a desktop prototype for this exergame platform: a paper silhouette of the user 'rests' on a miniature slide made of polystyrene. On the left, next to the arm of the researcher, one can see a black camera used to test the system for shape recognition. On the computer screen one can see Pascuza, the software used to calibrate the artificial vision system.*

This is one of the first meetings to talk about the slide project between the engineer [E] and the young student [S] who is going to design the interaction script and write the code. It takes place at the Lab. A round table lies in the middle of the room, near the main door entrance, and surrounded by diverse working points. In one of these points someone is working on what I think is the optimization of the detection system of an infrared pointing interface (a physical interface that captures the position and orientation of the arm through two cameras). Two robotic arms, which provide haptic-feedback, remain motionless on two pedestals. I recognize the wooden structure of the slide prototype and, just behind it, a large projection screen for interactive systems that enables the detection of the entire body. At the time of the meeting, the screen is not being used, so it looks like a large rectangular panel, grey and dull. Beyond the screen, I glimpse a small warehouse area with cabinets, boxes and crates. And just behind the screen, hidden from us, a projector is pointing at us from one corner of the room. We sit at the table. Someone has left a remote control and a large pair of scissors with blue plastic handles. The student adds an A4 notepad, a case for eyeglasses, a mobile phone and a packet of tissues. […]

Some verbatim notes about the conversation:

E: I thought about something that pops up from the floor and you have to play with it, like the water jets in Water Games [a previous project]. We should do something fun. We want to have some excitement, something that would look finished, not a laboratory experiment […] If you want to try something with them it must be something that is worth them spending some time on; then you can have them there for a while; it should be something that motivates them. If we bore them, they will fall asleep.
S: You say… we may start with something playable…
E: …something like a firecracker, that rises… and… [moving his arm up]
S: I thought maybe something that moves up and down… [swinging his hands]
E: Maybe horizontal and vertical cross-cutting activities… [crossing his arms]
S: I saw an installation… blocks appeared… that you had to jump over…

In this conversation, the two designers were imagining user bodily actions through their own body actions and based on other previous interaction experiences – both from designs for previous projects and from playing with someone else's project. Gestural movements involved connecting their own lives to those of others (Gunn and Donovan 2012: 5), but here, they were also imagining the user's engagement at the same time as their body actions and transitions were put in relation to code, machines, software tools and other devices. They were also imagining what kids would like most, looking for an exciting and meaningful embodied experience. The 'user' took different forms: sometimes she was a pattern of behaviour, other times a body motion, a curious child, a simple gesture, and so on. What they were also worried about was how to keep the users engaged in conversation with the system so they could get enough data for testing their non-intrusive tools for physical exertion measurement; this was one of the key issues of *the experiment*, as they called it.

For the ethnographer, the slide was like a shared space, an environment created and maintained by the host users, which at some point let the guest users in, in order to share and confront their own experiences. They wanted their guests to have a rich, full and pleasurable experience, as well as get some healthy exercise. But to achieve that goal, they first needed to test that the slide worked well; that the dialogue between actual living humans and the system was fluid and harmonious, like the symbiotic relationship of the flower and the bee.

The experiment

On 17 July 2008, the Euroscience Open Forum, under the slogan *Science for a Better Life*, was about to open its doors at the Fira de Barcelona exhibition centre. At the two stands of the Research Institute, people worked to get everything ready. The inflated Interactive Slide rose, slightly rounded, white, big and strong, occupying a significant area of the exhibition. Several components surrounded the big object: an air compressor that hummed endlessly, a workstation on a table, a crank-up tower holding a projector and a digital camera, an infrared light source, loudspeakers, empty packing boxes and many connection cables, leaving little room for other facilities. Nearby, there was an exoskeleton intended for arm rehabilitation treatments in front of a screen, a small robot that could learn how to find things, two force-feedback arms … and, separated by a corridor, others were testing another installation from the Institute, an interactive experience called 'Oracle'. In front of the slide, a team from the University of Torino was presenting a stand under the name 'Secrets of the Frontiers of the Mind and Brain', the bright lights of which seemed to impair the lighting conditions required for the slide. Around the slide, the engineer moved up and down, going over the details: placing warning tape to limit access here, adhesive tape to protect cables there, situating the loudspeakers. He then started to work on our laptop, using the large packing box of the exoskeleton as a table. On this improvised table, the ethnographer had placed the tripod holding the video camera which would record the experiment. A few steps away, the young designer was typing at the workstation that controlled the slide.

Later, the engineer, the young interactive designer and another student tested the slide themselves. They climbed the unstable and elastic ladder to the left side of the slide and positioned themselves on top of the upper cornice. Meanwhile, a scene of a virtual world was projected on the sliding ramp, where a mould in the shape of a robot called for pieces, surrounded by levers, gears and steam. A noise could be heard as if coming from a factory machine. At the top of the sliding surface, a moving chain of virtual clamps held virtual mechanical pieces while robot pieces moved across the projection. The three observed the projected scene from above, waiting for the right moment to jump, sliding down the ramp and trying to interact with the projected images. They jumped, hit and moved quickly. The three hardly ever stopped on the lower central position, unlike when the system was tested on the large screen back at the Lab.

After going up and down for a while, the team leader called a meeting. The three of them sat on the exit platform, the projected images illuminating their sweaty faces while they recovered their breath after all the exertion. Then they discussed the interaction tempo of the application and training for the user groups to come; the fastest tempo would only be tested with users who had used the slide before and only if there were more people waiting. Discussion completed, the young designer resumed testing on his own. For a long while he climbed, jumped, slapped... to check the response of levers, clamps and virtual valves. He turned the control screen around in order to see the black and white image generated by the tracking vision system at a distance from the slide... and he exclaimed: 'This is probably the most tiring application to test in history!'

Given that the Interactive Slide only existed in its complete form outside the laboratory, events like this were a unique opportunity for the designers to experience it with all its full-body functionalities. Since the team leader had already tested the physical structure of the slide and its technology-augmented nature at a previous event, on this occasion the goals were more oriented toward testing the new game experience and whether they could get users to play with the game and the slide as a single unit. Moreover, they were interested in having an initial view of whether and how users could adapt their play intensity – their physical activity – to the interaction tempo of the application. *The experiment* consisted basically of having consecutive groups of three or four children play with the physical and virtual devices and getting data on their activity recorded by the system. By doing so, in their own words, they wished to test whether their method for measuring the physical activity of groups of users worked adequately, whether the system could influence the amount of physical activity done by a group of users, and whether the system could modulate and automatically adjust to the amount of physical activity done by a group of players (Soler-Adillon, Ferrer and Parés 2009: 137).

For the Lab team, *the experiment* was an exciting moment to test the work done during more than half a year. Hence, after having tested that everything was working smoothly and ready for the play sessions of their guests, they got ready to put the system in action. For the visitors that were queuing to play on the slide, the 'experiment' was a promise of playful amusement and wonder – to experiment with the artefact. From the ethnographer's point of view, it was a unique opportunity to observe the host and the guest users using the Interactive Slide. The ethnographer had been recording the host users in their lab, talking about the slide, imagining the preferences of users and their body movements, programming the system, tuning the devices, drawing cards, cutting cardboard prototypes of the slide and user silhouettes, etc. Finally, there he was, recording the whole interactive system in action.

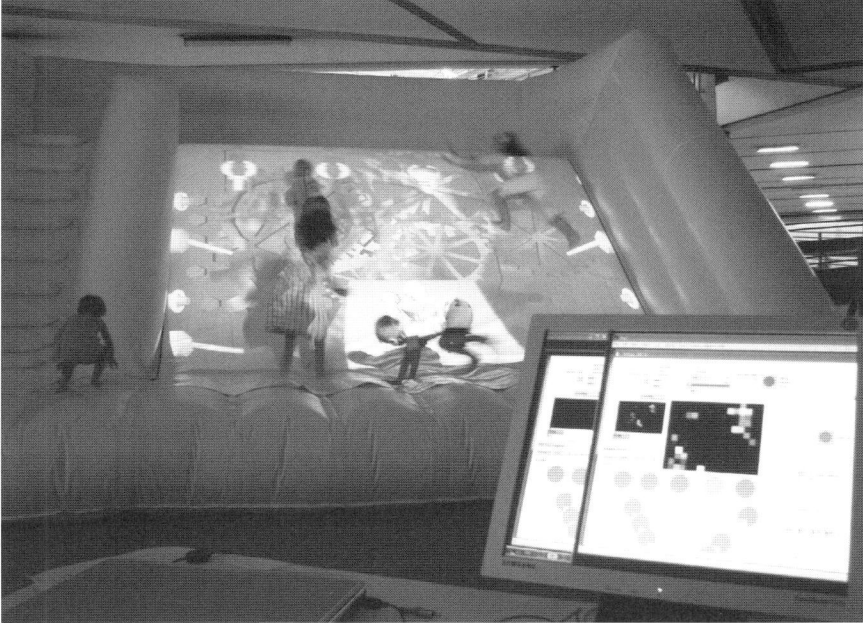

FIGURE 7.3 Robot Factory *with a group of very young children using the ramp to climb. In the foreground the screen shows the computer vision control system that the 'host users' use to verify that the activity of the 'guest users' is adequately tracked and that the elements of the virtual environment are being correctly activated by them.*

Based on the results of the consecutive sessions of play (the statistical automatic measurements and the qualitative and quantitative analysis of the visual records made by the dedicated ethnographer), the experiment was replicated in subsequent events, refining its parameters and adding new features. At every installation site, the ethnographer noticed that, when playing with the Interactive Slide, the host users played on it in a different way to that of the guest users and that subsequent adjustments to interactive system parameters to correct unexpected dysfunctionalities were also consistently and slightly 'subverted' by new, unexpected user behaviours. People usually used things in ways which were far beyond what the designers expected, but why? What were the kids doing?

Playing the right way

Expressions like 'playing well' or 'playing incorrectly' were frequent at the experiment event. The host users even commented in a humorous tone that the guest users were 'boycotting' the game. In the words of the young programmer, some players were not playing well, they were not playing the way they should, but nevertheless they were able to build robots, and this was the explicit goal of the game. Hence, what was actually going wrong?

Due to the disparity between the way some guest users played the *Robot Factory* game and the way the host users had expected, the data generated by the system during these play sessions did not follow the experimental criteria. Therefore, the data from those sessions had to be discarded, which partially weakened the experimental study. The activity detection system was designed for an 'ideal' behaviour, where players slide down and remain briefly at the base of the ramp, then climb back up again through the stairs and repeat the loop while interacting with the projected images. However, some of them stayed at the base of the ramp for a long time, while others stayed at the top. Moreover, some climbed the ramp instead of using the stairs (Figure 7.3). The issue was that some of these unexpected behaviours led to the robots being constructed with greater success. Based on a sample of the different groups, the statistical results showed that the best results, in terms of success in the game (making robots), were achieved (optimized) by those groups with 'misbehaving' players (whose physical movements took advantage of detection flaws in the activity detection system). These results were problematic, not only because they were associated with less physical activity during the play session, but also because this 'incorrect' way of playing interfered with the system's ability to record and regulate the activity. The fact that the game was 'well played' was a determining factor of the experiment's success and had an impact on the development of the whole project.

The observations made and interviews held by the ethnographer with children during the experiment sessions confirmed that they were playing and having fun. However, what kind of game were they playing? Did they play the same game as the host users?

The team did a thorough and systematic analysis of the video footage, concentrating on the players' changes on the surface of the slide throughout the play session. Different guests groups (three to four players for groups, four minutes of gaming each group, in twenty-nine play sessions) were analysed and results contrasted with the data obtained from the same careful analysis of the recordings of the host group (three players, in different rounds and sessions). We concluded that while the host group was playing the game in terms of individual physical activity, guest players were organizing themselves into collective actions to increase the probabilities of success in the game. The video recording and analysis not only confirmed these differences, but also provided documented evidence of different ways of managing space and time, as shown by a comparison of two extreme cases (see Figure 7.4.1 and 7.4.2).

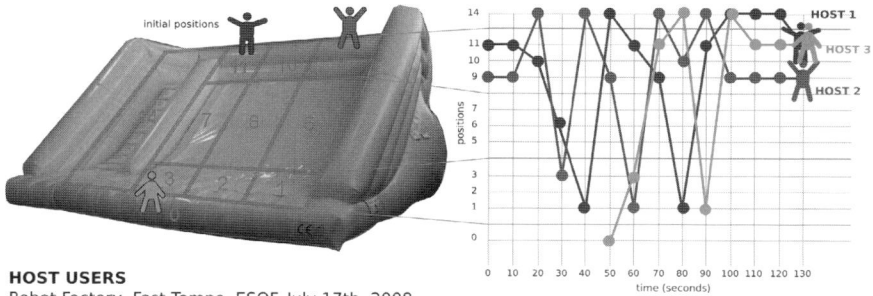

HOST USERS
Robot Factory, Fast Tempo. ESOF. July 17th, 2008

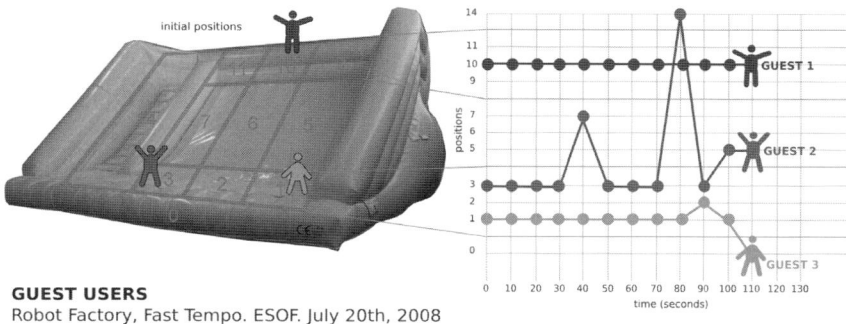

GUEST USERS
Robot Factory, Fast Tempo. ESOF. July 20th, 2008

FIGURE 7.4.1 AND FIGURE 7.4.2 Robot Factory: *Extreme examples where each group followed completely opposing strategies. Host users (top) moved up and down constantly and all the team players passed through all the zones and were synchronized, even though host user 3 joined the game later than the others. Guest users (bottom), however, barely changed their position (shortest arm and leg movements) and divided the space so that each one focused on 'their' territory. The interviews revealed that, in general, this organization could be both intentional, responding to a prior agreement between the participants, and the spontaneous result of a dynamic game where the guest players made no prior negotiations. Moreover, some were not even aware of the fact that they had followed an organized pattern.*

The analysis of the players' movements across the slide's surface revealed two different play strategies in relation to the physical surface of the slide and the virtual interactive system:

a) The movements of the host users followed a regular pattern, climbing up the stairs, sliding down while trying to interact with the virtual objects to create the robot, spending a short amount of time at the bottom of the slide's ramp and climbing back up again to repeat the sequence in a similar way.

b) The guest users did not use the stairs as often and they did not follow a regular pattern in relation to the surface of the slide (e.g.

alternating positions at the top or bottom), and often used the ramp to partially climb up to reach a virtual object. Essentially, they interacted with the virtual objects by standing at the bottom of the ramp and basically on both sides, and not only when sliding down.

Both groups of players (hosts and guests) interacted with the *logic interface* of the slide in a meaningful way – that is, they accomplished the task of building robots.

The ethnographer observed that these two different strategies could be explained by looking at how the users were giving meaning to their actions – that is, the way in which the host and guest users integrated the physical and virtual components of the game depended on their previous experiences and their knowledge of the rules and objectives of the game. In the case of the host users, when playing, they knew that the main objective of the game was to engage in physical activity. They knew that the system was measuring their physical activity in a very specific way, and, therefore, they followed the 'correct' path. Finally, they knew that 'building a robot' was only a fun component intended to keep the physical activity going. However, this ultimate goal of the interactive experience was not made explicit to the guest users. They were given some basic rules and a goal for the game: to build as many robots as possible and enjoy the game. Through their own experience of the game, they discovered that they could achieve better results if they organized themselves by tasks, with different expertise thus being developed among the players. Moreover, while waiting in the queue for their turn to play, they watched other players and hence engaged in a complex learning process that related physical activity with their understanding of the logic of the virtual system and with their ability to cooperate socially.

Some of the guest users became 'skilled practitioners' (Kilbourn, 2012). For example, in one of the sessions, there was one child who appeared to be extremely engrossed in the game. He had already played six rounds and when called to be part of an upcoming group of players, he refused to play with that group of children: 'No, I don't want to play in this group, they don't know how to play! They will do it like this little girl [pointing at a girl that was then sliding down]. They don't think!' A while later, he looked much happier. 'How is it going?' the ethnographer asked. 'Much better now, good team!'

To the ethnographer's eye, this and subsequent experiments, together with the analysis of his notes, interviews, recordings and graphics, point to the enormous importance of self-organization among the children during the game experience. This 'social factor' was something that was acting ineludibly as a disruptive force in every attempt by the designers to reconfigure the system to get the *desired attitude* of the user. Perhaps the results of *Robot Factory* were not those expected (especially in terms of promoting controlled, healthy physical activity), but the Interactive Slide proved to be a good tool for socialization among children and for learning collective action coordination. While the designers were studying the data in order to correct system 'errors' to get the desired results, the ethnographer's experience confirmed that the deeper he went into the analysis of the chore-ographic movements of the children playing with the evolving Interactive Slide, the more it appeared to him that he was trying to capture a fascinating elusive life form (Ingold 2011).

Between 2008 and 2011, the Interactive Slide evolved in different ways: from the different versions of *Robot Factory* to an almost entirely new appli-cation, *Balloons*. In these different prototypes, the main focus was on the development of a non-intrusive measurement system of physical activity and on the improvement of the interactive system to adapt its tempo to a desired amount of physical activity. Alongside the tasks of reprogramming, reframing and re-parameterizing the slide, the Lab team also developed new explicit game rules for the players (e.g. avoid task specialization). Hence, the playing style of hosts and guests was gradually converging into the same patterns. Between 2011 and 2012 the slide had a double life as a tentative platform for virtual learning environments based on embodied cognition (*Archimedes*) and as the already described system to foster physical activity through a new game, *Fishing*. This game was obtained as the result of a participatory design process with girls and boys.

A seasoned object

The slide was a tangible, touchable and measurable object. It could be traversed and manipulated (just like places, habitats, tools or vehicles). It was heavy, noisy, equipped with a crank-up tower, an infrared light source, cables, a projector, a computer, etc. It resembled a fairground attraction yet at the same time was simple and austere, as an enigmatic piece of industrial equipment. It also had another tangible side: the virtual environment that changed with each new experiment (the projected images that react at the rank of movements monitored by the vision system). Finally, there was its hard core, something profound and hidden, something almost ignored by the guest users but that was the subject of the fundamental work of its creators: its software. Different layers of code, with rules, scripts, tools, and utilities made sense of the whole assemblage, turning it into something interactive and alive, able to converse with bodies, movements and gestures – the 'thing' that engaged the kids in meaningful playtime.

FIGURE 7.5 *The installation of the mixed reality Interactive Slide.*

We could say that the Interactive Slide is a *coded object*; 'its materiality is reliant on software to perform as designed' (Kitchin and Dodge 2011: 5). The code is a constitutive element of the object because it shapes the materiality of the slide as well as its presence in the world, i.e. its ability to generate a response, a conversation with the bodies that walk through it, and be able to change its own behaviour accordingly. According to Kitchin and Dodge:

> Although software is not sentient and conscious, it can exhibit some of the characteristics of being alive [...] This property of being alive is significant because it means code can make things do work in the world in an autonomous fashion – that is, it can receive capta and process information, evaluate situations, make decisions, and, most significant, act without human oversight. (2011: 5)

Code enables a suite of 'understated' technologies, the environments of which become both extended and active (Thrift 2005: 464).

Our Interactive Slide was born in 2003 as an idea, an interesting engineering project with great potential for recreational and educational goals. Its inflatable body was developed during 2006 and first tested as part of an interactive experience in 2007 (*Virtual Mosaic*).[6] In its more than five years of existence, the Interactive Slide gained experience as a 'seasoned' coded object. During its life, in the iterative process of testing and improving the interactive system, it matured with each new host and guest user. It underwent transformations: parameters were adjusted, new code lines added, new images and aesthetic environments generated, game rules, etc. Thus, the slide embodies hours and hours of experience from the play sessions of host and guest users – and it is still an ongoing digital–material existence.

We have seen that host users play with the coded object in a very specific way: that is, checking that the system is working as they expected. What makes the slide a singular object is *the system*. While host users say they play with 'the system', some guest users say that they play with 'the slide', but more often it is with the 'video game'. Indeed, they seem not to take the object into account in their play experience. It is experienced as a game space – a made-up environment. The slide is experienced as an object neither by the guest nor the host user. The 'thing' is an experience for the host and the guest user but of a different kind. It is defined by its developers as 'the system'. The system is more than its physical components; ultimately it is the code that makes the system what it is. The system could then be understood as a specific kind of imagined alignment, integration and connection among things that cannot be reduced to a substantial or tangible unity. 'The integrity of a system has to be imagined, because it cannot readily be seen or articulated' (Mackenzie 2003: 369).

Designers play with the system mainly to detect program errors and debug them. Only on special occasions (the experiments) can they play with the whole object at hand and see how other users experiment with it; usually they play with emulator prototypes, alternatively testing different parts of the system. Designers play to ensure the system works well, and to ensure this they repeat fragments of conversation with specific meanings a hundred times, but they rarely complete full sentences. This is where the notion of experiment comes in; they need someone who can play the game, without being worried about the system. They need someone – the guest user – who converses with the coded object without taking every word into account, someone able to engage with the whole thing in a fluid conversational manner. Therefore, the guest users are more than mere users. In fact, they could be described as co-workers. Co-workers because they have a task to do when playing: they are helping the designers to test the robustness of the design as a whole. But can they be described as co-designers?

Why (co)design?

The concept of co-design is understood usually as a consequence of a collaborative effort in the creative side of design. For example, some authors define co-design as collective creativity that is applied across the whole span of a design process: 'We use co-design in a broader sense to refer to the creativity of designers and people not trained in design working together in the design development process' (Sanders and Stappers 2008: 4). Co-design is aligned with co-creativity, and creativity is considered here as an individual act of bringing something new into existence. Therefore, we might argue that the children who participated in the experiments were collaborating as co-designers because their unexpected ways of playing could be seen as a form of collective creativity that was challenging the host users' way of playing, revealing new possible rules and actions for the game, proposing new grounds for further applications, and thus contributing to the creation of new versions of the slide. But as for their participation in the design process of *Robot Factory*, since it was not based on their play expertise or on their own experience as players but rather was limited to their body activity, the guest users in this case cannot be considered co-designers (at least in Sanders and Stappers' sense), because they did not participate consciously either in the creative process or in the decision-making (Stirling 2008).

However, we feel that the role of the guest users in the slide design process must be understood as that of an active agent – not a passive user. They were a flow that could be sensed by the vision system and which was in dialogue with the code. Claiming their materiality is what allows us to say that the children 'danced' with the designers through the Interactive Slide and that their participation was as important as that of the designers themselves in the slide's configurations. Following Hodder, we can say that the guest users – in their materiality and flow – were pivotal to the Interactive Slide's existence and were incorporated into its experience. They had an important role in the successive transformations of the slide. Surprisingly enough, users are key co-agents – and co-designers, we would argue – in the design process because of its materiality and thingness. In terms of computer science, its agency happens in a deep layer between bits and atoms: in the modular flow of bodies in movement. As Hodder claims, humans are themselves complex things with a particular life form. Like any other thing, the human is a transient bounded entity through which energy flows, connecting it to other things (Hodder 2012: 219–21). Therefore, users and designers are caught up in the Interactive Slide entanglement in very specific ways that come about through complex material interactions. This position restores the gap between the 'human being' and the 'human factor' in traditional HCI design. Users become co-designers in their agency as things and are in dialogue with the code through their materiality, and code mediates the relationship between the co-designers.

If the agency of any living thing is acknowledged, the user's agency cannot be obliterated, and there is always (co)design, whether as a kind of thing or as a human with needs, expectations, and so forth. Even in co-design, participatory design or open design, there is a moment when the digital designer codes the object, and this intimacy with the system excludes her or him from experiencing it as a whole. Here, it is not an issue of different kinds of expertise, but of different kinds of experience. The interactive designer always needs a guest user, because 'the user' is the only one that has a holistic experience of the system, and it is through experimentation that he or she actively contributes to giving it its shape and has a decisive role in the design creation. Vindicating the material conditions of users allows us to understand user and designer as co-designers, opening generative ways of understanding design as a co-creation process between living beings.

8

Designing for the active human body in a digital–material world

Florian 'Floyd' Mueller

Introduction

Recently, there has been a trend in using technology to support the active human body. This contrasts with the prevalent focus of technology supporting desk-based work that has characterized the history of the field. For example, where most prior work on the design of interactive systems focused on developing software for desk-based computer systems, with advances in miniaturization and sensor advances came a new breed of interactive technologies that support interactive experiences beyond the desktop. Such interactive experiences are often not only encompassing other locations than a desk environment, they are also offering completely new interaction experiences and techniques. Typical game systems within this genre are the Xbox Kinect and Nintendo Wii that enabled new forms of digital play. Such 'exertion games' systems (Mueller, Agamanolis and Picard 2003) are offering exemplary interactive experiences that collectively have been assembled under the notion of the so-called third wave of human–computer interaction (Harrison, Tatar and Sengers 2007), which argues that our interactions with computers moved from mainframes where multiple people needed to share one computer, to individual desktops, to now many devices equipped with many sensors that support a more embodied-centric digital experience focus. Such a more embodied-centric digital experience focus originated from a view that the 'body' of the computer matters more than originally assumed; for example, the shape and form of a laptop does not only allow computers to be moved from place to place, but also affords new opportunities for interaction (Dourish 2001). Typical examples arose through the field of tangible interfaces (Hornecker and Buur 2006); these are new interfaces that highlight the physical form of the device people use to interact with when engaging with digital content. Extending this, new research has emerged that not only considers the body of the computer, but also the body of the user; for example, jogging apps on mobile phones support people being physically active as part of the digital interaction experience.

With these new opportunities to support the active human body comes an increased desire to understand how to design these new technologies to support interactions in which the human body actively engages with a world full of physical and digital materialities. Considering physical materialities is important, as the human body never acts in isolation or independent from its environment and social others, and digital materialities are important to consider as this chapter is concerned with the information processing of digital data as a result of sensor systems. However, it should be noted that there is no dichotomy between physical and digital materialities, but rather a constant quick back-and-forth of users engaging with physical and digital materialities as part of the bodily experience, which should become clear throughout this chapter.

Based on hands-on experiences of engaging ethnographic-informed design research on the topic of creating playful experiences for the active human body, we have derived a set of reflections on how to design interactive technology for an active human body. We use specific examples from our own research in the Exertion Games Lab (http://exertiongameslab.org) to illustrate this thinking.

This work on the design around the active human body is the result of having engaged with this topic for over a decade and having developed a portfolio of projects that demarcate the field. The projects make a contribution through their associated research-through-design (Zimmerman, Forlizzi and Evenson 2007) processes we engaged with, but they are also complemented by an ethnographic investigation that contributes towards further understandings in design knowledge by investigating possible future interactions with the technology. As such, these ethnographic investigations differ from other approaches such as those described by Pink et al. (Chapter 5, this volume), whereby ethnography is used to understand people's current practice when engaging with digital materialities in order to provide guidance for designers. In our work, we use ethnography to provoke future interactions to not only understand what is, but what 'should be', in line with a future-oriented approach to research, a strength associated with design research (Zimmerman et al. 2007). Therefore the projects presented combined with the research-through-design processes provide a perspective on the design of materialities for the active human body. Our investigation started with our early work on exertion games – digital games that require physical effort from players (Mueller et al. 2003; Mueller et al. 2011; Mueller, Gibbs and Vetere 2008). These exertion games are a key departure point for us to engage the active human body.

Related work

Prior work has previously investigated the role of the body in interactive technology design, which informed and guided the understanding of the body as digital materiality put forward in this chapter. Many of these previous investigations lean on phenomenology as a theoretical basis (see, for example, Fogtmann et al. (2008); Larssen et al. (2004); Loke et al. (2007); Moen (2006)). It appears a phenomenological view on people 'experiencing the world through their bodies being in it' (Fogtmann et al. 2008) often aids interaction design researchers to highlight the opportunities a consideration of the human body affords when interacting with technology. In particular, we believe Merleau-Ponty's view of phenomenology is relevant, as he puts forward a heightened sensitivity to the human body acting in the physical world filled with other human bodies, highlighting the consequential social aspect that comes with such a view (Merleau-Ponty 1945). Accordingly, we believe that designing for interactions with objects (see, for example, the works on tangible interfaces (Hornecker and Buur 2006)) is a different endeavour to designing for interactions with bodies. We hope our work provides initial guidance towards an understanding of the design of such interactions.

The design of bodily interactions has been particularly examined in the context of games, as probably driven by the emergence of the Nintendo Wii and Microsoft Kinect. For example, the investigations by Bogost (Bogost 2006, 2007) and Lehrer (Lehrer 2006) led to the idea that digital games that involve the body afford a different kind of gameplay from mouse and keyboard or gamepad games. Bogost proposes that the larger bodily movements the players engage in have an increased performative character that can attract and involve bystanders, expanding the social play experience of everyone involved. On the other hand, Lehrer draws on theories around emotions to argue that the increased bodily movements have the potential to alter the emotional state of players, and as such also afford different experiences that designers need to consider.

The work by Sheridan et al. highlights the fact that designers who consider bodily interactions need to give thought to the potential of physical materiality to support the body, and that these physical materialities often afford playful engagement with the body (Sheridan, Dix, Lock and Bayliss 2005). Dourish with his theory of embodied interaction brings together trends in interactive system development that have put an increased emphasis on the users' bodily interactions within the physical world (Dourish 2001); however, designers have lamented that his investigations are too conceptual to be put into design practice (Antle 2009). Responding to this, this chapter offers a design-focused view on the opportunities and challenges when it comes to digital materialities and the active human body. In the next section, we put forward our view on the role of the body in terms of digital materialities, how developments have evolved over the last couple of years and what shift in perspectives this has brought out. We then present a set of our own works to demonstrate our thinking on this topic in order to set out a direction for future work with the aim of advancing the field.

The body as digital–material

The argument put forward here is that prior work in interaction design mostly treated the active human body as a physical form of the user that interacts with digital materialities. Even more recent systems like the Microsoft Kinect afford a clear separation between the body and the digital–material – the body on one side of the living room, the screen with digital content on the other – that leads to the proposed view of seeing the human body as a new form of interface, replacing the traditional mouse and keyboard or gamepad interface. The next step forward suggested in this chapter is a non-separation between the active human body and the digital–material. As such, it proposes to see the body as a form of digital–material based on the findings from our ethnographic studies that suggest our participants often did not make a distinction between digital and bodily materiality. Consequently, the question then arises as to how interaction designers can support such a view of the body as digital–material. In order to provide a pathway to answer this question, this chapter presents a set of examples from our own work that aim to highlight how such a view can be approached in practice, and as such, attempts to provide an initial understanding towards a view of seeing the body as digital–material. We see our works as initial steps towards an enhanced knowledge about how to design interactions for the active human body and, as such, contribute to our understanding of digital materiality; however, we also acknowledge that these are only preliminary investigations at the beginning of an exciting journey. We also acknowledge that some of these examples follow this approach more, and others less, which is a natural consequence of them coming out of design practice with all its opportunities and compromises that designers need to make when aiming to realize functional systems using today's technologies. Furthermore, it is noteworthy to mention that this approach of seeing the body as digital–material is, and was, informed by the design practice reflexively, informing each other as the work progressed. We hope that the following examples offer the interested reader initial insights and serve as inspiration and guidance for future work that will extend and expand this field further.

Exemplary systems

Based on our past experiences of designing, evaluating and researching exertion games for over a decade, we now offer insights on the design process and how our studies involving everyday players contributed to their success. We begin with a description of a couple of digital experiences for the active human body that are relevant to understanding the idea of seeing the active human body as digital materiality. Together, they aim to present a wide range of diverse experiences. Nevertheless, as we are working in the field of game design (influenced significantly by the work of Salen and Zimmerman 2003), they focus on play. After the description of each system, we present reflections on how the interactive component of each play system contributed to the overall experience. We then describe how we arrived at this reflection based on our analyses of players' experiences. We did this through ethnographic-style studies in which we exposed users to the systems and observed how they interact in such a future scenario. We hope that with this reflective account we are able to guide others who are interested in understanding the design of materialities for the active human body and ultimately regarding the body as digital materiality. After this, the chapter presents two design tools we developed in order to support other designers who create experiences for the active human body; again, we focus here on exertion games. These tools are available online for free and we recommend their use when designing exertion games. They offer a structured approach when it comes to the design of such interactive systems and might offer initial guidance for readers interested in the topic. After the tools are introduced, the limitations and advantages of using an approach that reflects our personal design experiences are discussed. The chapter continues with discussing future work before concluding with a summary of the contributions.

In the next section, we begin with describing some of the exertion games coming out of the Exertion Games Lab at RMIT University in Melbourne, Australia. We articulate how we engaged with players of these games in order to understand their experiences as a way to contribute new knowledge and design better experiences in the future. In order to keep the contribution concise, we focus on one particular reflection and discuss its implication in depth in order to provide a comprehensive picture of our contribution to the field. Although the author describes them using the collective 'we', huge credit goes to the many members of the lab that designed and developed these systems.

Cart-Load-O-Fun

Cart-Load-O-Fun is a system that explores the intersection between play and commuting on public transport. We developed this system as part of our research practice and installed it in trams in Melbourne and on commuter trains in Sydney, Australia in 2013 and 2014. Travelling on public transport is often not an engaging experience, and in response, we designed Cart-Load-O-Fun to demonstrate that there is an opportunity to enrich the commuting experience by exploring play in this public space. This opportunity was explored by deploying a social exertion game designed for public transport in trams and trains. We then studied people's interactions with the game in-the-wild (Rogers, 2011) – i.e. not in simulated trains, but on actual trams and trains that ran as part of regular public transport timetables. The goal was to understand how people would interact with such systems in which the commuter's body is moving as a result of the train or tram moving, while the use of sensors in the environment affects the moving body and is affected by the moving environment. As such, the digital sensor data is drawing on the moving body but also the moving environment and how they interact with each other. In particular, we are intrigued by the fact that the commuter is part of a *moving* space, however he/she is often not moving very much at all. In response, we are interested in how game design can exploit this relationship.

The aim of the project was to provide guidance for designers who consider moving spaces such as trains and trams as a design resource to evoke playfulness in users of these spaces. In response, the result might allow for more engaging experiences for users of these spaces.

In Cart-Load-O-Fun two players collaboratively play together while commuting on a tram or train. We augmented existing bars in the carriage with pressure-sensitive sensors so that when holding onto the bars (as passengers often do for safety reasons, especially when standing), passengers are in effect operating a game controller. The two passengers control a single character from a top-down third-person perspective. One player controls the character's movement on the x-axis while the other player controls the y-axis. They do so by applying force through squeezing the bar. Squeezing the bar was chosen as input as passengers already tend to hold onto bars when travelling and grip harder when a tram is accelerating and decelerating. Players must work together to collect gems that randomly appear in the game, while avoiding enemy characters that bounce around the level. Each gem collected adds two seconds to the timer. A game usually lasts sixty seconds.

It is interesting to note that the act of commuting, i.e. travelling on the train or tram, actively contributes to the play experience: while the train or tram is moving, the passengers' bodies are also moved, often swaying and being rattled by the movement of the carriage. This affects their 'holding actions': when the train or tram accelerates or breaks, passengers need to hold onto their bars tighter, resulting in a different pressure of their grips. This in turn affects the outcome of the game. So players are in control of their game character through their gripping action; however, once the train or tram is moving, the movement of the carriage and resulting swaying of the passengers also affects the game. As such, players are continuously engaging with the varying levels of control that emerges as a result of their conscious grip actions and the grip actions resulting from being moved by the train or tram. So far, the game only supports two players; however, we can envision a future version of the game with additional sensors that support more players at the same time.

Reflection: Transform

Our work on Cart-Load-O-Fun highlights how interactive technology can transform commuting into a play experience. Passengers on public transport usually do not see commuting as a play experience. The introduction of the visual elements making up the gameplay experience allows players to see their holding-onto-bar activity as one of play, turning the activity of standing and holding-on into a playful experience.

We believe it is interesting to note that passengers are still standing and holding onto the bar while commuting, so the bodily actions appear (to an outsider) to be the same as when commuting without the game. Furthermore, the commuters are still achieving their goal of getting to and from work. Nevertheless, what we believe the interactive experience is facilitating is transforming the perception of the commuting experience. The commuting action is not just one of passively waiting until the destination is reached, it is now also an active means of playing: only by commuting are the players able to play the game.

Previous work has highlighted that managing levels of control can be an engaging game element, and that such management is particularly key for engaging entertainment experiences when it comes to the control of the human body (Marshall et al. 2011). Prior designs showed that controlling an artificial amusement ride bronco with a breathing sensor is engaging, as the

FIGURE 8.1 *Cart-Load-O-Fun on a train.*

players need to manage the control between not breathing too much, yet breathing some (in order to catch some air). Our Cart-Load-O-Fun complements this work by demonstrating the potential of using the management of control of the body as a game design resource for engaging game experiences. As a result, these game experiences have the potential to transform existing 'boring' commute rides into engaging play experiences, and as such, demonstrate one way in which the body can be seen as digital materiality: the moving body is part of the design enabled by sensor technologies embedded in the environment.

We see this opportunity of technology to transform the perception of existing non-engaging activities into playful activities as an interesting area to develop further. We argue that with advances in sensing technologies and reduced costs, there is a timely opportunity to transform existing activities (especially non-engaging ones) into playful experiences.

SweatAtoms

SweatAtoms is an interactive system we developed at the Exertion Games Lab to explore material representations of physical activity to support the experience of being physically active (Khot, Hjorth and Mueller 2014). SweatAtoms highlights the fact that technology can support a playful interaction around exertion through material artefacts; in our case, these material artefacts are coming out of a 3D printer.

SweatAtoms works in the following way: our system transforms physical activity data, such as people's heart rate, into 3D printed material artefacts. These artefacts aim to form an aesthetic and informative expression of physical activity data in a material format. By presenting the user with a material representation of his/her heart rate data (instead of the traditional graph on a screen), we believe there is an opportunity to engage the user in a different and novel way with the data that traditional representational media do not support, or at least do not lend themselves easily to. As such, we use the SweatAtoms system to understand something about how we can enhance the relationship between being physically active and the associated data that are available to us nowadays with the many wearable sensors currently on the market.

An in-the-wild study (Rogers 2011) whereby we deployed the system in six households revealed interesting insights into how people would use such a system (we work on the assumption that in ten years' time, 3D printers will be making their way into people's homes as did paper printers previously). In this study, the participants were able to experience five different material representations of their physical activity for a period of two weeks each. Our results suggest that the material artefacts were able to inspire a new interest in participants' involvement and engagement with physical activity. In particular, we were able to use the results to make three concrete design recommendations to support physical activity using material representations. We recommend seeing these representations of physical activity:

- as an opportunity to form an autotopography (González 1995), which refers to the understanding of the material artefacts as physical signs to spatially represent the identity of the user. For example, our participants used the material artefacts to decorate their rooms, pointing visitors to the fact that they represent personal data from specific achievements.

- as personalized rewards. For example, participants reported that they felt rewarded when the 3D printer produced a particularly intricate material artefact after a rather strenuous physical activity.

- for reflection and reminiscence. For example, our participants told stories about their activities to others using the material artefacts to guide their storytelling structure and used them to point out specific highlights of their physical activity journey.

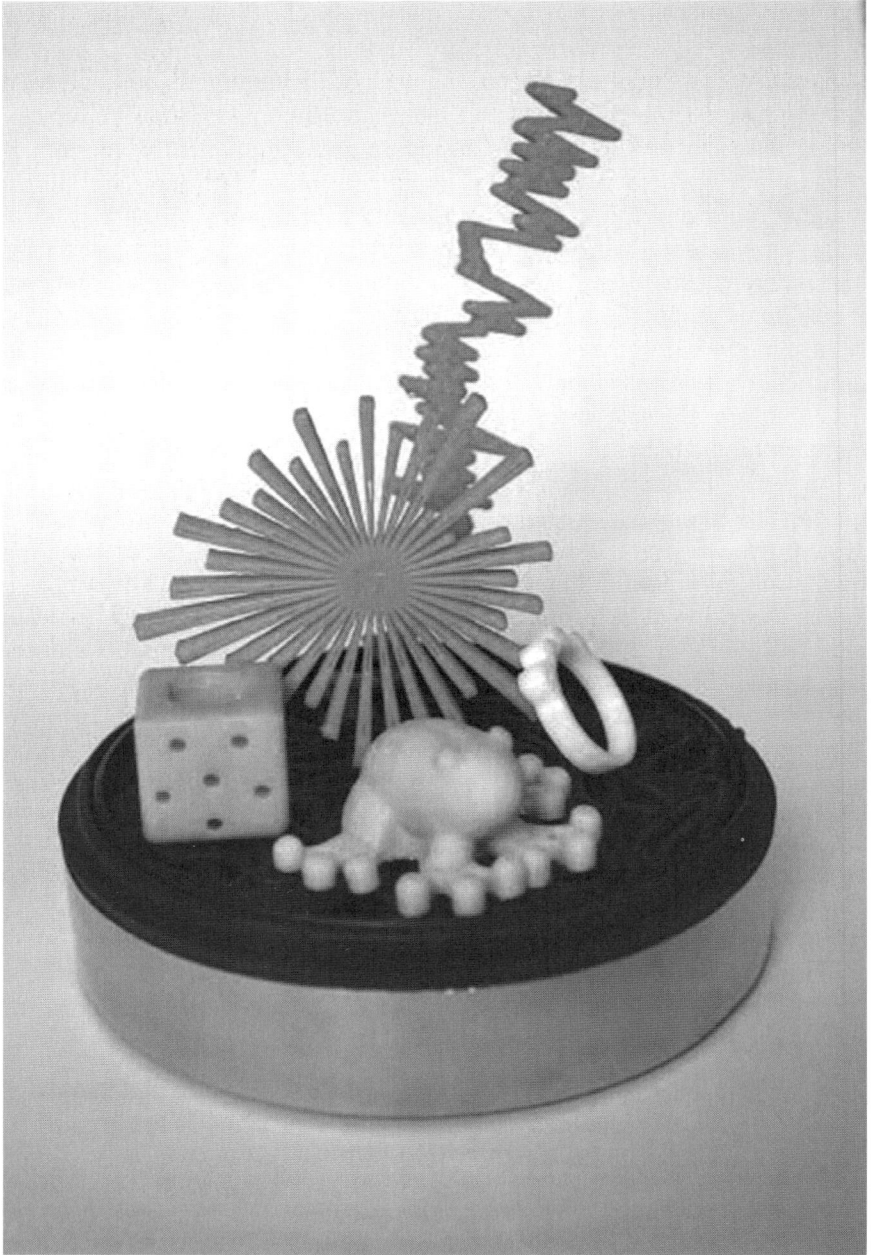

FIGURE 8.2 *Some of the material artefacts that the 3D printer produced based on people's heart rate data.*

FIGURE 8.3 *The SweatAtoms system in people's homes.*

Reflection: Alternative representation

We see SweatAtoms as an exemplar system representing some of the opportunities technology offers to reshape a person's engagement with physical activity based on an alternative representation of his/her activity data. By capturing exertion activity through some of the emerging wearable sensors, we have the possibility to present the resulting data in various forms, and digital fabrication tools provide unique opportunities to offer alterative representations. These alternative representations have the facility to reshape a person's engagement with physical activity, as our study suggests. As such, our work highlights that if we see the body as digital materiality, we have an opportunity to transform this materiality into other forms, complementing the original bodily experience in novel ways that were previously not possible, or at least difficult, without digital technology.

Musical Embrace

In the next section we describe Musical Embrace, again developed in the Exertion Games Lab. We developed this research vehicle in order to investigate the potential of the concept 'social awkwardness' as an intriguing game design element, in particular when it comes to social awkwardness facilitated by the body (Huggard, De Mel et al. 2013a, 2013b). Musical Embrace is a two-player game. The players need to control a sensor-equipped pillow suspended from the ceiling and falling at chest height with their torsos in order to collaboratively navigate a virtual world filled with sound sources. As such, the pillow functions as a controller that is only operable if both players coordinate their torsos together. The pillow is wirelessly connected to a screen positioned to the side to display the virtual world that the players need to traverse. The players do so by collaboratively applying pressure to the four sensors situated on the corners of the pillow-like controller. Each sensor is mapped to the four directional keys, i.e. up/down and left/right, of the controller. If players apply pressure simultaneously to the top sensors their viewpoint will move forward. If they apply pressure simultaneously to the bottom sensors their viewpoint will move backward. Tilting the entire unit to the left or right will rotate the viewpoint to the left or right. The use of hands is not permitted; however, in order to intensify the pressure, the players can use their arms to embrace the other player, hence the name Musical Embrace. The goal of the game is to move through the virtual environment with speed and accuracy to collect the most amounts of rewards, i.e. virtual coins. Audio cues guide the players to the virtual coins, increasing in volume as the player moves in the right direction. The players have one minute to complete the game and collect as many rewards as possible.

Musical Embrace helps us understand the potential of concepts such as social awkwardness for the design of engaging experiences. In particular, we believe it is noteworthy that social awkwardness has a traditionally negative connotation, however here it is a facilitator for an engaging experience. As such, this work adds to our understanding of uncomfortable interactions (Benford et al. 2012), a topic previously investigated from an interaction design perspective. In short, Musical Embrace is helping us understand the benefits of considering social awkwardness as facilitated by bodily interactions when designing interactive experiences.

FIGURE 8.4 *Musical Embrace.*

Reflection: Linking bodies together

The design process of Musical Embrace highlighted the opportunity of employing technology to link bodies together in a way that supports the emergence of what has been described as social play (Isbister, 2010). This contrasts with the majority of existing digital systems that support bodily social play, such as Kinect Adventures (contributors) and Wii Bowling (Nintendo n.d.), in which the players' bodies interact with the game independently from one another – in other words, the player's bodies do not interfere with one another. With Musical Embrace, however, the players' bodies are linked together through the affordance of the pillow. This results in an interpersonal bodily play experience that players appear to find engaging. The design of Musical Embrace, including the hard- and software, facilitated this interpersonal bodily play: the controller encourages a collaborative bodily approach by the players in order to successfully navigate the shared virtual world. In previous work, it has been highlighted that technology is particularly useful when it comes to linking bodies together over a distance through the use of networking technologies (Mueller et al. 2003; Mueller, Agamanolis, Vetere and Gibbs 2009; Mueller, Gibbs and Vetere 2009); here, Musical Embrace highlights the fact that technology offers opportunities to link players' bodies together that in turn can facilitate the emergence of bodily social play.

Tools for designing digital experiences for the active human body

Having presented several systems that exemplify how one can design materialities for the active human body, and pushing this idea even further by seeing the active human body as digital materiality, the question might now arise of how this perspective can inform future designs. In order to provide a starting point towards answering this question, we direct the reader to some of the design tools we have developed over the last couple of years. These tools were initially targeted at designers who want to create games and playful experiences for the active human body. They are available online and might guide people interested in creating materialities for the active human body and seeing the body as digital materiality. It might be useful to add that these tools have been evaluated previously in a design context and we have collected evidence (Mueller et al. 2014) that suggests they can actively support designers in their practice.

Exertion Cards

The Exertion Cards are a set of design cards aimed at facilitating the design process of creating interactive exertion experiences (Mueller, Gibbs, Vetere and Edge 2014). The Exertion Cards have been successfully used in workshops to facilitate the ideation process of exertion games; for example, students and professional designers have used the cards successfully in order to generate exertion game ideas (Mueller et al. 2014). The Exertion Cards present a series of dimensions that designers are encouraged to 'think about'. These dimensions represent a set of design choices which are neither 'good' nor 'bad', but rather aim to make the designer realize that making these choices will have implications on the resulting play experience.

For example, one of the cards asks designers 'to what extent is physical risk considered?', reminding him/her that physical risk is a key element when it comes to designing digital experiences where the body is involved. However, physical risk is not necessarily something to avoid, but can rather also be an interesting design resource. As such, the card asks designers to think about the extent to which physical risk is considered. If there is a low level of physical risk considered, there is in consequence a low level of injury to be expected. In contrast, if there is a high level of physical risk considered, designers might be able to facilitate excitement due to a risk–reward balance. As such, the card aims to make designers aware that: a) they should 'think about' physical risk; b) they should also 'think about' to what extent they consider physical risk; and c) the various levels of consideration can result in different user experiences.

There are fourteen Exertion Cards in total. They all feature the same structure in terms of aiming to make designers aware of what to 'think about' when it comes to designing for exertion. The dimensions for each card come from the Exertion Framework (Mueller et al. 2011), a conceptual theoretical framework for the analysis of exertion games, and represent a designer-focused approach to support the design practice of designers that is readily applicable.[1]

The Exertion Cards evolved out of our many years of research in this topic, especially from observing and immersing ourselves into the design work, where we identified the need for academic knowledge to be translated into practical tools for designers that suit their day-to-day operations. We think that translating academic knowledge into practical guidance for designers is also part of the academic discourse and should be considered as an elemental part of the investigation. We found that carefully studying and engaging with the target group – in our case, game designers – is an effective strategy to achieve this, and recommend to others to consider this in their work as we also find it personally rewarding.

Movement-Based Game Guidelines

In the following section Movement-Based Game Guidelines are presented, our result of extending thinking about the motivation that drove the Exertion Cards work. The Movement-Based Game Guidelines were developed after the Exertion Cards and are related, but target different stages of the design

FIGURE 8.5 *Four of the Exertion Cards*

process. Whereas the Exertion Cards are particularly useful for the ideation process, the Movement-Based Game Guidelines are meant to be used when designers already have an idea in mind and want to improve upon an existing design. In other words, the Movement-Based Game Guidelines are more aimed at 'checking' whether a designer's game idea has followed established principles.

There is also a website and accompanying paper (Mueller and Isbister 2014) describing the work on these Movement-Based Game Guidelines in detail. The guidelines were developed based on the combined experience of Florian 'Floyd' Mueller's work with the Exertion Games Lab and Katherine Isbister's Games Innovation Lab at New York University of designing exertion games for over twenty years. The resulting guidelines were refined through the feedback of fourteen experts in academic, indie and commercial game development fields with experience in movement-based game design.

By interviewing them about their experiences in their daily practice and enabling them to engage with the guidelines, an interesting dialogue emerged in which the designers became active participants in refining the guidelines. It might be interesting to point out that the dialogue often started with an elaboration by the designer about where in their practice they observed certain aspects of the guidelines before they moved on to actively shape and refine the guideline based on their practical experiences. Of course, we acknowledge that it might have helped that many of them had prior experience of exposure to academic contexts and were therefore knowledgeable about the process of knowledge creation.

The structure of the guidelines is based on design patterns (Björk and Holopainen 2005; Borchers 2001) and phrased in hopefully easy-to-remember wording that is aimed at being appealing to designers. Each guideline includes *Do's* and *Don'ts* as well as explanations and examples. The anticipated use of the Movement-Based Game Guidelines consists of going through the website and examining each guideline with the examples provided and considering whether the current game design idea could be improved by incorporating the guideline.

We note two key observations. First, although the guidelines also support the design of exertion activities, we chose to use the word 'movement-based' as our experts, although divided, thought that 'movement-based' has recently emerged as a common industry term. Second, the term 'guidelines' was extensively discussed. In a strict sense, what we are presenting are not rigorous guidelines; they are more like design patterns, an idea we originally departed from (building on the fact that design patterns have been previously used successfully by designers of interactive systems (Borchers 2001)). However, our experts pointed out that making a tool applicable to designers also needs to involve presenting it in the right form and format,

Search this site

MOVEMENT-BASED GAME GUIDELINES

Movement requires special feedback

Embrace ambiguity
Celebrate movement articulation
Consider movement's cognitive load
Focus on the body

Movement leads to bodily challenges

Intend fatigue
Exploit risk
Map imaginatively

Movement emphasizes certain kinds of fun

Highlight rhythm
Support self-expression
Facilitate social fun

Consider movement's cognitive load

Guideline

Moving can demand a lot of mental attention, creating a high 'cognitive load', especially when learning new movements, so do not overload the player with too much feedback.

Details

Developing movement skill requires not only bodily, but also cognitive attention, with attention being a limited resource. Initially, players will need to focus on learning a new movement (so focus the feedback on this), while when getting better at the movement, they can devote more cognitive attention towards more complex and nuanced forms of feedback. For example, first time you try to to pat your head and rub your belly at the same time, you probably cannot do much else, but when you get better at it, you can probably do something else simultaneously, such as having a conversation.

Examples

Dance Central 2	Ninja Shadow Warrior	Pac-Manhattan
Dance Central 2 provides multiple layers of feedback to players. Beginners can focus their limited attention on imitating the avatars. More advanced players can use the diagrams and score details to refine their moves.	In Ninja Shadow Warrior players are ninjas that need to fill out object silhouettes together to hide from evil, by 'becoming' objects. Figuring out the best positioning of multiple bodies takes a lot of attention, so the computer feedback is kept to a	Pac-Manhattan is a large-scale urban game that utilises Manhattan's grid to recreate a game of Pac-Man. As players run around the grid, their cognitive attention is focused on moving, so wirelessly connected controllers

FIGURE 8.6 *The Movement-Based Game Guidelines website.*

which includes identifying a suitable title. In consequence, many title varia-tions were discussed and it was decided that 'guidelines' most accurately matches both the intention behind the work as well as sounding appealing for practitioners in a way that motivates rather than discourages engagement.[2]

We can also add that we have trialled both tools in combination during a six-day game design workshop with students and staff interested in the topic of designing digital experiences for the active human body. The goal of the workshop was to enhance one's understanding of the topic by actively designing a bodily play system that demonstrates a particular aspect of the bodily focus. When asked about the cards and guidelines, participants reported that they found them valuable for their design process as they made them 'think about things they would not have thought of'. As such, it appears the tools were able to extend the participants' current practice by adding food for additional thought. Although a richer evaluation might reveal a more thorough understanding of the consequences of having used the cards and guidelines, we believe our initial engagement showed promising results which confirm prior engagements that were more formally evaluated. In consequence, we believe it might be interesting to consider both of these tools in further investigations concerning materialities for the active human body and examine how seeing the body as digital materiality is comple-mented by the implicit knowledge expressed in these tools.

Limitations

Of course, no such work is complete, especially when operating in the practical domain of design. As such, we acknowledge the following limita-tions of the work. First of all, the presented insights are derived from a personal view of the topic, since they are based on our experiences of designing exertion games. However, we believe this personal account can offer insights not available with other methods of reflection and as such provides a unique opportunity.

Secondly, in this chapter, we were able to present only a limited number of exertion games. By articulating several games, we tried to describe the wide range of contexts in which exertion games can play a role. However, by increasing the number of games, further contributions to design knowledge could be made. Including additional reflections on other games could also extend the contribution.

Thirdly, this work only scratches the surface when it comes to under-standing the analysis of the presented games. Such investigations would allow for deeper and more thorough understandings of the design process and user experiences, expanding our knowledge of what currently 'is' in order to inform what should 'be'. This future-oriented view matches with a research-through-design agenda (Zimmerman et al. 2007) which originally influenced our work.

In sum, we acknowledge that our work has limitations; however, we believe it provides a useful starting point for further work in the area of seeing the body as digital materiality and we therefore believe it could serve as a springboard for further investigations. In particular, we hope our work highlighted that a future-oriented approach can provide inspiration which allows for seeing materiality as a conceptual view that goes beyond current technology limitations. Ultimately, we hope we were able not only to answer some of the questions emerging from the field, but also to highlight unexplored areas that might inspire others to investigate further, essentially contributing to a better understanding of the field as a whole.

Future work

We aim to take this work further and note that this research can benefit from future investigations in terms of examining more and conceptually different systems to derive further insights. Furthermore, additional tools that support designers in subsequent stages of the design process and through alternative ways might also benefit the domain. For example, one avenue we find interesting to explore further is the idea of communicating knowledge about the design of exertion games not just through cards and guidelines, but by actively playing and designing them. We believe that playing games is one way of understanding games, and can hence lead to better game design. Similarly, designing games can help us understand something about the games. In essence, we believe these two aspects – understanding games and designing them – are interlinked; however, we also believe that this interlinking could be supported by tools. Creating such tools that support this interlinking is another avenue for future work that sounds appealing to us. We believe investigating this can not only significantly help us understand something about the field as a whole, but also support us in actively advancing and shaping the field. We are currently investigating ways to make this a reality.

Conclusion

We have presented in this chapter an early understanding on the design of new technologies to support interactions in which the human body actively navigates a world full of physical and digital materialities. Based on hands-on experiences of engaging with design research with a future-oriented focus on the topic of creating playful experiences for the active human body, we derived a set of reflections on how design can support a view of the body as digital materiality. We hope the work is able to offer a useful perspective that complements other work done in the field.

We proposed that there is no dichotomy between physical and digital materialities, but rather a constant quick back-and-forth of users engaging with physical and digital materialities as part of the bodily experience, and extending this, that the active human body, thanks to interactive technology advances, can even be seen as a form of digital materiality. To illustrate this thinking, we used specific examples from our own research practice. The examples made contributions through their associated research-through-design processes with which we engaged, but they were also complemented by ethnographic investigations that contributed towards further under-standings by investigating possible future interactions with the technology. These ethnographic investigations differ from other approaches that often aim to understand people's current practice, whereas we used ethnography to provoke future interactions to understand what 'should be'. Therefore the projects presented provide a future-oriented perspective on the active human body as digital materiality.

In sum, the goal is to inspire and guide others who aim to support the active human body in navigating a world full of physical and digital materi-alities by seeing the body as digital materiality, ultimately furthering our understanding of what it means to design for the active human body.

Acknowledgements

We wish to thank the many members of the Exertion Games Lab who made this possible for all the hard work they put in. In particular, we thank Jayden Garner, Amy Huggard, Anushka De Mel, Rohit Khot, Jeewon Lee, Chad Toprak, Katherine Isbister, Darren Edge and Object – the Australian Centre for Design. Image credits go to flickr users: sanAago_sa, bass_nroll, ilmv, 91651935@N00, braytonlaw, allenjaelee, trioculus, jasmic, microsoQ_xbox360_natal1, oblivion, tomeppy, sportswatchinformant, ben_lawson, teotwawki, mirsasha, romec1, drsam, Joan Guzman, mirsasha, sportsandsocial, shawdog. Florian 'Floyd' Mueller is the recipient of an Australian Research Council Fellowship (DP110101304).

PART THREE

Insider Design

9

Mobile intimacies: Everyday design and the aesthetics of mobile phones

Heather Horst

A few years ago, we decided to end our day of fieldwork in the town of Pedernales watching the sunset on the sea wall overlooking the Caribbean Sea. The spot is a favourite gathering point for Dominicans in this small but orderly town on the border of Haiti and the Dominican Republic. Occupied by groups of friends, couples sharing moments together and others looking for company, the wall sits at the end of a main road in the town. It is also near a small bar where local residents come to buy bottles of the local beer *Presidente*, listen to music played on the large sound speakers and hang out to admire the colourful and often form-fitting clothing donned by many of the women in the town looking to relax. For an ethnographer, it's a fantastic spot to spend time immersing oneself in the forms of sociality that constitute everyday life in the town, including the use and display of mobile phones. Indeed, one of the most striking observations I made sitting on the wall that evening was how frequently mobile phones were carried in people's hands as they moved to, from and alongside the wall, so much so that I started to count the number of people *not* carrying their phones in their hand – only five out of thirty-eight people over a period of about an hour. While carrying the mobile phone in one's hand was not a new phenomenon (it is present in all of my research in Jamaica, USA and Fiji), the sheer number of handheld devices inspired a greater consideration of the kinds of relationships and intimacies people have developed with their mobile devices across the world.

This chapter represents a humble attempt to address the kinds of questions I began pondering on that sea wall in the Dominican Republic, concerning the claims about the universalizing properties of mobile phones and the more anthropologically inspired work on the cultural specificity of mobile phone use, and the tensions around the everyday designs that emerge when looking at ways in which people, bodies and worlds become engaged in relationships with mobile phones (Horst 2012). Bringing together material culture studies approaches with the study of digital anthropology, design anthropology and mobile phone appropriation in the Caribbean (Clarke 2011; Drazin 2012; Horst and Miller 2005, 2006, 2012; Miller and Horst 2012), I explore the ways in which mobile phones become part of the aesthetic worlds of Jamaicans and Dominican-Haitians in the region. This chapter draws upon long-term ethnographic research in Jamaica beginning in 1999 (Horst 2004, 2006, 2008) and a shorter, collaborative engagement with Erin Taylor working on the border of Haiti and the Dominican Republic over three years between 2010 and 2012 (Horst and Taylor 2014; Taylor and Horst 2014). Given the forms of intimacy and personalization associated with the mobile phone, I begin with a brief review of the ways in which mobile phones enhance and work to illuminate various forms of intimacy. Drawing connections between different notions of mobile intimacies in the literature on mobile media and communication, I then turn to the ways in which vernacular designs (Galloway et al. 2004; Rapoport 1980, 1990) emerge in everyday engagements with mobile phones and devices, suggesting that these forms of mobile intimacies are just as meaningful as the communication that flows through these mobile technologies. I conclude by reflecting upon the relationships between mobile phones and their integration into the broader ecologies of design and pattern.

Mobile intimacies, mobile aesthetics

Since the mobile phone's introduction and mass appropriation in the 1990s, a range of scholars have commented upon how the mobile phone facilitates relationships between people, especially intimate relationships. Barry Wellman (2001), Rich Ling (2004, 2008) and others have examined the extent to which mobile and internet communication devices may be changing the nature of our social connections, especially with 'close' connections defined as spouses/partners, family members, peers and neighbours (Campbell and Parks 2008). Focusing upon the number of connections as well as the intensity of the relationships (e.g. frequency of calls), scholars have highlighted how mobile phones are primarily used for connecting with family and friends, often the same five people who are connected via place-based relationships and engaged in the micro-coordination of everyday life. In effect, people use mobile phones for developing and extending these relationships whether they are family-based, place-based or more ego-centred (Horst and Miller 2005, 2006; Pertierra 2006). Fortunati (2002) describes a similar process, what she terms 'nomadic intimacy', wherein people opt to use the spaces of 'downtime' to engage with their intimates rather than engage in 'small talk' with strangers on the bus or train.

Alongside defining who is involved in communication through mobile phones, mobile intimacies research emphasizes the quality of communication it facilitates between people. Ito, Okabe and Matsuda's (2005) notion of the 'full-time intimate community' acknowledges the ways in which the mobile phone and other technologies are used on the move to maintain connection to a small number of people, usually close ties and, in turn, to engage in 'selective sociality' with close friends, family and partners over the course of a day. The sharing of mobile phones and SIM cards, the practice of 'beeping', 'flashing' and missed calls, the development of codes and languages via SMS and micro-exchanges and gifting of airtime or credit all represent forms of communication between intimates (Donner 2007; Horst and Taylor 2014). Research by Hjorth (2009), Ito, Okabe and Matsuda (2005), Lasen (2010) and others has also called attention to the practice of sharing the intimate and mundane details of everyday life, such as displaying and discussing photos of families and pets saved on mobile handsets or sending MMS of what you are having for dinner as a form of 'intimate co-presence' (see also Hjorth and Lim 2012; Licoppe 2004). As a range of scholars have noted, these forms of co-presence have expanded with the integration of media – what Goggin and Hjorth (2009) termed the shift from mobile technologies to mobile media.

Finally, a spate of research has focused upon the ways in which smart-phones, in particular, are facilitating mobile intimacies in relation to work and professional lives (e.g. Wajcman, Brown and Bittman 2009; Wallis 2013). For example, Melissa Gregg (2010) writes about the role of technologies in the lives of workers in knowledge or creative industries. Alongside developing feelings of intimacy towards their work, Gregg outlines how the presence of work permeates into domestic life through the smartphones which provide workers with the ability to check their work email, respond to messages and be available around the clock – a phenomenon that she describes as 'presence bleed'. Others have examined the ways in which parents, especially mothers, use the mobile phones to maintain their family and domestic life. This may include managing rides for their children between home, school and after-school activities, checking to make sure their children have arrived home, and negotiating meals (Clark 2012; Hjorth 2011; Hjorth and Lim 2012). In all of this work, the mobile phone is viewed as facilitating intimacy between spheres considered separate domains.

In this chapter I wish to move away from a discussion of mobile intimacies as defined by how mobile phones are used to communicate between people considered intimate or the kinds of relationships formed between people;

these represent only one dimension of the ways in which the mobile phone creates and results in forms of connection and intimacies. Instead, I want to focus upon the *handheld* nature of mobile technologies, the implications of the hand for the kinds of mobile intimacies that develop, and the diverse practices and meanings that people attach to their mobile phones through an engagement with its materiality (Horst and Miller 2012; Miller and Horst 2012). In the following section I turn our attention to the ways in which mobile intimacies are formed in relation to bodies, body parts and other related objects – what we may term *mobile aesthetics*.

The aesthetics of mobile intimacies

This shift in emphasis from mobile phones mediating relationships between people towards the development of a mobile aesthetics requires attention to the mobile phones in the context of other intimate objects and practices and the ways in which aesthetic worlds are created in and through the 'intimate zones of everyday life'. In what is now a classic introduction to a special issue on intimacy, Berlant (1998) challenges scholars to consider intimacy as a process of attachment that is produced relationally between people, institutions, nations and an infinite range of other possible relations rather than a defined set of feelings such as love, friendship or connection (see also Zelizer 2006). As Berlant describes:

> Intimacy [...] does generate an aesthetic, an aesthetic of attachment, but no inevitable forms or feelings are attached to it. This is where normative ideologies come in, when certain 'expressive' relations are promoted across public and private domains – love, community, patriotism – while other relations, motivated, say, by the 'appetites,' are discredited or simply neglected. (1998: 285)

Berlant further notes that these normative ideologies and the narratives that emerge around them are enacted in the 'intimate zones of everyday life'.

In order to understand the ways that normative ideologies, patterns and practices of handheld mobile devices are played out in the intimate zones of everyday life across two national contexts, I also wish to draw upon Ron Eglash's (1999) work on indigenous design, patterns and African fractals. Eglash's attention to fractals, or patterns that move across various domains, is a particularly useful framework to understand the integration of the mobile phone across two different contexts. Looking across different domains, Eglash demonstrates that the patterns and designs that are used are often not the products of explicit or formal knowledge systems, or even, in the case of artisans, the result of 'explicit thinking' (1999: 7). Rather, by tracing how designs move across contexts and scales, he identifies the processes through which an aesthetic emerges in relation to a particular group or place. In this first section I will draw upon material that has emerged through my long-term ethnographic engagement in Jamaica, particularly over the past decade (Horst 2004, 2006, 2008, 2014a). The longitudinal nature of this engagement – one that mirrors the discipline of anthropology's concern with holism (see Horst 2012) – and interest in mobile phones created an opportunity to see how everyday design has emerged over time and how different handheld devices have become integrated into the everyday aesthetics of attachment.

The aesthetics of display

One of the striking features of mobile phone usage in Jamaica over the past decade is its visibility. While some people make an effort to keep their phone(s) hidden in bags, pockets or other locations for fear of theft or loss, a significant proportion of Jamaicans actually travel with the cell phone in the palm of their hand, an act that brings the materiality of the phone into a fundamental relationship with the hand and body and both creates and makes evident the process of design among everyday mobile phone users. To understand how mobile aesthetics are created through the intimacies of everyday design, I want to begin with the story of Kacey, a twenty-five-year-old Jamaican woman whom I have known for a number of years. When I first met Kacey as a teenager in 2004 she was lovingly holding her first cell phone in her hand – a pink clamshell flip phone (a cutting-edge model at the time) – that she had recently received from her boyfriend, who attended a prestigious high school in Kingston, Jamaica. The phone for Kacey was itself an important external symbol of the seriousness of the relationship and the kinds of intimacies associated with purchasing a costly new model mobile phone. Yet, it was also an object that Kacey viewed as a vehicle through which she would create and negotiate her own sense of self in the world through aural and visual means. For example, Kacey's boyfriend's gift was very strategically selected through a series of visits by Kacey and her boyfriend to mobile phone stores and vendors over a period of a few months, during which Kacey held or posed with various models before stating a preference for the clamshell model mere weeks before Valentine's Day. In anticipation of her gift on Valentine's Day, she selected a soft pink dress to wear for their evening dinner at a local Chinese restaurant. Alongside her dress she rallied her cousin to paint her fingernails bright pink, a colour that she later noted would complement the clamshell case. However, once Valentine's Day was over, Kacey returned to everyday life and the royal blue uniforms she was required to wear at school. Kacey did not feel that these were especially complementary, yet continued to want to call attention to her 'sexy' new mobile phone. Alongside making or arranging phone calls in the spaces between classes or after school, she managed to convince her cousin (who wanted to be a beautician) to give her nails acrylic extensions and an elaborate design of pink and white swirls which would be on display every time she flipped open the phone to answer a call or look at her phone. While Kacey was not the only young woman in high school who managed to acquire this phone model, she developed a reputation as being someone who 'wears her phone' well.

Over the past decade, Kacey has moved on from her boyfriend and the clamshell phone; she has owned four other phones since this time, including a prepaid Blackberry which she states was one of her favourite phones despite its limited ability for customization. Now that there are more phone models available and a wide range of smartphones that differentiate status, Kacey is older and much less concerned with the status she enjoyed through her phone as a student. Her most recent phone, a Huawei with an Android operating system, has more 'on the inside' with apps and photos that enable her to customize her phone. Yet – and somewhat remarkably – the aesthetic she has maintained over the past decade is a commitment to pink and the flipping motion associated with that initial phone she worked so intentionally to feature in her high school years. Anyone who has seen a Huawei smart-phone is aware that the normal model does not have a flip phone feature. Kacey, however, managed to arrange a delivery from her auntie who was coming to Jamaica on a visit from Florida; the delivery was a pink Huawei Y330 flip phone case. It took a few months to obtain the case, but once acquired, the phone enabled Kacey to return to her preferred colour and gestures that have come to constitute her mobile aesthetic. And to commemorate the arrival of the new case, she added new acrylic nails with a pink and white nail design with clear, white imitation crystals embedded in each nail polish. For Kacey, the application of painted acrylic nails (with the latest design) worked to integrate her mobile phone with her body.

While Kacey's aesthetics of display was tied to her performativity while answering or talking on the phone, another very common form of display – and the play between displaying and concealing – revolved around where the phone was carried. An exemplar of this kind of playfulness is Veronica, a woman in her early thirties who lives in Marshfield, an area of Portmore, Jamaica (Horst and Miller 2006). Veronica had her first child with her high school boyfriend when she was seventeen and now has a son with her current boyfriend. While her eldest son was in high school, she started her university degree. Although she receives some support from her son's babyfather for her elder son's school fees, she had to move into a place with her auntie and two cousins to be able to manage both sets of school fees

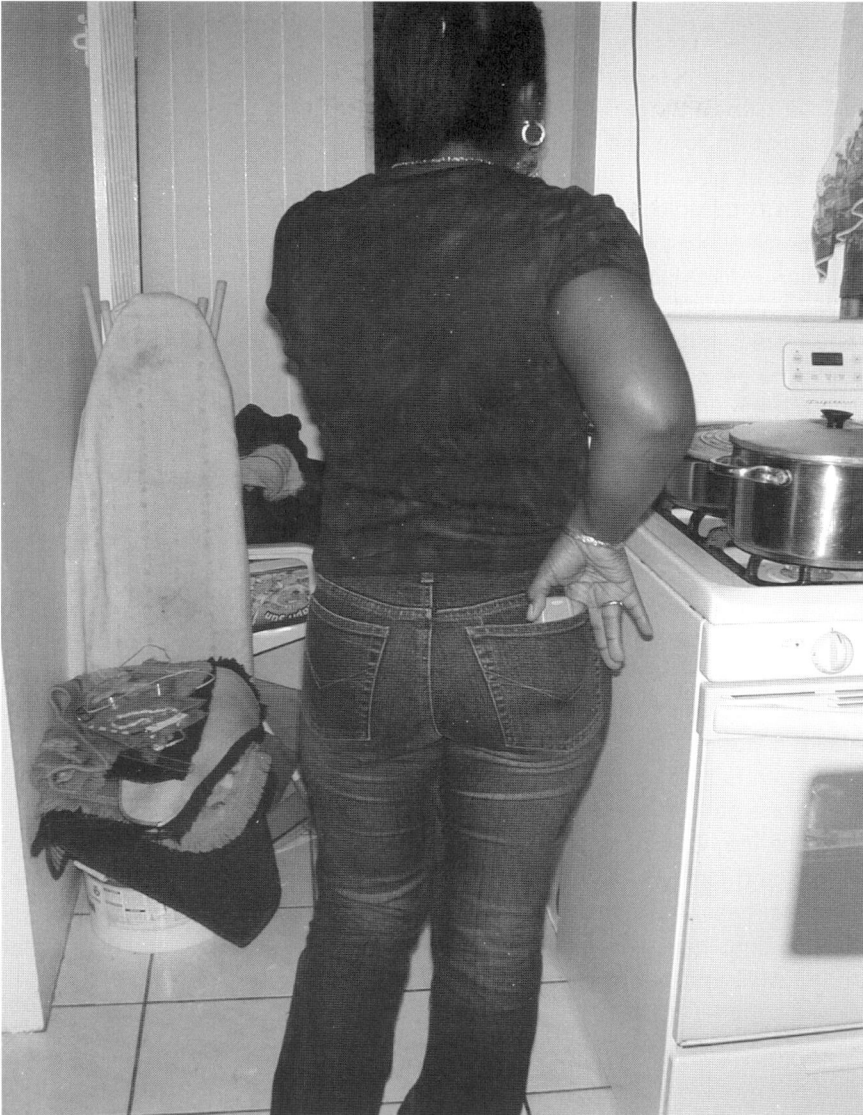

FIGURE 9.1 *Veronica's phone. (Heather Horst 2004)*

and to receive some help with the care and coordination of her family. Her current boyfriend's main contribution was the purchase and maintenance of three phones – one for Veronica and two for her sons.

Veronica's entrance to university as an older student has meant that she feels quite conscious of the time she has spent away from school, so she works quite intentionally to appear 'young and sexy'. While no longer the 'slim' young schoolgirl she used to be before she had her two children, Veronica tries to stay 'fit' and wear clothes that feature her curves.[1] This typically includes tight, figure-hugging blue jeans and a range of black, purple, fuchsia pink or turquoise V-neck teeshirts or collared tops that complement her dark skin tone and cleavage. She also likes to wear bright pink lipstick, a series of gold necklaces and large gold hoops earrings (real gold, or at least 24 carat gold; the latter were a gift from her boyfriend). When it came to selecting her phone, a 'young and sexy' aesthetic also dominated her decision. At the store Veronica went through the process of picking up the phones and holding them in her hand to assess how light they felt, how slim they were and if they fit into her back pocket. When she narrowed down her final choices, she then posed with the final three options in her back pocket. Without a mirror she had to trust her boyfriend to assess if the phone in her back pocket looked 'right'.

Once home, she used a mirror to determine the right placement of the phone around her 'backside' curves in different jeans, and practised walking in front of her close friends who confirmed the walk, poses and gaits through which she achieved maximum sexiness. The phone needed to be prominent enough to notice, small enough that she could wedge her fingers in the side and remove it when wanted, but not loose enough that others could steal it. The snugness of her jeans guaranteed that theft would be difficult for others, as the phone was to all intents and purposes attached to her body. But it also meant it was not particularly easy to extract the phone from her back pocket herself. In fact, she often missed phone calls because she could not wiggle the phone out of her back pocket fast enough to answer the ringing phone. Veronica did not see this as necessarily a negative feature and, in fact, her friends and family knew to call her back twice as she rarely returned calls, given her economic situation (Horst and Miller 2005). For Veronica and others like her, tight jeans allowed her to both aesthetically integrate and display her phone while mitigating the risk of theft or loss.

The aesthetics of modesty

The aesthetics of display apparent in many Jamaicans' use of mobile phones contrasts significantly with the aesthetics of modesty that emerged in our study of mobile phones and mobility among Haitians living on the border of Haiti and the Dominican Republic. Throughout this project, Erin Taylor and I explored the ways in which objects, bodies, commodities, money and other cultural forms circulated across the national border and what Rowlands (2006) termed the 'relative materiality' of these objects (see also Miller 2006). Rowland's concept of relative materiality attends to the ways in which power emerges in, through and around particular forms of material culture and how what becomes 'material' is directly tied to who has the power to define. In a context like the border of Haiti and the Dominican Republic, Haitian bodies are both highly visible but are often seen to matter less, as we see in a recent ruling to deport Haitians back to the Dominican Republic.

In a region where bodies are politicised, we have to acknowledge the constraints and affordances of different forms of material culture as well as the social and cultural dimensions of objects, bodies and commodities wherein the materiality of the objects and infrastructures that support them are effectively subsumed within their broader social purpose. To this end, we attempted to understand the materiality of the border in terms of the objects, their role as part of a 'set' of objects, and the broader material ecology in which they exist and through which repertoires of practices and meanings emerge. Through a study of the everyday portable kits (Ito, Okabe and Anderson 2009), we focused upon the mundane items that border residents carried with them as they lived, worked and socialized in and around the border region, which typically consisted of objects such as mobile phones, keys, currency, ID cards, bibles, hand cloths, forms of currency; papers, IDs and money were often viewed as the most important items to facilitate migrant mobility. Contextualized within the study of life in the region we initiated in 2010, our aim was to understand the relative significance of intimate mobile items in light of the different currencies, citizenship status, telecommunications infrastructures, languages, economic opportunities and power relations that distinctly shape the ways in which mobility and movement is possible.

While many of the participants had been living in in the region for some time, movement and mobility remained a fact of life for border residents, and this shaped the ways in which they thought about mobile phones and a range of other objects. Indeed, the importance of the phone (and the right phone, given the different carriers in the region) meant that the way they were carried mattered a great deal. In the case of Bronte, a woman born in the Dominican Republic but raised in Haiti, she views the phone as a functional rather than a personal item and always invests in the least expensive model she can find. For the past decade Bronte has worked as a cleaner and receptionist in a hotel outside of Pedernales. Indeed, her employer at the hotel facilitated her acquisition of her first mobile phone in 2006. Since then, she has gone on to own three more phones, including one which works in Haiti which she uses to keep in touch with her relatives there.

While Bronte makes very little effort to learn about the features of her phone – she often asks her husband or sister to help her use certain features, such as checking her credit balance or how many 'call me' messages she has left – her phone still remains very important in her day-to-day life. In our interviews Bronte identified her phone as being one of the most important things she carries because it allows her to stay in contact with her husband and family. She will send her husband a text or a 'call me' message if she remembers something she needs from the shop. Bronte will also talk often with her mother, who travels from her hometown in Haiti to Pedernales twice per week to buy goods in the local stores to resell in the market. However, Bronte's challenge is that the hotel where she works only permits employees to take a very small bag to work. As she describes:

> In my work they don't permit bags any larger than this. I only carry my documents so that if I have any problem I don't have to leave in a rush. If I have to go to the hospital, I grab my bag and I go to the hospital. I walk around with my phone, my social security card, and my bag. For example, this bag doesn't fit anything within it, only my things for work, because they don't accept larger bags … Because there are clients who bring panties or bracelets and maybe they think that you're going to take them. They have reason to think this … because in a big one you could fit a towel, a blouse, many things fit there, and they prohibit it.

What this means is that her mobile phone must always be small enough to fit comfortably with her other items, and any time that she requires a new phone she tests whether the phone will fit in her simple black wallet which zips around three sides and comfortably fits in her hand. The wallet itself is packed tightly with the most functional items, such as money, carefully placed in an accessible location so that she can conceal the most important items. This creates a simple, streamlined aesthetic that goes with her neatly pulled-back hair and small gold-plated earrings; the only thing she wishes she could bring (but will not, given possible confusion with the guests) is a small face powder to keep herself looking neat and clean before and after work.

Yet even when she is home she notes that she keeps the most important items in a small bag. In fact, Bronte pointed out that her house was *not* the most logical or 'safest' place to keep important or valuable items. Instead, Bronte and most of our participants who lived on the border were more likely to carry with them what they deem to be important items. Some of the items she carries with her relate to her own health and that of her children, including the family's health care cards, her hospital receipts, prescriptions, and an article that she saved. And even when she is at home, she keeps a small bag inside a larger bag in the bedroom where there is less traffic. In a sense, she views this bag as an extension of her body which, when not constrained by work, accompanies her whenever she leaves the house. For Bronte, the key is that these items fit in her nondescript black handbag – an item that defines her simple and largely pragmatic aesthetic.

FIGURE 9.2 *Image of Bronte's wallet: Mobiles, Migrants and Money Project. (Heather Horst and Erin Taylor, 2012)*

Like Bronte, twenty-three-year-old Sandra also describes her style as 'simple'. Sandra was living with her family in Pétionville, Haiti (just outside of Port-au-Prince) when the earthquake of January 2010 occurred. After the loss of family members and their home and a few months sleeping in a park in their old neighbourhood, her family packed up and made their way to Anse-à-Pitres, on the Haitian side of the border. Six months later the family moved across the border to Pedernales, where they now reside in a sparsely furnished rental home in the middle of the town near Sandra's sister (who married a Dominican) and cousin's house. Sandra received her very first phone in 2004 from her grandmother, which she still has to this day – an amazing achievement, since so many things in her life were destroyed in the earthquake. While a notably old model, the small black phone is clean and well maintained. She also now owns two other phones – one almost brand new; one is with a Dominican carrier (Claro) and the second phone, with a carrier in Haiti (Digicel), is shared with her mother and used when she goes to Anse-à-Pitres. Despite having so many phones, Sandra does not spend much money or time calling people, and most of the people she calls are family members. The one exception is her use of the phone for her work evangelizing in Haiti. Her task is to use the phone to record the number of people who want to study with the Jehovah's Witnesses, and to keep track of the hours that she has spent evangelizing. For this reason she keeps her phone in her shoulder bag, which contains a serious of other religious items.

Sandra bought her bag in the border market a few months before our interview and likes it because it fits a lot of pamphlets and magazines that she brings when she wants to evangelize. Indeed her bag contains many religious pamphlets sent from New York to give to people, a Creole Bible and a guide on how to evangelize. Two of her most important items are Jehovah's books called 'Las Despiertas' and 'Las Atalayas'. Sandra notes that she tries to read the Bible every evening for between thirty minutes and an hour. Her favourite part of the Bible is Psalm 30.3: 'O LORD, you have brought up my soul from Sheol; you restored me to life from among those who go down to the pit.' She has identified with this verse since the earthquake.

While she grew up in the religion, Sandra noted that she used to go to discos and drink, but now she avoids bars and does not dress like she used to. She says that she wasn't happy before she found Jehovah, but now she doesn't need anything else to be happy. Nothing and no one can disturb her now, because she is at peace with Jehovah. However, not all of the vestiges of her life before her recent return to religion have disappeared. She has a face powder that a fellow witness living in Canada sent her, which she always

FIGURE 9.3 *Image of Sandra discussing her portable kit. (Heather Horst and Erin Taylor, 2012)*

carries. The bag also contains other make-up, hand sanitizer, asthma medicine and lip gloss that she uses to look *acicalada* (pretty), in the name of Jehovah. A testament to her simple, pretty, modest aesthetic is that she has never had to pay a bribe to the guards on her way to Santo Domingo, or to the two border guards who charge money for people to cross, because they let people who look like they are evangelizing (*predicar*) cross for free.

Everyday aesthetics: Designing across intimate zones

The development of an individual aesthetic takes place within a broader social and cultural context and cultural logic. As noted elsewhere, this cultural logic no longer 'occurs within long-term customary orders of things given by history [...] with the pace of change connected to digital media and technology, the same processes can be remarkably effective within only a couple of years' (Miller and Horst 2012: 29). Yet, what has not been widely discussed in the literature is how these aesthetic practices extend beyond the phone and its associated paraphernalia. Mobile phone aesthetic practices are not limited to customization, branding, or even mobile infrastructure. Rather, phones are part of an aesthetic ecology through which repertoires of practices and meanings emerge. At times they are a central part of the broader aesthetic, and at others they fall into the background as other objects take on the work of creating, contesting or maintaining aesthetic worlds (Horst and Taylor 2014).

In the first two examples in urban Jamaica, the aesthetics of display emerges through the integration of the mobile phone with other intimate objects. Whereas Kacey's particular form of everyday design involved creating aesthetic continuity between her nails, phone colour and the flip gesture of opening the phone, other women developed their design aesthetic through coordinating the colour of their clothing, handbag, glasses and even their hair with the external features of the phone. In Veronica's case, the mobile phone became part of her 'sexy' aesthetic, with the value of the phone in this aesthetic being less about the external features of the phone, such as colour, and more about its contour and size. In fact, the only real act of customization she made to her phone was to add a ringtone with her favourite R&B song (Gopinath 2014; Horst 2014b; Licoppe 2011) which she and others could hear as she tried to wiggle her phone out of her pocket. Kacey effectively designs her aesthetic through normative values of display created through attention to contours and lines of the body that can be featured through intimate objects such as clothing, make-up, jewellery and mobile phones. While phones, jeans, earrings, make-up and other objects are all designed and imagined as products by various firms, people are the ones who design these items into their own worlds.

The second set of examples on the border of Haiti and the Dominican Republic reveal how the mobile phone can also be integrated into a broader aesthetics of modesty. In the case of Bronte, we see how the wallet's aesthetic is created in relation to the constraints of her workplace that restricts the size and volume of bags carried by workers and, in turn, the objects that can be contained within them. Bronte's choice of a mobile phone is impacted by this constraint. Yet for Bronte the aesthetics of modesty – basic black mobile phone lacking customization, simple black wallet, nondescript black bag, hair simply pulled back into a small bun at the back of her head, neatly ironed shirt and skirt and small earrings in the shape of a ball – all work together to create a sense of discretion and humility. These aesthetics have become a uniform for Bronte and are what many would see as a key asset for someone of Haitian descent living in the region. Sandra also creates an aesthetics of modesty, but one that is influenced by her religious commitments. While there is an element of display involved in carrying a large bag and multiple phones, the aesthetics of display are not necessarily about expressing her individual status, as we might have seen in the examples of women in urban Jamaica. Rather, the bag and the items contained within it, the way she dresses and the modest way she applies face powder or other make-up, work together to communicate her membership in the Jehovah's Witness community. This, in turn, provides her with unfettered passage across the border and within the Dominican Republic. Yet in both cases the constant possibility of movement and mobility dominate. Bronte always has her most important items packed and ready to go in a bag, despite the fact that she had one of the most stable residential situations of all the individuals we interviewed. And Sandra is constantly on the move, evangelizing, in her efforts to rebuild the religious foundation of her life in the wake of a national and personal crisis.

While expressed differently as forms of display or modesty, people and individuals define how mobile phones and other intimate objects become part of everyday aesthetics through the kinds of surface ontologies common in the Caribbean (Horst forthcoming; Miller 2013). As Miller (2013) discusses, with surface ontologies 'true selves' are not viewed as occurring on the 'inside', as posited by most psychological theory that draws upon Western theory and contexts. Rather, for those who hold a surface ontology, the 'true self' emerges in and through attending to the outside and on visible surfaces – what those who have an ontology of the inner self might define as superficial. But in places like Jamaica and other parts of the Caribbean where surface ontologies are valued for a variety of historical and contemporary reasons, it is what one makes of oneself that matters rather than the 'inside' determining what should and/or can be revealed on the 'outside'. The work that people like Veronica or Bronte do to create an aesthetic works to then design their own experiences and movements in their everyday life.

Conclusion

In this chapter I have focused upon the ways in which mobile aesthetics are created through practices of everyday design, with particular attention to the role of materiality in the creation and maintenance of aesthetic worlds. Through four detailed examples of women in the Caribbean and their creation of two different aesthetics, I reveal how an already designed and mass-marketed object like the mobile phone becomes part of broader designed and material worlds, creating mobile aesthetics. Mobile aesthetics can be forged through the application of acrylic nails with particular designs, the wearing of a particular type of jeans or the acquisition and use of particular kinds of wallets and handbags. Attending to the contextual ways in which mobile phones become part of the wider designed and material worlds, we begin to see how the values and norms around display and modesty are played out through the integration of mobile phones through the hands.

In addition to wider norms and regimes of value (Myers 2002), we can also see the central role of pattern in the process of crafting and re-crafting mobile aesthetics. In Kacey's case, we see how repeating and complementary colours are used to integrate Kacey's nails and phone, which, combined with particular gestures, work together to create an aesthetic. Similarly, Sandra's attention to simplicity and modesty in her black bag which carries religious material signals her aspiration and identity as an evangelist who navigates the border of the Dominican Republic and Haiti. While mobiles are only tangentially used in the work of counsellors and evangelists to call and/ or send messages, the mobile and its relationship to the bag and religious material aesthetically links the two practices which are reflected in the material worlds created by participants such as Sandra. As Makovicky's (2010) work on lace and Graeme Were's (2010) work on Pacific patterns highlights, pattern plays an important role in 'the forging of connections between what some may consider altogether different styles' (Were 2010: 26). As is argued in the introduction to this book (see Pink, Ardèvol and Lanzeni, Chapter 1), through the process of designing an aesthetic, mobile phones become part of a wider configuration of objects, things, processes, biographies, identities and intimacies.

Time also plays an important role in understanding the process of creating and maintaining aesthetics of modesty and display. In the case of Kacey, we can see how multiple mobile phones have been designed into her life over time and how people continue to design mobile phones and other digital media technologies as new functionalities, possibilities and life stages redefine their meaning (see also Horst 2009). As material culture studies scholars have argued, the everyday design of digital media technologies we see emerging in these examples – and the digital materialities embedded in this process – merely represent one form in the broader processes of materialization (Buchli 2005; Eglash 2006; Kopytoff 2006). While the examples I have introduced generally stress continuity, all of the participants are actively concerned with 'moving forward' in life and view the mobile as one of a configuration of objects that contributes to these forms of possible change, if we see aspiration as a non-linear process (Horst forthcoming). We also see instances of participants like Sandra actively working to change her situation and life through a rupture with her past, such as the subtle differences between how she dressed before and after actively returning to her faith. Given our commitment to maintaining our research relationships with particular people and places over time, disciplines such as (digital) anthropology have a particularly important role to play in producing and sharing these kinds of longer-term insights and perspectives.

The ways in which people use objects to design and redesign their lives through such aesthetic practices, the level of intention that goes into designing aesthetics (Gell 1998), and general attention to the ways in which continuity and change occur through mobile aesthetics in different cultural and social contexts (e.g. for women who occupy a particular economic position, or in a place where mobility and movement is regulated), demonstrates the role that individuals play in shaping, designing and intervening in their aesthetic worlds. This often moves in directions that are orthogonal to the kinds of ways (behavioural) change is inscribed into objects by designers, engineers and others through design specifications, materials, code and algorithms, and the methods by which marketers mediate this process in their branding strategies. This chapter therefore illustrates how mobile aesthetics are dynamic and intervene in other active social and design processes that are in constant creation and re-creation.

10

Designing for the performance of memory

David Carlin

Introduction: A Living Archive for a circus

I write here neither as an anthropologist nor as a designer, but as a writer and practitioner in the arts. In my practice, which has threaded its own eclectic path between creative writing, the performing arts and media, a recurring preoccupation is with the vicissitudes and materialities of memory, and the different ways that memory circulates in how we perceive and fabricate the world through practices of making such as storytelling. Being human, as digital anthropologists Horst and Miller remind us, 'is a cultural and normative concept' (2012) – as for that matter is being nonhuman. I am interested in exploring micro-sites in which these everyday processes of normative acculturation, as well as counterflows of resistance, can be observed and documented, approaching this making-work of storytelling as an attempt in itself at resistance. Such micro-sites need to be assemblages of material circumstances (including history) in which, to appropriate Barthes's (1981) notion of the punctum, something punctures or wounds me. Other metaphors for this puncturing action that come to mind include haunting, infecting and seducing: each in its own way denotes an affective charge that draws in and implicates the observer so that he/she/I cannot maintain a fantasy of detachment. Instead, he/she/I participates in what we could think of as an ethics of care. Family is obvious as such a site (Carlin 2010). Another, as in this case, is a circus.

I have had some association with this circus, the leading Australian contemporary company, Circus Oz, for over thirty years, first as a teenage fan, then as a member of their complex and messy extended family (see

Carlin 2011 for gory details), later as a show director, writer and videographer. Circus Oz emerged from the vibrant Australian theatrical scene of the 1970s. It began as a radical collective in 1978, aiming to both subvert and celebrate the popular traditions of circus. It has grown and matured into a 'national treasure' (Syke 2014), but has managed to maintain its inclusive, collectivist, politically attuned and conceptually sophisticated aesthetic into the new century. Since 2008 I have led the Circus Oz Living Archive project team, a multidisciplinary effort to develop a platform for a digital archive for Circus Oz. The project can be conceived of as a digital intervention. It is attempting to intervene in cultural practice, and specifically the practices of an internationally significant performing arts company, investigating the costs and benefits for such a company of designing a system to make legible the knowledge and experience embodied in its cultural memory. At the same time, the project has another agenda: to intervene critically in the concept of the 'archive' itself by asking what kind of archive does a circus want and need – be it 'radical' (Geismar 2012), 'participatory' (Huvila 2008), or 'animated' (Burdick et al. 2012) – and what is involved in designing such a thing?

My aim in this essay is to revisit the trajectory of the development of this digital archive platform and to trace a number of key moments – meshes between the digital and the material – within that trajectory, which help to reflect not only on how and for what purpose community (digital) archives might be made, but also upon the ways in which the approach to making such an archive has influenced what can and will be made. The proposition I want to suggest is that digital archives afford opportunities for communities and organizations to develop what I am calling new *platforms for the performance of memory*. Platforms for the performance of memory, in the way I will use the expression, are what Assmann (2008: 98) would characterize as 'institutions of active memory [that] preserve the past as present'. But, more than this, they are provisional dynamic sites which stage the complex and multithreaded interplay between past and present, memory and experience, and do so in a way that helps us both to orient ourselves in relation to the past and to open up 'lines of flight' (Deleuze and Guattari 2004) into the future.

The project, broadly speaking, aimed to build something practical in the 'lifeworld' (to borrow anthropologist Tim Ingold's word (2011: 2)); namely, an interactive digital archive built upon the 2,000-plus-hour performance video collection accumulated over the thirty-seven-year history of the internationally acclaimed Australian contemporary circus, Circus Oz. As a research rather than commercial undertaking, the project sought to investigate the technical, cultural, design and organizational issues around the making of such an archive, with the agreed premise that success was to be measured by the extent to which the archive could contribute to the ongoing life and culture of the circus now and into the future. It was assumed that the knowledge generated would be applicable more widely in the performing arts sector and beyond to other organizations holding potentially valuable archival collections.

The project team was large and multidisciplinary: a diverse, productive mix of artists, designers, media and performance scholars and computer scientists (see archive.circusoz.com/credits), including staff, current and former artists of the circus itself. The project began in 2008 with a proposition: the 'Living Archive'. Drawing enthusiastically from the then-current rhetoric of Web 2.0 (O'Reilly 2005), online 'collective intelligence' (Levy 2007) and 'knowledge communities' (Jenkins 2008), we situated the project as:

> interrogat[ing] the intersection between the raucous circus space that welcomes audience interaction in the ring and the online 'living archive' that welcomes interactive participation – creating a socially mediated online space where Circus Oz information/creation can be augmented, annotated, explained, mashed-up and (re)created, engendering new material for the live show, which will find its way into the online circus space. (Carlin and Mullett 2010)

From 2010–14 the videos were digitized and the Living Archive itself was built in a series of prototypes collaboratively designed in a process led by PhD candidates Reuben Stanton and Lukman Iwan. It was 'soft launched' online in 2013 (see archive.circusoz.com) and handed over by the research team to the circus, where, as of 2014, it was operational and in use both for repertoire development and marketing purposes.

Elsewhere, myself and project colleagues have discussed and theorized the Circus Oz Living Archive project through a variety of lenses, most notably in the book *Performing Digital: Multiple Perspectives on a Living Archive* (Carlin and Vaughan 2015), as well as in articles focusing on design methods (Vaughan et al. 2013) and the tensions between notions of archive and reper-toire (Carlin 2014). Here I want to consider the notion of the 'platform' that implicitly underpins this digital archive project, thinking about it in the context of the opposition Ingold draws between classification and storytelling. How can the platform for a digital archive engender storytelling, not simply classification?

A knot of stories

A platform, according to the *Oxford English Dictionary*, is 'a surface, or area, on which something may stand'. Platforms are typically flat, so that things upon them can stand and not slide or topple off; they are typically elevated, so that what is stood upon them is more visible or more distinguishable from its surroundings. Platforms can also be grounds or foundations for ideas, the basis for actions.

For anyone with a theatrical background, the notion of the platform brings that of the stage irresistibly to mind. The stage – or in a circus tent or arena, the ring – is the platform for performance: at once a surface for things (actors, animals, stage scenery and apparati), ideas and actions. But on a stage or in a circus ring these things do not so much stand as move; they flow through the medium of time.

Performances occupy their chosen platform (stage, ring) for a certain length of time, flowing onto it at the beginning and off again at the end. By being placed on or occupying a platform they are designed to attract attention as focused instances of what Ingold calls 'a knot of stories' (Ingold 2011: 154). Ingold lays out a persuasive theoretical framework for thinking about how humans apprehend and help to shape the world, starting with the premise that, as inhabitants of the lifeworld, our knowledge flows from enmeshment in that world, across time, as 'wayfarers' (2011: 155). It is by wayfaring through the lifeworld that we pick up knowledge. Ingold argues that the classificatory splitting of the world into a panoply of discrete subjects and objects, bounded and fixed, material in their thing-ness, is a misapprehension:

> For inhabitants, things do not so much exist as occur. Lying at the confluence of actions and responses they are identified not by their intrinsic attributes but by the memories they call up. These things are not classified like facts, or tabulated like data, but narrated like stories. And every place, as a gathering of things, is a knot of stories. (2011: 154)

Natural language, for instance, is not a set system passed on by parents and teachers to children, to be built up chunk by chunk into an edifice, an armature of knowledge, but rather an ever-changing stream of sounds, words, grammatical conventions, sentences, intonations, puns, jokes, etc. into which each of us, as infants, floats and gradually learns to navigate (Ingold 2011). We might forgive Ingold if he resorts to a somewhat clunky neologism to express how inhabitants integrate knowledge neither vertically, as in systems of classification that link discrete objects through classes of similarity and difference, nor laterally, as in networks connecting points on a grid, but 'alongly' – along the way of the inhabitant's movement through the world, weaving together its elements, each of which is in constant flow as well. He calls this 'the alongly integrated knowledge of the wayfarer' (2011: 155). In opposition to classification, Ingold positions the activity of story-telling. Classification works by separating out the characteristics of things independent of context, but 'stories always and inevitably draw together what classifications split apart' (2011: 160). It is through story that we constitute the world and the world constitutes itself for us as inhabitants: 'the things of this world *are* their stories, identified not by fixed attributes but by their paths of movement in an unfolding field of relations' (2011: 160, italics in original). Stories are organic mechanisms for the retracing and sharing of paths of movement through the world, techniques dexterous enough to convey – to choose an arbitrary example – the fluttering death-throes of a moth on Virginia Woolf's desk along with the pulsing empathy of the author herself as she observes the little creature along with the clouds scudding above the fields beyond her window and the panorama of animals, plants and birds framed therein (see Woolf, *The Moth*).

Archives, historically, have been understood as sites of storage and preservation, within which archival units known as records are classified and catalogued. However, as Mike Featherstone and many others have argued, the move from physical to digital archives changes fundamentally what the archive can do and how we understand it. In a digital archive, as Featherstone puts it: 'the notion of immediate access and feedback replaces the former data separation (the file in the box on the shelf) which created the differences out of which archive order was constructed and reconstructed' (2006: 596). The new digital archive, instead of being fixed and closed to all but the initiated, is, in Featherstone's words, 'fluid, processual, dynamic' (ibid.).

In this move, the place of the archive in meaning production and in story-telling has changed. The classical post-Enlightenment archive was the place where the past lived in silence. As Caroline Steedman vividly describes it, 'nothing happens to this stuff, in the Archive [...] It just sits there until it is read, and used, and narrativised' (1998: 67). It was by agency of the historian that the archive was 'made to speak' (1998: 69); the historian who uncovered and pieced together stories from its traces. By contrast, the digital archive holds the promise that now the archive itself can become a knot of stories, a live site of meaning-formation. This is what I am edging towards with the concept of a platform for the performance of memories, which can help to weave what Ingold calls 'the meshwork of storied knowledge' (2011: 168).

The performance event and its recording

A platform for the performance of memory, I would like to propose, is made through the mediation and remediation of a minimum of three types of event. These we can call the performance event, the memory event, and the performance of memory event. (In saying this I run the risk, I realize, of introducing a reductive classificatory schema; bearing this risk in mind, I offer the schema as a designer would a sketch, as a shorthand for thinking through the connections amid a meshwork of materials, digital and otherwise.)

In this instance, where the platform is for a circus, the performance event is usually quite literally a circus performance, although it might also be a rehearsal or a backstage/offstage activity such as the performers putting on make-up in their dressing room, the audience assembling outside the venue, or the company embarking on a regional tour. Circus performances, like their performing arts cousins in theatre, dance or live music, rely on a highly charged mesh of relations between performers, stage technicians and audience members. Each performance arises out of a long continuum of what Roland Barthes (2011) would call 'preparations', which might include, for the performance makers, years of training, rehearsal, travelling, construction, scriptwriting and choreography, and for the audience members, acculturation through reading and other informal research, conversation and participation in previous performance events.

The next ingredient is that the performance event must be recorded in one medium or another. Until the advent of photography and, later, phonographic sound recording, performances were recorded, if at all, through first-hand written accounts, drawings and paintings. The advent of widely affordable video recording technologies in the 1970s made it possible for the first time to regularly record full-length live performances (previous celluloid film technologies were expensive and restricted to ten-minute film reels). Circus Oz, which began performing in 1978, was one of many performing arts companies that quickly took advantage of the new video technologies, using (typically) a single camera from a fixed position among or behind the audience. These recordings, made on a variety of videotape formats, including U-Matic, VHS and later, Mini-DV, were stored by the circus in its optimistically named 'archive room'. They were accessed and viewed within the company from time to time using VCRs and televisions, most commonly by performers and directors wanting to review performances for show development purposes.

These recordings were made notwithstanding the widely held view of practitioners and performance scholars (see Phelan 2004; Auslander 2008) that the essential force of live performance derives from its very liveness and ephemerality, the precious sense that it can only be experienced 'in the moment' at the time of the event and that it therefore always disappears, resisting any attempt to 'capture' or 'store' it. A live performance occurs and remains in the realm of what Taylor calls 'the repertoire' of a culture: 'embodied memory: performances, gestures, orality, movement, dance, singing – in short, all those acts usually thought of as ephemeral, non-reproducible knowledge' (Taylor 2003: LOC 607).

Bearing these ideas in mind, it follows that video recordings of a live performance such as those of Circus Oz should not be seen as re-presentations of the performance, or, in other words, attempts at a mediated restaging, for as such they will always fall short. However, such recordings do have forensic value as documentary evidence, and can be particularly useful in this regard not only for circus practitioners but for scholars and students interested in studying performance and cultural history, as Varney and Fensham (2000) have noted. This scholarly and, so to speak, dispassionate use for performance video recordings should be remembered in the design of digital archives collecting and presenting those recordings, and it formed one scenario of use that the Circus Oz Living Archive prototypes were designed to enable.

But insofar as our interest here lies in the development of a platform for the performance of memory, the video recordings perform a function as mnemonic prompts. Their power lies in their indexical ambiguity as traces of the performance event. The materiality of the video recording format – its pixellations, glitches, colour approximations and tints – as well as that of the conditions and operations of filming – the placement of the camera and the attention or lack thereof of its operator to matters such as framing, focus and the following of action – serve to distance the recording from correlation with the embodied memory of the event retained by a person who was there (this applies even to the memory of the camera operator herself, as anyone who has been in that position would attest). At the same time, their photographic effects of verisimilitude – the capacity of video to render details of colour, movement, gesture, voice, atmosphere and many other elements of the performance – draws in the viewer to examining their surfaces. It is the tension between the distancing effect – this is not the same as the live performance I experienced – and the drawing-in effect of recognition, for the viewer of the video who has previously experienced the live event recorded or one similar, that infuses these audiovisual archival documents with their potential to contribute to memory-work. The viewer is confronted by an uncanny rerunning in the present of an event that is recognizable as having been experienced in the past but at the same time that is critically divergent from the viewer's at-that-time-existing embodied memory of that event. (In saying this, of course, we have to be careful to remember that embodied memory is itself constantly in a dynamic process of becoming: forgetting and revision.)

Ingold defines storytelling thus: 'to tell a story is to relate, in narrative, the occurrences of the past, bringing them to life in the vivid present of listeners as if they were going on here and now' (2011: 161). In this sense, video recordings of performances are nonhuman storytellers, bringing the past to life as if it were going on here and now – and yet clearly inflected with an idiosyncratic and nonhuman (in this instance, machinic) bias in the telling: telling a story that points towards but is distinctly different from the past as it was lived.

The memory event (1): Digitizing, Kim and her notes

The second event that a platform for the performance of memory needs to facilitate is this moment of confrontation and subsequent interweaving between the materiality of the machine memory (the disembodied recording, in this case on video) and that of the embodied memories of the humans implicated in some way in the original event. This can be called the memory event.

In the design and development of a digital archive, the first opportunity for the memory event occurs with the digitization process. Current techniques for the digitization of video recordings requires that they take place in 'real time' – the originating analogue video must be spooled through a machine displaying its electromagnetic contents in audiovisual form so that these can be digitally analysed, encoded and stored as digital data by a software program. Facilitation of this process requires attention to such details as tape cleaning and configuration of video file formats: the purview of a technician. This is a long, expensive and tedious procedure.

However the Circus Oz Living Archive project demonstrated the benefits of treating digitization as more than a technical chore. Participation in the AusStage consortium, a group of Australian universities and performing arts companies working together to develop the AusStage online database for performance research, gave us access to a mobile laboratory. This was a bespoke set-up incorporating state-of-the-art SAMMA video digitization machines and designed to be packed up into roadcases so that it could be physically shared by companies and universities facing the common finite problem of digitizing a performance video collection. As first users, we set up the AusStage mobile lab in situ at Circus Oz for six months in 2011. Moreover, we made the crucial decision to employ Dr Kim Baston to run the digitizing process – not a technician but rather a circus scholar, circus musician and longtime Circus Oz fan, and hence coming to view the videos across, as it were, several storeys of interest.

Baston and her equipment were situated in a small room next to the music rehearsal room, with a door onto the courtyard where company members leave their bicycles. While to begin with she was left alone for the most part by Circus Oz staff and performers, as the months went on she found that people would drop by to check out what she was up to, watch and comment upon the videos. Circus Oz is a performing arts organization with a very idiosyncratic culture and history. Many individuals have long and complex histories with the company. Baston found that Circus Oz staff and performers began to engage with the videos on the laboratory screens in a variety of ways: discovering footage or acts they hadn't previously known about, remembering their own performances, contributing impromptu anecdotes in response to the scenes they were viewing. This informal inter-action between Circus Oz members, Baston and the digitization laboratory helped the researcher, in some instances, to clarify the details of the dataset (correcting dates, identifying performers or venues in particular videos). More fundamentally for the future prospects of the project, it began to embed the reality of the nascent 'living archive' process within, or at least contiguous to, the daily practice of the company. This memory event of digitization was itself recorded by Baston herself in the form of an idiosyncratic but highly valuable set of notes, documenting the process. These notes not only record technical information such as glitches and sound problems but also Baston's detailed personal commentary on the videos as she is watching them. For example:

> Wayne electrocuted. Musical number .---- 2 Poles erected. Swirly electronic music, audience clapping along. 10 performers up poles. ---------Missed a bit due to phone call and now I'm completely mystified. Torch song parody. (Baston, 2011, '1985 – Albury, Australia, Big Top, Howell Tree Reserve – 12 Dec')

Baston's digitizing commentary, known as 'Kim's Notes', has been incorpo-rated into the online Living Archive.

The memory event (2): The Barrel of Memories

Once the digitization process was underway it became possible to start to use the digital files created to produce more memory events, even before a sophisticated online platform could be prototyped. An attempt to create a digital archive from a collection of community records will always prompt questions of ownership and curation: who gets to say what records will be accessible and to whom, and what interactions with those records will be invited? For performing arts companies, where performers' livelihoods and reputations are at stake, these questions are acute. Circus Oz holds copyright over their performances, with a few negotiated exceptions (including some pre-existing acts brought in to the show, and of course all copyrighted music). However, since at the time the video recordings were made the performers in many cases could not have foreseen that they might one day potentially form part of an online 'living archive', the issue of moral rights arises. Circus Oz made endeavours to contact all past and present performers and techni-cians and to invite any with objections to come forward. At the same time, a number of community events were held to introduce and discuss the concept of the living archive and thereby build a spirit of trust and inclusiveness. I will briefly describe here the first of these, held at Circus Oz's Melba Spiegeltent venue in Melbourne in May 2011, and how it functioned as a memory event.

About seventy-five people attended at the Spiegeltent – current Circus Oz artists and staff, past performers, and their families. The research team dressed in white labcoats in a playful and ironic nod to their status as 'performers of research' on the project. Tim Coldwell hosted a 'Lucky Barrel of Memories Dip' to introduce the proposed 'random access capacity' of the digital archive. We had assembled on a laptop computer a set of a half-dozen short clips of circus acts drawn from the newly digitized video recordings. Audience members drew from the barrel ping-pong balls, each of which was labelled with a given act. As the ball was drawn out and the act announced, it would be played on the big screen, as if (tongue-in-cheek) it had been conjured miraculously from the still-to-be-built living archive.

Afterwards the audience was invited to split into small groups in booths in the Spiegeltent. In each booth a laptop was loaded with a small set of Circus Oz show videos as raw digital files that could be viewed or scrubbed through using Quicktime Player. These sets were themed: for example, 'The early days', 'The 90s', and 'Kim's classics' – the latter an eclectic collection of Kim Baston's favourites as observed during the digitization process, underlined the idea that the act of curation in this developing archive platform could be informal, playful and open to any user.

Importantly, this was a social memory event. New performers discovered the former feats of their older, now-retired colleagues, who were sitting

FIGURE 10.1 *The Barrel of Memories.*

FIGURE 10.2 *The community 'memory event'.*

alongside them; children watched the younger incarnations of their parents performing for the first time. And those confronted by their own memories, as performers or audience members at the original event, responded with a palpable affective intensity, as can be seen in the documentary footage of the Spiegeltent evening.

Participatory community events such as this one proved crucial, not just for sharing information and ameliorating moral rights concerns, but also for affirming the affective power of the video recordings as storytelling devices.

To 'record', Ross Gibson tells us, means to 'bring back to the heart' (2013: 252). The word 'record' (re-cord) comes from the same root as cardiac and the French *coeur*. 'A record well stored and well retrieved', he continues, 'can bring life in its connection to the larger body of present knowledge' (ibid.). This, I would say, rather than for instance simply nostalgia, describes and explains the energy of the Spiegeltent event: here, the forgotten, partially forgotten or unremembered past is brought back to the heart of the community whose members lived it, with all of its accompanying implications and allusions for the future.

Designing for the online memory event

To create a playful live simulation of elements of the Living Archive proved, it goes without saying, much easier than constructing a functioning online digital platform that could facilitate memory events. In order to facilitate the performance of memory, and thereby the continued flow of storying in and around an ongoing activity of circus-making, cultural techniques of random access are required that enable large amounts of memory-data (the performance videos) to be 'served up' on the platform. Compared to text, and even to audio and photographs, digitized video files are large and cumbersome. Moreover performance video recordings are, let's remember, typically shot from a single camera without cuts. This renders the task of making them 'granular' and thereby 'porous to the network' (Miles 2013) that much more difficult. 'Porousness describes the way in which the objects within networked media need to be open to each other internally and externally' (ibid.). Porousness is facilitated by granularity. The more granular a dataset is – by which is meant the more finely grained it is possible for the units of that data set to be defined as and therefore to be findable, retrievable and in other ways meaningfully interacted with – then the more porous it becomes. The circus performance videos of ninety minutes' duration or so were objects frustratingly lacking in granularity. The original metadata told us the date and location of the recording but one had to scrub through on a video timeline to discover or relocate anything there in particular that one wanted to view in that performance.

Live circus performances do have an inherent granularity in themselves. They are made up of acts – usually between fifteen and twenty in a complete show, with each act around three to five minutes long. Each act is in turn made up of a succession of tricks: physical and verbal feats and gags. However, in discussion with Circus Oz, we decided that the basic initial granular level of their video archive should be the act. A three-minute video clip is much more like the standard length of a YouTube clip, and it was felt that acts, with accompanying metadata such as the Circus Oz act name, the circus skills or apparati involved – such as tightwire, flying trapeze, etc. – and the featured performers, would be of wide interest to a diverse city of archive uses and users.

This in turn raised a number of interesting problems. These included: 1) how to divide the videos into acts; 2) how to systematically name the acts; and 3) most fundamentally on a conceptual level, what data model should be designed that would best lend itself not only to porousness and granularity but also to encouraging discovery and representation of the multiplicity of possible connections or facets (to return to Adrian Miles' three properties of networked media) that the things in the archive 'present to each other'. These problems have been addressed through a number of multidisciplinary strategies. Space does not permit me to discuss them here, but the interested reader can refer to the work of Stanton (2015), Iwan (2015) and Thom (2015).

Through months of workshops, discussions, sketching and prototyping, we developed the concept of the clip as the basic level of record in the archive. A clip is a discrete artefact with its own URL. A clip references and in effect annotates a particular section of a video. According to Stanton:

> the living archive is not made up of a collection of videos, each with a complex, singular metadata record. Instead, the living archive is made up of a collection of many metadata records (clips), each referencing a video object. Because the annotations are digital, not physical, there is no theoretical limit to the number of annotations that are possible on any one video object: this leads to a potential 'layering' of records, where multiple clips can exist that point to a single object in the archive. (Stanton 2015: 50)

As Stanton points out, this clip structure is a form of what Ted Nelson called 'transclusion' – the inclusion of digital content into another context not by copying the original artefact but by referencing or, if you like, quoting it. So each video, or section of video, can appear in a potentially infinite number of contexts in the living archive and hence, outside it too: some of these, such as 'acts', can be decided by Circus Oz, but others users are invited to contribute.

With the database architecture in place, Stanton could design interfaces so that within the dense thicket of data presented by the many hours of raw video, users could now discover and isolate individual circus acts defined in the database as clips. Furthermore, inspired by Mitchell Whitelaw's theory of the 'generous interface' (2012), Stanton and our team designed interfaces (see Figure 10.3) that visualized the video data in patterns. These patterns were sometimes simply geometrical, querying the clip database to return and visualize representative samples of videos, acts and stories. On other occasions, elsewhere in the platform, they envisaged the chronological spread of videos, or the array of circus act types over time. These generous interfaces were designed to instantiate new forms of procedural, computational storytelling arising from database structures – what Wolfgang Ernst calls 'telling by counting' (Ernst 2013; see also Carlin 2015 for further discussion). They tell stories of the archive itself: its extent, the texture, range, scope and gaps within its records – as well as of the circus: the development and recurrence of acts and act types, the flow of tours around the world. But furthermore, these interfaces facilitate serendipitous pathways of discovery for the user (again: random access).

All the time these design moves were made in the context of a multitude of material constraints, including labour and skills, time, bandwidth, access to software programs and coding languages, video and audio quality on the recordings, as well as the intellectual property issues already discussed. The multidisciplinary design team, like the artist Ingold writes of, is 'ever caught between the anticipatory reach of the imagination and the tensile or frictional drag of material abrasion' (Ingold 2012b: 11). Nevertheless, it was now possible at a basic level for users accessing the prototype Living Archive online to come face-to-face with the traces of a given moment in a Circus Oz performance. And therefore, also, for memory events to occur.

The distinctive qualities of social networked media artefacts are that they can be remediated by users – manipulated, annotated – and that, by virtue of their porosity, are 'spreadable', to borrow Jenkins' (2013) term, across

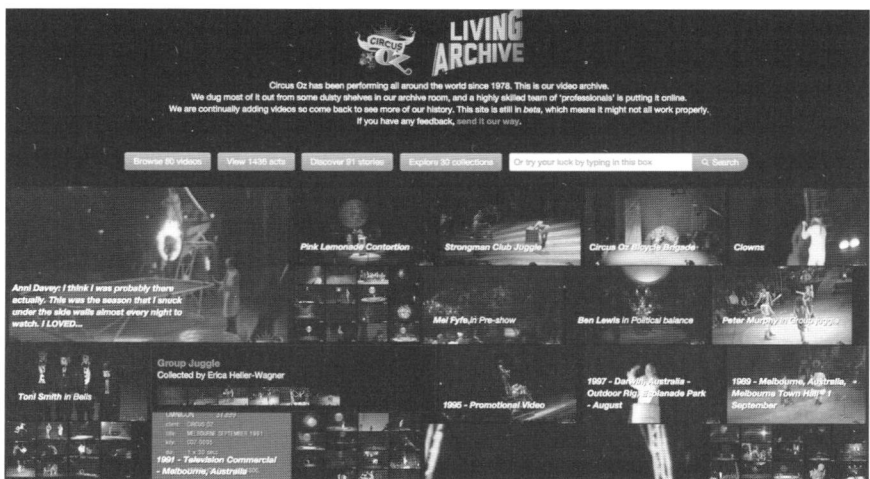

FIGURE 10.3 *The Living Archive homepage: a 'generous interface'*

networks. The circus Oz Living Archive incorporates basic facilities for clips to be shared on external social networks such as Facebook and Twitter. Likewise, facility for users to leave responses to clips, as they can do on many other websites in the form of 'comments', seemed like an obvious thing to do. However, here, we attempted to shift time by inviting user responses not as 'comments' but as 'stories'. These stories would be threaded interconnection with particular video clips through a choice of two framing prompts offered up on the interface: 'I was there and...' or 'I wasn't there but...' Each story contributed by a user in this form becomes in itself a clip in the database, with its own unique URL, so that it becomes more than peripheral marginalia to the videos; rather, user stories and videos alike are all different types of story, each adding to the multistoreyed construction (pun intended) of the digital archive.

This user story space is one site where traces of the online memory event can be recorded. Perhaps unsurprisingly, to date the users motivated to contribute stories have been almost without exception people with a close association with Circus Oz. A founding member responded to footage of a TV interview with her from 1982:

> I was there, and... I don't remember doing the interview – but I do remember the hours and hours of practice that went into the ring juggle. And the lengthy collective meetings. Good to know that I was hopeful that Circus Oz would continue. (http://archive.circusoz.com/clips/view/47405)

And a long-serving company board member responded to footage of a scene featuring the mechanical Eric the Dog in the 2004 *Blue Show*:

> I was there, and... The *Blue Show* was supposed to be adults only but just behind me was a father with his 5-year-old son. Initially the little boy was saying 'Dad the dog is swearing', then 'Dad that dog said a rude word' and the Dad was trying to keep the little boy quiet saying 'Sshh it is OK' etc. At the end of the act the little boy turned to his Dad and said 'Dad, where can we get one of those dogs?' (http://archive.circusoz.com/clips/view/48982)

Stories range in style from the anecdotal to the reflective, the analytic to the discursive, and the casual to the considered.

The performance of memory event

The third event in the schema I'm sketching here for a platform for the performance of memory is at the second level of recursion. After the performance event and the memory event comes the performance of memory event. This is an occasion for a user/viewer connected to digital networks, whether physically alone in front of a digital device or in some other situation, to encounter and respond to the stories told by early users, who are themselves responding to the original performance. The online visitor to the digital platform finds there not only the traces of the original performances but also, in the digital 'story' annotations, traces of thoughts and feelings triggered in other users who are in some way invested in the memory of the performances. If the video recordings are, in their own way, stories about the live performances, then the user stories are always testament to the ambiguous experience of conjunction and disjunction between the video memory and the embodied memories stirred up in the encounter.

The technical conditions for a flourishing of memory work activities existed already in the public version of the Circus Oz Living Archive operating by 2014. In theory at least, it was possible for the Circus Oz community and radiating circles of interested wayfarers (past and future audience members, circus peers, students, scholars) to generate the polyvocal open-ended and non-linear storying of this circus envisaged in the Living Archive proposition. To a limited extent this has happened and is now visible on the site. But, for the most part, the potential remains yet to be activated. This is due, in large part, to limited resources. Anecdotal evidence suggests some users were deterred by the lack of social network (e.g. Facebook) login or by the speed at which videos would load – issues addressable through investment. Further, the circus, understandably occupied with its core business of live performance, has not been able to invest in curatorial resources that would help to more fully activate the site (cf footnote re archive/repertoire).

However, the design of the platform has facilitated other novel approaches to the performance of memory event. In June 2014, we invited twenty-three performers who had each played a significant role across the history of Circus Oz into a TV studio at RMIT University, for a creative experiment we called the Memory Booth. For each performer we selected three clips from the online Living Archive: three significant acts in which that performer had participated. We gave each perform a rough idea of what would be happening but didn't reveal the specific clips to them in advance. For about forty-five minutes each performer sat in front of a teleprompter machine. This allowed us to film them gazing directly towards the camera while actually watching their former selves perform on the teleprompter screen. We gave some headphones and invited them to voice their responses to the videos – to speak along with and across the flow of sounds and images streaming at them from the screen.

This, as it turned out, constituted ideal conditions for both staging and documenting a memory event. The studio set-up, in which the camera and the operators were masked behind the mirror of the teleprompter and

FIGURE 10.4 *The Memory Booth, featuring Lu Guang Rong and Toni Smith.*

surrounding curtains, heightened the effect that the performer/participant was alone in the space face-to-face with the video recording of their own live performance from ten, twenty, thirty or more years previously. Some performers reacted by watching mutely; others immediately began to 'commentate' on what they were seeing. Many had not ever seen the video clips before and had forgotten about their existence. The nature of a Circus Oz performance is that it is constantly evolving over time, with new elements improvised in front of audiences and successful ones incorporated into the ongoing act. This meant that the performers in the Memory Booth could not be sure exactly which version of an act had been recorded – often they commented that their memory of the act diverged from what they were seeing on the screen; at other times they had simply forgotten ever having performed a given trick or gesture. Sometimes we would show the same clip to a performer twice so that after the initial shock they could be given a chance to respond more reflectively to the experience of viewing the clip, and to narrate stories that occurred to them in the viewing. One performer, watching herself perform a group pole-climbing act, pinpointed the exact moment in the act when, on a subsequent occasion, a piece of equipment had broken and she had fallen and broken her neck during a technical rehearsal. A founding member, watching herself doing a subtle clown routine in 1979, recalled how the early performers, working without directors, had to develop the skill of seeing their own performance from the outside. Another performer broke down and cried after watching an ensemble act that was one of his final performances in 1993; he found it difficult to articulate what made the experience so emotional.

The Memory Booth video recording sessions were conducted with a view to making a media artwork of the same name for inclusion in a gallery exhibition called *Vault: the nonstop performing history of Circus Oz.* (This exhibition, which I conceived and made together with Reuben Stanton and Chris Marmo of the design research company Paper Giant, premiered at the 2014 Melbourne Festival.) For the exhibition, a number of television screens each showed a series of splitscreen videos, in which a circus act from the Living Archive was paired with the video image and audio of the performer watching and responding to that act. The exhibition attendee is invited to put on headphones so as to be privy to the intimacy of the Memory Booth, witness both to the performance event and at the same time to the memory event of the performer in the studio reencountering the mediated traces of her performance. This opens up an affectively rich new layer of storying built upon the platform of the digital archive, in which observers (whether in the gallery or subsequently online, woven into the fabric of the archive), who might be remote from the experience of the original performance event, can be drawn into storied knowledge of it through the mediation of someone whose body remembers being there. It is memory performed here, memory as a dynamic and complexly mediated flow of stories connecting past, present and future. The dynamics of the performance of memory can nowhere be observed more strongly than in the human face. The performers in the Memory Booth watch from across the chasm of time these traces of their former intensely lived activities (the performance videos). At the same time, I would argue, the affective evidence of their faces – eye movements, breath, involuntary expressions – suggests that they are projecting themselves back into the bodies they are watching: their bodies remember the lived experiences documented in the recordings. They themselves, like the screen images, are split – between embodied present and embodied past. This therefore performs, in a heightened, doubly theatrical manner (being both the theatre of the circus and of the studio), that which we think of as the common everyday lived experience of memory.

Conclusion

The question I began with in this chapter followed from the opposition posited by Ingold between storytelling and classification, between ideas of wayfaring with materials versus the pinning and fixing of objects: how might a digital archive platform enable storytelling above and beyond simply classification? I have proposed the concept of the *platform for the performance of memory* as a way to describe the recursive layers of engagement with memory and archival materials that can facilitate and trigger such storytelling activities, and thereby activate the potential of community archives to become part of the ongoing life of their communities. Kate Eichhorn has talked about the radical idea of archives as a genre, which 'may be understood as collections and spaces where readers and writers are permitted to dwell amongst documentary remains, crafting new narratives and new genres' (Eichhorn 2008: 10). It is just such opportunities for dwelling and crafting, distributed widely within diverse communities, which we are seeking to encourage here.

Acknowledgments

This research was made possible by an Australian Research Council Linkage grant (LP LP100200118 – 2010–14) led by RMIT University with partners Circus Oz, Australia Council for the Arts, Arts Centre Melbourne and La Trobe University. Our work was collaborative and multi-disciplinary: I would like to thank all of the members of that research team, including Adrian Miles, Peta Tait, Laurene Vaughan, James Thom, Reuben Stanton, Lukman Iwan, Kim Baston, Jane Mullett, Laetitia Shand, Patricia Stokes, Nick Herd, Peter Williams as well as Mike Finch, Linda Mickleborough, Tim Coldwell, Lou Oppenheim, Robin McGregor and Clare McKenzie from Circus Oz.

11

Digital interventions in declining regions

Ian McShane, Chris K. Wilson and Denise Meredyth

FIGURE 11.1 *The Big Merino, located just off the Hume Highway exit ramp at the southern edge of the city of Goulburn, welcomes visitors. (Photo Corrie Barklimore; flickr (CC Licence)) (held here https://www.flickr.com/photos/corrieb/3247619320/in/photolist-5WYU5y-5WUBsc-5WYVXo)*

Introduction

Goulburn's Big Merino stands around three storeys high, big even by the standards of Australia's outsized tourist kitsch. Built in 1985, the one-hundred-tonne sprayed concrete statue of a prize local Merino ram was installed in a paddock on the edge of the southern New South Wales city, a gigantic souvenir of Goulburn's glory days when local economic prosperity was underpinned by the wool industry.

Goulburn fell on hard times in the late twentieth century. In 1991 the Australian wool industry collapsed (Massy 2011). In December 1992 the city was bypassed by a new section of the Hume Highway that connects Sydney to Canberra and Melbourne, diverting more than 20,000 vehicles per day from city centre retailers and service providers (*Goulburn Post*, 1992). The drought that ravaged much of Australia in the 1990s and again through the first half of the 2000s was felt severely in Goulburn. By 2005, household water consumption was limited, the city managers turned off fountains and closed the public swimming pool, and the elegant city of 20,000 sweltered (Marino 2005). The local council looked to halt development in the town at this time and Debbie, the council's economic development officer, told us that

FIGURE 11.2 *Goulburn, Australia: A regional city with a population of just over 20,000 located in the New South Wales Southern Tablelands, 195 km south-west of Sydney and 90 km north-east of Canberra. (Photo Tim J. Keegan; flickr (CC Licence)) (held here: https://www.flickr.com/photos/suburbanbloke/5003371926/in/ photolist-8C8BFy-8C8Aad)*

an international reputation 'as the city that nearly ran out of water' has been difficult to shake and continues to impact on local investment.

In 2007, even the Big Merino was called upon to help reinvigorate the city's fortunes. The ram, which prior to the highway bypass had attracted up to forty busloads of tourists to Goulburn each day, was moved to greener pastures – a prominent location at the highway's southern exit ramp (Harte 2007). Unfortunately, while the relocated Big Merino and the golden arches of its fast food neighbour have managed to draw a substantial number of travellers off the highway, most resume their journey after a quick break, slipping back onto the open road without making their way into Goulburn's city centre.

Around the time of the Big Merino's move, the Australian government was developing plans to build a national broadband network (NBN), a AUD$43 billion infrastructure project that would deliver fast broadband through a combination of fibre, fixed wireless and satellite technologies. For Goulburn, and many other rural settlements around Australia, the bold announcement promised new and transformative economic and social opportunities, a boost to regions suffering from digital disadvantage. The NBN roll-out was planned to take a decade or more, but when the timetable was announced Goulburn was not on the roll-out schedule at all. New South Wales' oldest inland city was off the highway and off the broadband map.

The NBN decision was a significant blow to some Goulburn residents who saw digital communication technologies as a key part of Goulburn's future. Dissatisfied with market and state responses, they embarked on their own DIY digital intervention. This chapter analyses the work of community activists The Goulburn Group (TGG) in rigging up a wi-fi[1] network, providing free internet access to the public, in Goulburn's main street. We offer a narrative based on interviews, site observation and project document analysis. We tell it here as a local story with wider resonance. Part of the story is about how our own involvement on the site and interaction with participants challenged our assumptions about digital civic activism.

It began as a story about a rare Australian example of community wireless activism. Community wireless projects, common in other countries, are sometimes described with homely metaphors such as 'barnraising' (for example, Godwin, 1998), connecting traditional community values and digital enterprise. For some writers, the availability of low-cost wi-fi LAN (Local Area Network) equipment operating in unlicensed spectrum meant 'it was just a matter of time' before wireless communities emerged (Frangoudis et al. 2011: 206). However we share Postill's (2011) scepticism about the association between the spread of digital tools and the reinvigoration of community. The argument we make in this chapter, as it turns out, is not a story of community building and digital transformation, but one of loose civic and commercial alliances, linked more by opportunism and interest than by either vision or technology.

In examining the actors, strategies, texts and infrastructure associated with public wi-fi development in Goulburn, we argue that the important point of the intervention was not in directly enabling new forms of community or commerce in the city, but in enacting an ethos of local innovation, collaboration and entrepreneurialism, captured by the promotion of a 'progressive' Goulburn. The concept of progressiveness, for TGG, was hands-on and project-oriented, evident in TGG-initiated events such as solar power workshops and a small-scale urban regeneration project. This type of performativity (modelling desired social and economic behaviours) has been interpreted by economic geographers with a particular interest in regional development in Bourdieuian terms, as building symbolic capital to attract new residents and new economic activity (Spigel 2013). However, an anthropological lens provides a sharper focus on TGG's public wi-fi project itself, providing insight to the agency and relationship of the human, material and institutional actors constituting the network, adding to the few published studies in the emergent subdiscipline of digital anthropology that analyse user-initiated products and innovations at the physical layer of telecommunications infrastructure (van Oost et al. 2009).

Theorizing digital networks

In proposing a set of founding principles for digital anthropology, Horst and Miller (2012) reject any sense of digital exceptionalism by emphasizing the inherently cultural and material attributes of digital technologies. While making the case for an anthropological framing of how the digital is becoming a constitutive part of what makes us human, these authors also call attention to the political economy, institutions and infrastructures that shape the digital world. This work echoes earlier calls within the field of sociotechnical studies (STS) for greater attention to the interaction of infrastructure and human organization (Star and Strauss 1999). STS's conception of infrastructure as an entanglement of technical and human elements also rejects a priori distinctions between the technical and the social that render infrastructure 'invisible', surfacing only when it ceases to function. However, a singular conception of infrastructure has itself been queried by analysts who suggest that developments as diverse as open source software, the DIY and hacker movement, and cheaply deployed off-the-shelf networking equipment signal a fundamental challenge to the modernist conception of infrastructure as centrally provided large-scale technical systems such as electricity and water utilities. This development has been conceptualized as *inverse infrastructure*, or infrastructure which is typically user-driven and self-organized (Egyedi et al. 2012). Inverse infrastructures may be enterprise-level responses to state or market failure, such as municipal broadband, or less formal citizen-based activities such as community wireless networks. Circling back to Postill (2011), though, community-level initiatives are not necessarily demonstration sites of civic affiliation or bespoke provision. Instead, the published literature includes discussion of competing political interests, wavering volunteer commitment to mundane activities such as repair and maintenance (Verhaegh and van Oost 2012; Graham and Thrift 2007) and numerous disruptions caused by the behaviour of physical environments and other humans (Jungnickel 2013).

This chapter draws on field research and interviews with key actors in Goulburn, including the perspectives of members of TGG, local officials and business figures who supported the enterprise, as well as the views and rationales of those who opposed the development. Our research focused on the network's materiality: the physical site, the equipment, the design artefacts used by TGG to indicate both network coverage and support for the enterprise. It also saw the civic, commercial and association transactions associated with the enterprise as material, mappable and complex.

In addition to its human and material elements, the network was significantly shaped by political and institutional settings. Goulburn's wi-fi network can be understood as an adaptive response to well-established telecommunication and broadband policy settings and concomitant business models. As we describe below, the TGG network makes use of surplus data capacity purchased by participating main street businesses as part of their broadband or bundled telecommunication plans. Australia is distinguished internationally by the aggressive use of data bit caps by broadband and mobile retailers. The typical configuration of retail broadband plans encourages over-purchasing by business customers, with the fear of cost and/or network speed penalties for exceeding data limits influencing their choice from a small range of broad and exponentially increasing data caps (typically stepped at 50GB, 250GB, 500GB) (Given 2008; OECD 2014; Telstra 2014). In Goulburn's case, most of the participating businesses have purchased data caps well in excess of their needs, and donating the unused portion carries no avoidable costs.[2] Understanding this changes the story: rather than supposing that the community is an alternative to state planning or to markets, here community and local commercial interests use the affordances of the market, working within existing market structures to create a commercial commonality in the public interest. Participating businesses contribute to community-making from the sunk cost of their broadband plan, gaining civic credentials and perhaps increased custom by displaying a TGG wi-fi sticker in their windows. Community, in other words, appears in this story as market-engaged and entrepreneurial – a broad, joined-up conceptualization that underpins TGG's community development mission and strategies.

The Goulburn Group

TGG was established as a 'not for profit community think tank and action group' in 2008 by a number of residents and business people who, according to Urs, the group's founding and current president, felt Goulburn was 'really not where it could be' – that the city wasn't making 'use of the potential they have' (TGG 2014). The group is 'committed to sustainable economic, social and environmental development in the Goulburn Region', which it considers to be impeded as much by entrenched conservatism among the local government, businesses and residents as by the available stock of resources and infrastructure (TGG 2014). This formulation calls for sophisticated action, as the group of self-identified progressives seeks to change the local culture. The group has been both forthright in its criticism of the municipal government and active in seeking its reform through the endorsement of a political independent who served a term as the city's mayor in 2010–12. But it is through a series of research-based and professionally communicated development projects that the group has primarily sought to demonstrate the pathway to what it views as an alternate and more productive future for the city and region.

   A cursory look at the TGG website would suggest that the group is primarily concerned with environmentally sustainable futures. The *Goulburn Connects* sustainability festival, *Goulburn Goes Solar* energy promotion and *Goulburn Wetlands* urban wasteland regeneration projects are all foregrounded (TGG 2014). TGG is clearly committed to environmental change. It is, for instance, a 'crucial requirement' for those wishing to become members to accept human-induced climate change (TGG 2014). But its approach is not simply grounded in the politics of environmental sustainability. Instead, through its development projects, TGG views environmental sustainability as a market opportunity, underpinning the creation of 'an enriched social and economic community' (TGG 2014). According to Urs, the group would like to see Goulburn emerge as 'a hub for sustainable industries', particularly energy-efficient building products. He told us: 'We would like to become a host town for these kind of industries ... not just production ... but development.'

   TGG's strategic vision for Goulburn also embraced population change. 'Treechangers' such as Urs (he relocated from Sydney in the mid-2000s) brought new ideas to the city, and they also introduced greater ethnic and cultural diversity to a largely Anglo-Celtic population. Urs, a Swiss national conscious of his insider/outsider position within Goulburn, was clear about TGG's advocacy role in this area: 'The promotion of progressive thinking, like multiculturalism and showing how important multiculturalism is and what it can bring economically, is also a very important job of ours.' Goulburn's archaic telecommunications infrastructure, though, was ill-suited to the work of social and economic revitalization. It is in this broad context that TGG's digital intervention is situated.

Why wi-fi?

Telecommunications is a politically sensitive issue in regional Australia. In the late twentieth century, the provision of telecommunications was liberalized by partly privatizing the legacy public monopoly Telecom and introducing market competition. Where Telecom's universal service obligations meant that the Australian population had broadly equitable access to basic telephony, privatization and the introduction of new services encouraged the patchwork provision or cherry-picking of market segments, a pattern that Graham and Marvin (2001) famously characterized as 'splintering urbanism'. Thus, according to TGG, Goulburn's telecommunications have failed to keep pace with larger Australian centres, and the delayed and uncertain roll-out of the NBN means this gap is unlikely to be closed any time soon.

The poor state of telecommunications was a particular concern for Urs, who works as a foreign correspondent covering south-east Asian affairs for the Swiss public broadcaster and German business press. When, at our first meeting, he told us that public wi-fi was one of 'the earliest ideas I had after I started the Goulburn Group', we thought he aspired to build a high-speed wi-fi network to improve his lot and that of others seeking to engage in communications-dependent economic activity. Certainly, regional Australian local government authorities (LGAs) have increasingly engaged in direct action in the telecommunications field on the grounds of levelling the economic playing field with their urban cousins. These actions include investing in fibre networks, stumping up funds to extend the NBN fibre footprint, making a convincing case for priority NBN hook-up, or, in one case, obtaining a telecommunications carriers licence (Connolly 2014). However, Urs emphasized that the network was 'not wi-fi for the business people'.

Rather, TGG promoted a range of reasons for investing in public wi-fi, a common strategy adopted by civic and government public wi-fi developers seeking broad community support (McShane et al. 2014). In addition to direct use-benefits for the city's residents and visitors, TGG emphasized the economic benefits accrued from public wi-fi. Like other towns and cities with the prospect of attracting travellers, TGG felt that public wi-fi would 'boost tourism and foot traffic in the CBD' [central business district] and thereby 'benefit local retailers and increase the likelihood of a stopover visit' (Sebo 2013a, 2013b). Prior to the opening of the Hume Highway bypass in 1992, the city had been an important stopping point for travellers between Sydney and Canberra or Melbourne, and TGG claimed that free internet would encourage people to pull off the highway and come into town where they might 'stop for coffee and cake perhaps, or lunch and other meals, and to purchase incidentals such as newspapers or stationery, or petrol' (Sebo 2013a; Anson 2008: 9). Although these types of functional benefits have typically won political and community support for public wi-fi promoters, TGG have a more complex, symbolic rationale for public wi-fi investment.

As with its environmental projects, TGG felt that in developing public wi-fi it would model local innovative and entrepreneurial potential, with the aim of inspiring such behaviour in a wider set of local residents and businesses. The network would 'send a signal to the tourist industry and business generally that Goulburn is moving into the future' and encourage (note, not facilitate) 'business in Goulburn to take advantage of online services and applications to change the way they conduct and manage their business, [extending] their activities beyond Goulburn and the region' (Anson 2008: 9). Moreover, TGG argued that wi-fi would be 'very important as a marketing tool' for promoting Goulburn 'as a place with its eyes on the future, able and ready to attract more people to the city' including 'people looking for a "tree change" in a city not languishing in its past, and new business investment from within and outside the region' (Anson, 2008: 9). Urs explained how the network, symbolizing progressiveness, might attract likeminded new residents and help to build the critical mass necessary to overcome the conservatism that TGG feel is holding back the development of the city:

> If we can have a wi-fi network, just along Goulburn Street here … and promote it on the Hume Highway and through the media… then that could help in bringing people into town who would otherwise just pass. They come in, they look at the town, they think, 'it's quite nice here, you know … these people are quite progressive'.

As it turned out, TGG had to work very hard to overcome the conservative tendencies of local government and business to build its symbol of progressiveness.

Building the network

Wi-fi commonly operates in the 2.4 GHz band of the radio spectrum. This band was reserved as an experimental and research space by the International Telecommunications Union (ITU), as its original designation as an Industrial, Scientific and Medical (ISM) band signals. To encourage innovation, the ITU recommended a class-level licensing regime. Low-power wireless devices operating in this band required licensing, but bandwidth users did not. While the band soon became crowded as the manufacturers of consumer electronics took advantage of this regulatory freedom, the decision gave rise to the development of the IEEE 802.11 wi-fi protocol, and in the early 2000s manufacturers of computers and mobile devices began offering wi-fi technology as a standard inclusion (Gow and Smith 2006).

Wi-fi technology revolutionized household computing and communication habits and was subsequently adapted to facilitate portable computing in public spaces via hotspot access points (APs) that, in accordance with the low-power protocol, only distribute a short-range signal (Jungnickel and Bell 2009; Gow and Smith 2006; Van Oost 2009). Subsequent improvements in the ability of wi-fi device connections to be automatically transferred between geographically distributed APs with overlapping signal coverage has enabled the use of wi-fi for roaming/mobile communications. Demand for this type of access, previously the sole domain of cellular networks operating in the licenced spectrum bands (commonly signified as 3G/4G), has grown rapidly with the uptake of smartphones and tablet mobile devices.

The absence of regulatory constraints and spectrum access costs combined with the release of low-cost off-the-shelf wi-fi networking systems has opened up opportunities for a range of institutions, commercial, government and civic, to engage in wi-fi network provision. The relationship between institutional players in this space is dynamic and evolving. Internationally, the provision of public wi-fi networks by civil society groups and municipal governments has been closely scrutinized by higher governments and telcos, sensing rivalry with the commercial cellular mobile market (cf. Dunbar-Hester 2014: Chapter 7). Both telcos and governments saw a need to protect their investment in licensed spectrum, a major infrastructure cost for telcos and revenue source for governments. However, continued growth of the mobile device market, combined with a continuous escalation of data demand from mobile applications (ITU 2014), has encouraged telcos to themselves explore options for investment in wi-fi networks in a bid to offload data, decongesting their cellular networks to improve quality of service (fundamental for customer retention), while potentially increasing cost per data unit margins. As the low-power limitations of wi-fi necessitates access to a substantial number of geographically distributed APs to create effective roaming/mobile wi-fi networks, telcos have increasingly sought to work with government authorities in public–private partnerships that make use of government's distributed physical infrastructure, such as light poles, to mount APs (McShane et al. 2014). It was with a similar proposition that TGG approached Goulburn Mulwaree Council in 2008.

Lacking networking expertise, TGG engaged Orb Consulting to create the public wi-fi plan they presented to council as providing a unique opportunity for Goulburn 'to become the first free wireless city in Australia' (Anson 2008: 3). Orb recommended the development of a wi-fi mesh network. This network architecture enables access to one or more internet connections (internet gateways) to be distributed across a geographic area through a series of AP signal repeaters. Essentially, an AP connected to an internet gateway distributes a signal to end users as well as to other APs positioned inside a radius of 50 to 100 meters. The APs in this zone capture and relay the signal to further end users and APs, thereby creating an overlapping digital mesh. Network coverage can be expanded quickly and easily by adding APs, while enhancing network capacity is made possible by adding additional internet gateways. By 2008 this flexible network architecture had become very popular, underpinned by the emergence of companies, such as Meraki, that provide easy to install and operate off-the-shelf wi-fi mesh AP hardware and software (Middleton and Potter 2008).

Orb proposed the deployment of six outdoor APs and an unspecified number of indoor units. Three of the outdoor APs would be located at council facilities, with siting of the other three to be determined (little detail was provided about the location of indoor units). Council was asked to fund procurement and installation of the infrastructure at a cost of AUD$10,000. The three council AP sites would also serve as internet gateways, with the council asked to fund internet access through these at an estimated annual cost of $6,000 although, in accordance with TGG's entrepreneurial outlook, the proposal suggested a commercial ISP might opt to provide free access in return for promotion through the network interface. The plan suggested that the network be administered by council staff, a sensible proposition given that council was essentially providing all of the network resources and, like many Australian LGAs, had some experience with public internet provision through the municipal library service (Anson 2008: 4; Australian Library and Information Association 2013).

To TGG's disappointment, council rejected the wi-fi plan on the basis of 'various concerns, including legal implications' (*Goulburn Post*, 2010). As a relatively small council, the proposed network carried relatively significant sunk costs and risk of unpredictable ongoing costs relating to network admin-istration, maintenance and ISP fees. But it was security and legal fears that

TGG felt had sunk the proposal. Urs attributed such fears to poor technical understanding among councillors at this time and to the risk-averse briefing provided to them by the Chief Information Officer (CIO), which Urs characterized in these terms:

> He put the fear of God into these people … along these lines: 'Osama bin Laden, if he lived here, he could come to the Roses Café, log onto our internet, create a new 9/11 and we will then be liable.

Debbie, the council's economic development officer, agrees that within council there was 'some nervousness' about taking on the responsibilities of being an internet provider, finding 'the implications of this … a bit scary'. She confirmed the CIO's opposition, suggesting his response to council being involved in public wi-fi would be 'you're kidding, aren't you?'.

For TGG, council's rejection of public wi-fi was a typical encounter between old and new Goulburn. The Goulburn city council's conservative instinct had recently been strengthened by a merger with the surrounding rural Shire of Mulwaree. This merger brought new financial stresses and political sensitivities. As one council officer put it, the city folk don't want to pay for the rural roads, and the farmers don't want to pay for city services. While Goulburn's elected councillors customarily describe themselves as independent or non-aligned (political party affiliation is frequently masked in Australian local authority elections), the region has traditionally elected conservatives to the state and national parliaments. In 2010, TGG may have been hopeful that the new set of elected councillors would be more receptive to the public wi-fi plans,[3] but were again disappointed.

Following council's second rejection, TGG's wi-fi plan went dormant. In 2012 it was revived when Alex, the director of a Canberra IT company, became a member of TGG. Alex's technical expertise would prove vital to the successful establishment of the TGG public wi-fi network without council assistance, as would his connection to Goulburn's small business community. Alex had lived in Goulburn for ten years. His family operates a hairdressing salon on the main street and prior to working in Canberra he had established and operated an IT café business in Goulburn. Alex had even previously explored opportunities for local wireless internet provision in the town, telling us that, during his time with the IT café,

> I became involved with the local internet service provider, and we went down the path of setting up a commercial wi-fi network for the purpose of a wireless ISP. Back then, the laws for licensing were not as friendly to wireless ISPs as they are today, but anyway … I learnt a lot about wi-fi.

Although Alex retained the wi-fi mesh architecture outlined by Orb Consulting, he made a number of adjustments that reduced the cost of network development, and removed the reliance on council for access to AP locations and ISP gateways. Alex chose to use Openmesh hardware and software, an offshoot of Meraki (which had come to focus on high margin enterprise level wi-fi deployments since its acquisition by Cisco in 2012) (Constine 2012). The cost of the Openmesh APs including installation is just AUD$300, and they are centrally controlled using cloud-based software which simplifies network set-up and maintenance. Even AP software updates can be automatically distributed.

Alex solved the problem of securing multiple geographically distributed AP locations and internet gateway access by enlisting the support of local businesses. Convincing business owners to host an AP was the least taxing part of the project. The APs are mounted on the roof or awning of the business premises and are small, innocuous devices that do not require a planning permit or permission from the Australian Communications and Media Authority to install. Installation takes little time and, once set up, the cloud-based software control system means that TGG rarely have to access them physically. The cost to the local business is the power to operate the device which, as Alex explains to the businesses, is less in a year than 'you would spend … [on] having a light on for an hour' (Sebo 2013a). In return for such low-cost participation the business can display the TGG Free Wireless sticker at their premises, which for some retail and service businesses may yield increased patronage. Alex's process of convincing local businesses to provide internet gateway access was more difficult and innovative. Aware that, like his family's hairdressing salon, local businesses tended to be signed up to retail broadband plans that provided data caps far in excess of their needs, Alex speculated that these businesses might donate the unused portion of their monthly allocation without cost implications. In addition to his own family business, which provided the first internet gateway for the network, Alex examined the billing trends of a number of local businesses to establish a conservative estimate of monthly excess data capacity; he convinced some of these businesses to provide the excess capacity to the network.

Alex anticipated a range of risks that might dampen the enthusiasm of local businesses to participate in the network and used his IT expertise to address these. The biggest risk was financial, for if network use in a given month exceeded the data allocation of an internet gateway provider, that business would be liable for over-plan charges. To deal with this, Alex developed a software program that constantly monitors use-data extracted from the Openmesh network cloud controller and warns of any possible overrun. But some impediments to participation arose that Alex did not foresee.

One concern that surprised TGG was the spectre of the cafe 'lingerer'. Confident that public wi-fi would enhance trade, one of the first businesses Alex approached was a café located on the perimeter of the main street city park that did not currently offer wi-fi to its customers. He told us:

on the other side of the park there was quite a popular little café … and I thought, [public wi-fi has] got to be a no-brainer for them … After the initial meeting they came back and said 'no, we're not interested' … They were concerned about people just getting onto the free wi-fi and ordering one cup of coffee and staying at their shop all day and running their business from the shop.

While encouraging people to linger in Goulburn's central business district had been framed and promoted as a benefit of network investment by TGG and was considered 'a good thing' by the council's economic development officer, Alex's experience highlighted the need to carefully consider the impact (real or perceived) of the network on stakeholders. The encounter, according to Alex, 'got us thinking that we needed to think about the use of the wi-fi and limiting time and limiting speed and all that kind of stuff'. This wasn't, then, simply a story about realizing technical potential, of enhancing local communication capacity and speed. Instead, it was a combination of speeding up and slowing down. Negotiating the politics of speed and mobility – setting network speed and functionality, calculating the appropriate length of time that visitors should linger in local cafés, and how impressed they should be with network quality – was, we found, the most exacting part of the enterprise.

When the network went live in March 2013 it was throttled to enable email, web page and social media access, but was of little value for over-the-top services such as Skype (Sebo 2013a). Alex told us when we spoke in December 2013 that the 'sweet spot for use versus abuse' had been calculated at a download speed of 128 kbps and upload speed of 64 kbps. At this speed, he said, 'the types of things that people will want to do on the network is reduced, you're not going to want to go sit in a park and download a movie because it's going to take you about a month, it's easiest to go and buy it'. But when we used the network at this time we found it frustratingly slow, even for the most basic browsing and web-based email services.

TGG's caution in relation to network speeds seemed to contrast with their approach to network security and risk. Following some research on how other public networks handled risk and liability issues, Alex modelled terms and conditions on those used by Brisbane City Council, and distilled these as 'basically just a one-page terms and conditions which is very easy to understand by anyone who would read it'. The community enterprise was not bound by risk or quality of service expectations. Urs suggested that if anyone misused the network, the plan was simply to take it down.

The Goulburn initiative is not necessarily a model for public wi-fi provision. It certainly began life as a risky and fragile enterprise, capable of falling apart at any time through malicious action, regulatory/contractual legal challenge,[4] or changes to retail broadband plans. The term 'public' sits uneasily here too, in that public telecommunications provision is customarily associated with accountability and quality of service measures. Certainly, some community and municipal wi-fi networks have weathered such risks and defied their reputation for fragility or exclusiveness, outlasting commercial communications networks in emergency situations (Poblet et al. 2014). In the same way, Goulburn's network, technically and politically jerry-rigged as it is, continues to surprise its organizers and supporters with its political resilience and its durability.

Twelve months on

When we first visited Goulburn in late 2013 we were not confident of the longevity of TGG's public wi-fi network. This was partly because of our understanding of the field and assumptions about the resilience of community wi-fi networks. We were aware of the broader literature on the difficulty of sustaining community-based digital enterprises and interested in wider discussions of the neglect of mundane routines of infrastructure repair and maintenance, a challenge magnified for volunteer organizations (Verhaegh and van Oost 2012). It took some time to understand that the point of the TGG network was to build symbolic and human capital, not simply digital capital. In the first instance, TGG's network did not fit the model of municipal wi-fi we were looking for: its tactical use of wi-fi, the seemingly fragile coalition of business and political interests, and the group's preparedness to simply shut the network down in case of trouble did not promise durability. We found the functionality of the network to be limited and more likely to frustrate users than leave them with a feeling that Goulburn was a progressive community.

Twelve months on, though, the network was thriving. When it was launched in March 2013, Alex's main street business provided the only internet gateway and two other businesses provided APs only (Sebo 2013a). By September there were five businesses providing a combination of APs and gateways (Sebo 2013b). After twelve months, network coverage had expanded along the main street, with twelve APs and gateways in operation, and Alex told us of a number of new sites where negotiations are close to concluding (Dubber 2014). An AP installed at a rehabilitated rubbish dump some distance from the main street, which was now a wetlands – another of TGG's projects – was still functioning too. While Urs joked that these were the only ducks in the world with wi-fi, connectivity in this location is proving important to school and public visitors.

Along with network expansion, usage had also risen. On a public holiday in June 2014, Alex recorded 8,624 individual connections to the network (Dubber 2014). On our first visit to Goulburn we were informed that the network's busiest day was 80 logins. TGG had markedly improved the quality of service by increasing the network speed (download speeds were now four times faster at 512 kbps), and this is also likely to have affected network use. Certainly our experience in using the network during a visit in November 2014 was a much better one than a year earlier.

TGG had also developed new mechanisms to encourage business participation. Gateway providers now have the ability to promote their business on a customized part of the common splash page. They can also provide their customers with vouchers giving them higher network access speed. TGG had also investigated whether they could monetize the network's business model itself to generate a revenue stream for other TGG activities (Urs). However, the group has concluded that such a route raised philosophical and practical difficulties. Alex told us:

> Well yeah, I mean the thought had crossed our mind and we have received interest from other parties. We're … I suppose not really in a position. The Goulburn Group is a non-profit organization, so we have to be a little bit careful about how we go down the path of commercializing; but I mean realistically, we do want to help other groups and we are currently in negotiation with a couple of other groups – to show them how we've done it and to possibly do it for them.

Perhaps the most important development since the network's launch has been the increasing involvement of council. The council agreed to contribute AUD$9,000 over three years for network maintenance and expansion and, in late 2014, erected signs at the highway exits advertising the service (2GN 2014). The change in council's attitude was chalked up as a significant achievement by TGG. As Alex said:

> When we proposed the current implementation of the wi-fi project … [a] lot of the councillors … recognized that … public wi-fi is something that's very attractive to visitors and very attractive for people when they're looking for destination locations, it actually was something they saw as very much positive, whereas the first time that it went to council, it was quite the opposite, they just looked at the negative, you know, 'What could go wrong?'

Urs put it this way:

> this whole thing really started to change. We did it, then we started very
> early to involve the mayor ... who is – he says it himself – an arch-conserv-
> ative ... Every time he sees me he says, 'You have done a good job, but
> it doesn't mean I'm now more left'. He always assures me that he is not
> going bad, going to the left, because he approves of what we think ... he
> has very strongly supported us because he could see we deliver, we don't
> just talk.

Some within council clearly acknowledged that TGG's approach of modelling
progressiveness to encourage cultural change for local residents, businesses
and government had worked. Debbie told us that although council does 'want
to be seen as being awake and in this century' and 'should have been a little
bit more innovative and gotten on board in the beginning', 'sometimes the
bravery that's required [is] a little slower in coming through'. However, Debbie
suggested there were pitfalls in expecting council support for civic initiatives,
with residents sometimes assuming the council is 'a bottomless pit of money
and people and energy and so forth and it just isn't ... I mean, the projects
that have been the most successful are when people say stuff council we'll
go and do it anyway'. Referring to council's change of mind to support the
public wi-fi initiative, Debbie suggested:

FIGURE 11.3 *In 2014 Goulburn Mulwaree Council erected signs at the highway
exits advertising the town's Free WiFi service. (Photo C. K. Wilson (CC Licence))*

I think that they were pushed into a corner. And I mean that in the nicest way because you have to do that sometimes, but I think it's – I think we were almost shamed into it.

Interestingly, the council seems to have also taken up TGG's 'progressive' moniker to promote the region. Discussing a recent regional marketing campaign, council's acting manager of strategic marketing, Jessica Price told Melbourne's *The Age* newspaper:

The aim is to promote Goulburn as a destination to visit, live, work and invest in, and to change people's perceptions of the region. We are trying to position Goulburn Mulwaree as a progressive and innovative community that offers attractive lifestyle choices. (Strachan 2014)

Over time, we came to understand that what we were seeing in TGG was a resilient network and initiative that might look unlike more romantic conceptions of organic community cooperation and bottom-up innovation, but that from a pragmatic point of view was delivering a civic–commercial–voluntary hybrid capable of sustaining civic infrastructure.

Conclusion

Our narrative and analysis in this chapter is different from the standard human–technology story of heroic communities that build a network and are transformed by it. This is a more pragmatic story about a bottom-up project to build public wireless broadband infrastructure that has both functional and symbolic aspects. The main street network provides a visitor attraction, enticing travellers away from the free wi-fi available at McDonalds on the fringe of town. However, the basic functionality of the network in its early days suggests its symbolic role, as a demonstration site for an alternative Goulburn future.

When we first encountered TGG's public wi-fi project we were disposed to think the network had a limited future, because of the group's description of the network as a marketing tool, its seeming disregard for network functionality, and the preparedness to 'take it down' in the event of misuse or legal threat. The jerry-rigged character of this civil society initiative contrasted dramatically with the emphasis on service standards and accountability that underpins regulated commercial telecommunications ventures.

The success of the venture in its first year can be attributed to some local contingencies. The 'hybrid community' (Callon, 2004) that is TGG, comprising a range of political, communication and technical skills, was a prime factor in framing the project, garnering business support and setting up the network. Urs's subjectivity as an outsider, a self-described 'wog' not bound by Goulburn's social and political conventions, able to articulate and defend an alternative economic path for Goulburn, was a crucial input. Alex's technical skills and his donation of many hundreds of billable hours to the social enterprise was also a key input.

A range of structural factors also contributed to the project. The calibration of commercial broadband plans, encouraging businesses to sign up to data bit caps far in excess of usage, ensured availability of unused capacity to support the project. The absence of constraints in regulatory and planning regimes and the declining cost and increasing ease of deployment of mesh wireless equipment were also important factors.

However, perhaps what we identify as TGG's tactical use of wi-fi is not a weakness, but a strength: it may be the project's key innovation. This pragmatism speaks to an increasing familiarity with wi-fi, to its incorporation within a suite of tools available to civil society groups to promote alternative development paths for local communities. TGG may have embarked on the project as a political ginger group, but it succeeded in developing a new business model for Goulburn's economy. As the former Australian Labour government's vision of a national broadband network loses political commitment, significantly impacting on the thin telecommunications markets of regional Australia, it seems likely that we will see increasing 'bottom-up broadband' activism in coming years. Stories such as TGG's, if it survives, will be helpful in framing expectations of what can be done, and in prompting a more pragmatic understanding of emergent initiatives.

Notes

Chapter 2

1. http://bitsavers.informatik.uni-stuttgart.de/bits/Xerox/Alto/simulator/salto/salto-0.4.2/ [accessed 18 August 2014].

2. http://jamesfriend.com.au/pce-js/ [accessed 18 August 2014].

3. http://ascii.textfiles.com/archives/4546 [accessed 27 January 2015].

4. At the risk of further clouding an already complicated distinction, I will note in passing here that emulation is strongly related to the practice of 'virtualization' common in cloud computing and computer utility services. I'm not immediately concerned with virtualization here, but with virtuality – the idea that when we deal with digital objects, material manifestations are unimportant.

5. 'A1' might not look like a number, but it is. Hexadecimal numbers, i.e. numbers in base-16, are conventionally written using A–F for the positional digits representing decimal values of 10–15. Expressed conventionally in base-10, A1 is 161.

6. Pipelining is a technique for taking the various steps that a processor has to go through to execute an instruction, and break them down into separate units so that the processor can essentially be executing multiple instructions 'at the same time', all at different stages of completion. A more heavily pipelined processor architecture breaks instruction execution down into more steps – creating more parallelism but also requiring more complicated synchronization.

7. https://www.youtube.com/watch?v=2H2BPrgxedY

Chapter 3

1. http://www.nature.com/news/environmental-science-pollution-patrol-1.16654#sensors

2. Open source hardware is hardware whose design is made publicly available so that anyone can study, modify, distribute, make and sell the design or hardware based on that design. The hardware's source, the design from which it is made, is available in the preferred format for making modifications to it. Ideally, open source hardware uses readily available components and materials, standard processes, open infrastructure,

unrestricted content and open-source design tools to maximize the ability of individuals to make and use hardware. Open source hardware gives people the freedom to control their technology while sharing knowledge and encouraging commerce through the open exchange of designs, http://www.oshwa.org/definition/

3   https://www.kickstarter.com/projects/acrobotic/the-smart-citizen-kit-crowdsourced-environmental-m [accessed 16 January 2015].

4   Do-It-Yourself refers to the activities of repairing, creating and making something without professional training or assistance under one's own initiative. DIY refers also to a collective organization around these activities in order to encourage people to engage with this modus operandi. (Source: Merriam-Webster)

5   The idiom imaginary has to be understood as social shared common understanding carried out by images, stories, legends, writings and speeches (Tylor 2004). It is a floating meaning that is held by large groups of persons and put into effect to legitimize and inform people's concrete practices.

6   *Nature*, news feature, 7 January 2015, by Kat Austen.

7   IoT social platforms are the interfaces through which people connect and build up projects in common, such as meet-up groups, discussion groups or magazines.

8   PACHUBE (see COSM now XIVELY) is a carrier-grade cloud platform to connect IoT devices and services. It is for private customers as well companies. The change of name has occurred as a result of its acquisition, by different companies. https://xively.com/ [accessed 14 November 2015].

9   *Kickstarter* is one of the world's largest funding platforms for creative projects, https://www.kickstarter.com/projects/edborden/air-quality-egg [accessed 16 January 2015].

10   Air Quality Egg crowdfunding campaign, https://www.kickstarter.com/projects/edborden/air-quality-egg [accessed 16 January 2015].

11   Research and experimental centre in Visual Arts and Technology subsidized by Catalan local government.

12   Cisco Systems, Inc. is an American *multinational corporation* that designs, manufactures and sells *networking equipment*, http://en.wikipedia.org/wiki/Cisco_Systems [accessed 2 May 2015].

13   http://share.cisco.com/IoESocialWhitepaper/#/0/6 [accessed 22 May 2015].

Chapter 4

1 Parts of this chapter draw on material from the following book: Strengers, Y. 'Smart energy technologies in everyday life: Smart Utopia', 2013, Palgrave Macmillan, reproduced with permission of Palgrave Macmillan.

2 For some occupants, the smart home market also aims to provide health and well-being benefits for people who require assisted living (Balta-Ozkan et al. 2013).

Chapter 7

1 Interactive playgrounds is an interdisciplinary field of research that focuses on the development of digital products aimed at creating play and playful experiences as a way to promote children's welfare. Many of these products are aimed at reducing obesity and providing an alternative to sedentary computer games. This has resulted in initiatives such as the Centre for Playware in Denmark, the DigiWall by the Sonic Studio of the Interactive Institute in Sweden, the Hybrid Playground project by the Lalalab group at the University of Valencia in Spain, and Reactive Playgrounds and Space Explorers for Kids from MIT Media Lab groups, among others. (See also Mueller, Chapter 8, this volume.)

2 The Interactive Systems Lab belonged to Universitat Pompeu Fabra in Barcelona and its principal researcher was Dr Narcís Parés (http://www.dtic.upf.edu/~npares/projectes/InteractiveSlide/ InteractiveSlide.htm). This lab is currently the Full-Body Interaction Lab and Prof Parés still heads it.

3 This chapter is based on a PhD thesis project and this narration in third person is about the learnings and troubles of Jaume Ferrer, constructed in dialogue with his PhD thesis supervisors and the co-authors of this text (Elisenda Ardèvol, the anthropologist and Narcís Parés, the engineer who was, at the same time, the leader of the design team subject of this study).

4 Such as the EU-funded project *Mediate*, an interactive multisensory environment for children with severe autism and no verbal communication (2001–4), *Jocs d'Aigua* (Water Games) for the international event *The Forum of Cultures*, Barcelona 2004, *Interaction with Virtual Water* for the international event *Expo2008* (2006–8) and *Connections* (2007) an interactive multi-user installation for teens (14–18) to bodily explore and experience how science and knowledge are structured for the *CosmoCaixa* science museum in Barcelona.

5 This was the call announced on the university website, for Master's degree students' research project thesis in 2007.

6 In the *Virtual Mosaic* project, Miquel Soler, Anna Carreras and Martí Utset were other student collaborators who worked with the principal investigator.

Chapter 8

1   The Exertion Cards are available to download and we encourage users to print them out as tangible tokens during design sessions. The URL is: http://exertiongameslab.org

2   Like the Exertion Cards, the Movement-Based Game Guidelines are also available online. The URL is: http://exertiongameslab.org

Chapter 9

1   Miller and Sinanan (forthcoming) also note that in Trinidad, women focus upon remaining 'sexy' after the birth of their children, a pattern that differs from the practices of mothers in a small English town in the UK.

Chapter 11

1   Although Wi-Fi is a trademark (registered in 1999), it has become a broad signifier for wireless connectivity under a specific set of IEEE (Institute of Electrical and Electronics Engineers) protocols and is now commonly expressed using the lowercase 'wi-fi' (Dunbar-Hester 2014).

2   Note, however, that the data use trend analysis conducted by TGG in the process of negotiating partnerships with new businesses could in some cases assist these businesses to select a lower cap and thereby reduce their broadband costs.

3   The basic elements of the proposal were unchanged, although the costs had been revised upwards to AUD$20,000 (perhaps to account for inflation) (*Goulburn Post*, 2010).

4   Telcos could, for instance, attempt to alter contracts with their business customers to preclude the type of surplus data sharing upon which the Goulburn network is based.

Bibliography

Chapter 1

Akama, Y. and A. Prendiville (2013), 'A Phenomenological View to Co-designing Services', *Swedish Design Research Journal* 1 (13): 29–40.

Akama, Y. and S. Pink (2015), *Un/Certainty*, iBook (RMIT University).

Appadurai, A. (2013), *The Future as Cultural Fact* (London: Verso).

Ardèvol, E. and Gómez-Cruz, E. (2014), *Digital Ethnography and Media Practices*, The International Encyclopedia of Media Studies, Vol. 7 (Hoboken, NJ: John Wiley & Sons).

Baym, N. (2000), *Tune In, Log On. Soaps, Fandom, and Online Community* (Thousands Oaks: Erlbaum).

Bennett, J. (2009), *Vibrant Matter: A Political Ecology of Things* (Durham and London: Duke University Press).

Bennett, J. (2010), 'A Vitalist Stopover on the Way to a New Materialism', in D. Coole and S. Frost (eds), *New Materialisms: Ontology, Agency, and Politics* (Durham and London: Duke University Press).

Boellstorff, T. (2008), *Coming of Age in Second Life: An Anthropologist Explores the Virtually Human* (Princeton, NJ: Princeton University Press).

Bratteteig, Tone (2010), 'A Matter of Digital Materiality', in I. Wagner, T. Bratteteig and D. Stuedahl (eds), *Exploring Digital Design: Multi-disciplinary Design Practices* (London: Springer), 147–69.

Brauchler, B. and J. Postill (eds) (2010), *Theorising Media and Practice*, vol. 4 (Oxford: Berghahn Books).

Clarke, A. J. (2010), *Design Anthropology* (New York: Actar).

Coole, D. and S. Frost (2010), *New Materialisms: Ontology, Agency, and Politics* (Durham and London: Duke University Press).

DeLanda, M. (2004), 'Material Complexity' in N. Leach, D. Turnbull and C. Williams (eds), *Digital Tectonics* (London: Wiley), 14–21.

Dourish, P. and G. Bell (2011), *Divining a Digital Future: Mess and Mythology in Ubiquitous Computing* (Cambridge, MA: MIT Press).

Dourish, P. and M. Mazmanian (2013), 'Media as Material: Information Representations as Material Foundations for Organizational Practice', in P. Carlile, D. Nicolini, H. Tsoukas and A. Langley (eds), *How Matter Matters: Objects, Artifacts, and Materiality in Organization Studies* (Oxford: Oxford University Press), 92–118.

Drazin, A. (2012), 'Digital Anthropology in Design Anthropology' in H. Horst and D. Miller (eds) *Digital Anthropology* (London: Bloomsbury).

Drazin, A. (2013), 'The Social Life of Concepts in Design Anthropology' in W. Gunn, T. Otto and R. C. Smith (eds), *Design Anthropology: Theory and Practice* (London: Bloomsbury), 33–50.

Ewart, I. J. (2013), 'Designing by Doing: Building Bridges in the Highlands of Borneo', in W. Gunn, T. Otto and R. C. Smith (eds), *Design Anthropology: Theory and Practice* (London: Bloomsbury), 85–99.

Fuller, M. (2005), *Media Ecologies: Materialist Energies in Art and Technoculture* (Cambridge, MA: MIT Press).

Gabrys, J. (2011), *Digital Rubbish: A Natural History of Electronics* (Ann Arbor: University of Michigan Press).

Ginsburg, F. (2012), 'Disability in the Digital Age', in H. Horst and D. Miller (eds), *Digital Anthropology* (London: Bloomsbury), 101–26.

Ginsburg, F. D., L. Abu-Lughod and B. Larkin (eds) (2002), *Media Worlds: Anthropology on New Terrain* (Berkeley, CA: University of California Press).

Gramazio, F. and M. Kohler (2008), *Digital Materiality in Architecture* (Baden: Lars Müller Publishers).

Green, L. and S. Pink (2015), 'Using Digital Interventions to Engage in the Everyday', in *Media International Australia* 153: 73–7.

Gunn, W., T. Otto and R. C. Smith (eds) (2013), *Design Anthropology: Theory and Practice* (London: Bloomsbury).

Halse, J. (2013), 'Ethnographies of the Possible', in W. Gunn, T. Otto and R. C. Smith (eds), *Design Anthropology: Theory and Practice* (London: Bloomsbury), 180.

Haraway, D. (1991), A cyborg manifesto: science, technology, and socialist-feminism in the late twentieth century. *Simians, cyborgs and women: the reinvention of nature*, 149–82.

Haraway, D. (1999), The biopolitics of postmodern bodies: Determinations of self in immune system discourse. *Feminist theory and the body: A reader, 1*(1), 203.

Henare, A., M. Holbraad and S. Wastell (eds) (2007), *Thinking Through Things: Theorising Artefacts Ethnographically* (London: Routledge).

Hine, C. (2000), *Virtual Ethnography* (London: Sage).

Hine, C. (2007), 'Connective Ethnography for the Exploration of e-Science', *Journal of Computer-Mediated Communication* 12 (2): 618–34.

Hodder, I. (2012), *Entangled: An Archaeology of the Relationships Between Humans and Things* (Hoboken, NJ: John Wiley & Sons).

Holbraad, M. (2011), 'Can the Thing Speak?', *Open Anthropology Cooperative Press, Working Papers Series* 7.

Horst, H. A. and D. Miller (eds) (2012), *Digital Anthropology* (London: Bloomsbury).

Ingold, T. (2008), 'Bringing Things to Life: Creative Entanglements in a World of Materials', ESRC National Centre for Research Methods, NCRM Working Paper Series, 1–15.

Ingold, T. (2011), *Being Alive: Essays on Movement, Knowledge and Description* (London: Taylor & Francis).

Kopytoff, I. (1986), 'The Cultural Biography of Things: Commoditization as Process', *The Social Life of Things: Commodities in Cultural Perspective*, 68: 70–3.

Latour, B. (2005), *Reassembling the Social* (Oxford: Oxford University Press).

Law, J. (2004), *After Method: Mess in Social Science Research* (London: Routledge).

Leander, K. M. and K. K. McKim (2003), 'Tracing the Everyday "Sitings" of Adolescents on the Internet: A Strategic Adaptation of Ethnography Across Online and Offline Spaces', *Education, Communication and Information* 3 (2): 211–40.

Madianou, M. and D. Miller (2013), *Migration and New Media: Transnational Families and Polymedia* (London: Routledge).

Maxwell, R. and T. Miller (2012), *Greening the Media* (Oxford: Oxford University Press).

Miller, D. and H. A. Horst (2012), 'The Digital and the Human: A Prospectus for Digital Anthropology', in H. A. Horst and D. Miller (eds), *Digital Anthropology* (London: Bloomsbury), 3–35.

Miller, D. and D. Slater (2000), *The Internet: An Ethnographic Approach* (Oxford: Berg).

Moores, S. (2012), *Media, Place and Mobility* (London: Palgrave Macmillan).

Nakamura, L. (2002), *Cybertypes: Race, Ethnicity, and Identity on the Internet* (London: Routledge).

Parikka, J. (2011), 'FCJ-116 Media Ecologies and Imaginary Media: Transversal Expansions, Contractions, and Foldings', *The Fibreculture Journal* 17.

Parikka, J. (2012), 'New Materialism as Media Theory: Medianatures and Dirty Matter', *Communication and Critical/Cultural Studies* 9 (1): 95–100.

Pinch, T. (2008), 'Technology and Institutions: Living in a Material World', *Theory and Society* 37 (5): 461–83.

Pink, S. (ed.) (2005), *Applications of Anthropology* (Oxford: Berghahn).

Pink, S. (ed.) (2007), *Visual Interventions: Applied Visual Anthropology* (Oxford: Berghahn).

Pink, S. (2013) *Doing Visual Ethnography*, rev. and exp. 3rd edn (London: Sage).

Pink, S. (2015) *Doing Sensory Ethnography*, 2nd edn (London: Sage).

Pink, S. and K. Leder Mackley (2012), 'Video as a Route to Sensing Invisible Energy', *Sociological Research Online*, February 2012, online at http://www.socresonline.org.uk/17/1/3.html [accessed 3 October 2015].

Pink, S., K. Leder Mackley, V. Mitchell, C. Escobar-Tello, M. Hanratty, T. Bhamra and R. Moroşanu (2013), 'Applying the Lens of Sensory Ethnography to Sustainable HCI', *Transactions on Computer-Human Interaction* 20 (4), article no. 25.

Pink, S., H. Horst, J. Postill, L. Hjorth, T. Lewis and J. Tacchi (2015), *Digital Ethnography: Principles and Practice* (London: Sage).

Smith, R. C. (2013) 'Designing Heritage for a Digital Culture' in W. Gunn, T. Otto and R. C. Smith (eds), *Design Anthropology: Theory and Practice* (London: Bloomsbury).

Suchman, L. (2005), 'Affiliative Objects', *Organization* 12 (3): 379–99.

Suchman, L. (2011), 'Anthropological Relocations and the Limits of Design', *Annual Review of Anthropology* 40: 1–18.

Thrift, N. (2005), 'From Born to Made: Technology, Biology and Space', *Transactions of the Institute of British Geographers* 30 (4): 463–76.

Tunstall, E. D. (2013), 'Decolonizing Design Innovation: Design Anthropology, Critical Anthropology, and Indigenous Knowledge', in W. Gunn, T. Otto and R. C. Smith (eds), *Design Anthropology: Theory and Practice* (London: Bloomsbury), 232.

Turkle, S. (1995), *Life on the Screen* (New York: Simon and Schuster).

van Dijck, J. (2004), 'Composing the Self: Of Diaries and Lifelogs', *The Fibreculture Journal*, 3. http://three.fibreculturejournal.org/fcj-012-composing-the-self-of-diaries-and-lifelogs/ [accessed 14 April 2015].

Wagner, I., T. Bratteteig and D. Stuedahl (2010), *Exploring Digital Design* (London: Springer).

Wasson, C. and C. Metcalf (2013), 'Bridging Disciplines and Sectors: An Industry-Academic Partnership', in W. Gunn, T. Otto and R. C. Smith (eds), *Design Anthropology: Theory and Practice* (London: Bloomsbury), 216.

Willmann, J., F. Gramazio, M. Kohler and S. Langenberg (2013), 'Digital by Material', in S. Brell-Cokcan and J. Braumann (eds), *Robotic Fabrication in Architecture, Art and Design* (Vienna: Springer), 12–27.

Chapter 2

Blanchette, J.-F. (2011), 'A Material History of Bits', *Journal of the American Society for Information Science and Technology* 62 (6): 1024–57.

Brubaker, J., G. Hayes and P. Dourish (2013), 'Beyond the Grave: Facebook as a Site for the Expansion of Death and Mourning', *The Information Society* 29 (3): 152–63.

Dourish, P. (2014), 'NoSQL: The Shifting Materialities of Database Technology', *Computational Culture* 4.

Dourish, P. (2015), 'Protocols, Packets, and Proximity: The Materiality of Internet Routing', in L. Parks and N. Starosielski (eds), *Signal Traffic: Media Infrastructure and Globalization* (Champaign, IL: University of Illinois Press).

Dourish, P. and M. Mazmanian (2013), 'Media as Material: Information Representations as Material Foundations for Organizational Practice', in P. Carlile, D. Nicolini, A. Langley and H. Tsoukas (eds), *How Matter Matters: Objects, Artifacts, and Materiality in Organization Studies* (Oxford: Oxford University Press), 92–118.

Heddaya, M. (2014), 'Warhol Computer Art Discovered on 1985 Floppy Discs' http://hyperallergic.com/122381/warhol-computer-art-discovered-on-1985-floppy-discs, April 24 [accessed 18 August 2014].

Hiltzik, M. (1999), *Dealers of Lightning: Xerox PARC and the Dawn of the Computer Age* (New York: HarperCollins).

Johnson, C. (2013), 'Thanks to an online archive, here's a Karateka review in 2013', *Ars Technica* http://arstechnica.com/gaming/2013/10/playing-apple-iic-games-30-years-late-through-an-online-emulator-museum [accessed 18 August 2014].

Leonardi, P. M. and S. R. Barley (2008), 'Materiality and Change: Challenges to Building Better Theory about Technology and Organizing', *Information and Organization* 18: 159–76.

Montford, N. and I. Bogost (2009), *Racing the Beam: The Atari Video Computer System* (Cambridge, MA: MIT Press).

Orlikowski, W. J. (2007), 'Sociomaterial Practices: Exploring Technology at Work', *Organization Studies* 28 (9): 1435–48.

Orlikowski, W. and S. Scott (2008), 'Sociomateriality: Challenging the Separation of Technology, Work and Organization', *The Academy of Management Annals* 2 (1): 433–74.

Schön, D. (1984), *The Reflective Practitioner: How Professionals Think In Action* (New York: Basic Books).

Smith, R. (1986), 'Experiences with the Shared Reality Kit: An Example of the Tension Between Literalism and Magic', *IEEE Computer Graphics and Applications* 7 (9): 42–50.

Thacker, C., E. McCreight, B. Lampson, R. Sproull and D. Boggs (1979), 'Alto: A Personal Computer' Technical Report CSL-79-11, Xerox Palo Alto Research Center (Palo Alto: Xerox Corp).

Turing, A. (1936), 'On Computable Numbers, with an Application to the *Entscheidungsproblem*', *Proceedings of the London Mathematical Society* 42 (2): 230–65.

Chapter 3

Anderson, B. (2007), 'Hope for Nanotechnology: Anticipatory Knowledge and the Governance of Affect', *Area* 39 (2): 156–65.

Anderson, B. (2010), 'Preemption, Precaution, Preparedness: Anticipatory Action and Future Geographies', *Progress in Human Geography* 34 (6): 777–98.

Appadurai, A. (2013), *The Future as Cultural Fact* (London: Verso).

Chun, W. H. K. (2004), 'On Software, or the Persistence of Visual Knowledge', *grey room* 18: 26–51.

Coleman, G. (2009), 'Code is Speech: Legal Tinkering, Expertise, and Protest among Free and Open Source Software Developers', *Cultural Anthropology* 24 (3): 420–54.

Diez, T. (2014), 'Distributed and Open Creation Platforms as key enablers for Smart Cities', *Journal Peer-to-Peer production,* http://peerproduction.net/issues/issue-5-shared-machine-shops/editorial-section/distributed-and-open-creation-platforms-as-key-enablers-for-smarter-cities/.

DiSalvo, C. (2009), 'Design and the Construction of Publics', *Design Issues* 25 (1): 48–63.

Dourish, P. (2010), 'HCI and Environmental Sustainability: The Politics of Design and the Design of Politics', in *Proceedings of the 8th ACM Conference on Designing Interactive Systems* (ACM), 1–10.

Dourish, P. and G. Bell (2011), *Divining a Digital Future: Mess and Mythology in Ubiquitous Computing* (Cambridge, MA: MIT Press).

Elías, N. (1998), '¿Cómo pueden las utopías científicas y literarias influir sobre el futuro?' in *WEILER, Vera (compiladora): Figuraciones en proceso, Santafé de Bogotá*, 15–44.

English-Lueck, J. A. (2002), *Cultures@ Silicon Valley* (Stanford, CA: Stanford University Press).

Galloway, A. (2013), 'Emergent Media Technologies, Speculation, Expectation, and Human/Nonhuman Relations', *Journal of Broadcasting & Electronic Media* 57 (1): 53–65.

Gaonkar, D. P. and E. A. Povinelli (2003), 'Technologies of Public Forms: Circulation, Transfiguration, Recognition', *Public Culture* 15 (3): 385–97.

Graeber, D. (2005), 'Fetishism as Social Creativity, or, Fetishes are Gods in the Process of Construction', *Anthropological Theory* 5 (4): 407–38.

Graham, S. and N. Thrift (2007), 'Out of Order: Understanding Repair and Maintenance', *Theory, Culture and Society* 24 (3): 1–25.

Gunn, W. and J. Donovan (2012), 'Design Anthropology: An Introduction', in W. Gunn and J. Donovan (eds), *Design and Anthropology* (Surrey: Ashgate).

Gunn, W., T. Otto and R. C. Smith (eds) (2013), *Design Anthropology: Theory and Practice* (London: A&C Black).

Halse, J. (2013), 'Ethnographies of the Possible', in W. Gunn, T. Otto and R. C. Smith (eds), *Design Anthropology: Theory and Practice* (A&C Black).

Kelty, C. M. (2008), '*Two Bits: The Cultural Significance of Free Software* (Durham and London: Duke University Press).

Kinsley, S. (2010), 'Representing "Things to Come": Feeling the Visions of Future Technologies', *Environment and Planning A* 42 (11): 2771–90.

Kinsley, S. (2012) 'Futures in the Making: Practices for Anticipating "Ubiquitous Computing"', *Environment and Planning A* 44 (7): 1554–69.

Leach, J. and L. Wilson (2014), *Subversion, Conversion, Development: Cross-cultural Knowledge Exchange and the Politics of Design* (Cambridge, MA: MIT Press).

Lemert, C. (2006), *Durkheim's Ghosts: Cultural Logics and Social Things* (Cambridge: Cambridge University Press).

Leonardi, P. M. (2010), 'Digital Materiality? How Artifacts Without Matter, Matter', *First Monday* 15 (6).

Light, A. (2014), 'Citizen Innovation: *Active*Energy and the Quest for Sustainable Design', in M. Ratto and M. Boler (eds), *DIY Citizenship: Critical Making and Social Media* (Cambridge, MA: MIT Press).

Lindtner, S. (2014), 'Hackerspaces and the Internet of Things in China: How Makers are Reinventing Industrial Production, Innovation, and the Self', *China Information* 28 (2): 145–67.

Marwick, A. E. (2010), *Status Update: Celebrity, Publicity and Self-branding in Web 2.0* (Doctoral dissertation, New York University).

Moore, H. (1990), 'Visions of the Good Life: Anthropology and the Study of Utopia', *Cambridge Anthropology* 14 (3): 13–33.

Moore, H. L. (2004), 'Global Anxieties: Concept-metaphors and Pre-theoretical Commitments in Anthropology', *Anthropological Theory* 4 (1): 71–88.

Nam, T. and T. A. Pardo (2011), 'Conceptualizing Smart City with Dimensions of Technology, People, and Institutions', in *Proceedings of the 12th Annual International Digital Government Research Conference: Digital Government Innovation in Challenging Times* (ACM), 282–91.

Nielsen, M. (2011), 'Futures Within: Reversible Time and House-building in Maputo, Mozambique', *Anthropological Theory* 11 (4): 397–423.

Pink, S. (2009), *Doing Sensory Ethnography* (London: Sage).

Pink, S. (2014), Digital–Visual–Sensory Design Anthropology: Ethnography, Imagination and Intervention, *Arts and Humanities in Higher Education*, 1474022214542353.

Pink, S. and J. Morgan (2013), Short-term Ethnography: Intense Routes to Knowing', *Symbolic Interaction* 36 (3): 351–61.

Ratto, M. and M. Boler (eds) (2014), *DIY Citizenship: Critical Making and Social Media* (Cambridge, MA: MIT Press).

Suchman, L. (2011), Anthropological Relocations and the Limits of Design', *Annual Review of Anthropology* 40: 1–18.

Suchman, L. (2012), '4 Configuration', in C. Lury and N. Wakeford (eds), *Inventive Methods: The Happening of the Social* (London: Routledge), 48.

Taylor, C. (2004), *Modern Social Imaginaries* (Durham and London: Duke University Press).

Zandbergen, A. D. (2011), *New Edge: Technology and Spirituality in the San Francisco Bay Area* (Doctoral dissertation, Institute of Cultural Anthropology and Developmental Sociology, Faculty of Social and Behavioural Sciences, Leiden University).

Chapter 4

ABIresearch (2013), *Wi-Fi to Play Dominant Role in the $25 Billion Smart Appliance Market* (ABIresearch, London, 9 January).

AEMC (2011), *Issues Paper: Power of Choice – giving consumers options in the way they use electricity* (Australian Energy Market Commission (AEMC), Sydney).

AEMC (2012), *Overview Summary: Power of Choice Review – giving consumers options in the way they use electricity* (Australian Energy Market Commission (AEMC), Sydney).

Akrich, M. (1992), 'The De-scription of Technical Objects', in *Shaping Technology/ Building Society*, W. E. Bijker and J. Law (eds) (Cambridge, MA: MIT Press), 204–24.

Aldrich, F. K. (2003), 'Smart Homes: Past, Present and Future', in *Inside the Smart Home*, R. Harper (ed.) (London: Springer-Verlag), 17–39.

Ausgrid (2012), *Smart Home Update: Energy Analysis* (Ausgrid and Sydney Water, Sydney).

Balta-Ozkan, N., R. Davidson, M. Bicket and L. Whitmarsh (2013), 'Social Barriers to the Adoption of Smart Homes', *Energy Policy* 63 (0): 363–74.

Berg, A. J. (1994), 'A Gendered Socio-technical Construction: The Smart House', in C. Cockburn and R. Furst Dilic (eds), *Bringing Technology Home: Gender and Technology in Changing Europe* (Buckingham: Open University Press), 165–80.

Berry, M., M. Gibson, A. Nelson and I. Richardson (2007), 'How Smart is "Smart" – Smart Homes and Sustainability', in A. Nelson (ed.), *Steering Sustainability: Policy, Practice and Performance in an Urbanising World* (Burlington, VT: Ashgate), 239–52.

CEA (2011), *Unlocking the Potential of the Smart Grid – A Regulatory Framework for the Consumer Domain of Smart Grid* (Consumer Electronics Association (CEA), Arlington).

Clear, A., A. Friday, M. Hazas and C. Lord (2014), 'Catch my drift?: Achieving comfort more sustainably in conventionally heated buildings', paper presented to *Proceedings of the 2014 Conference on Designing Interactive Systems*, Vancouver, BC, Canada.

Climate Group (2008), *Smart 2020: Enabling the low carbon economy in the information age*, Global eSustainability Initiative, Brussels.

Control4 (2013), *Residential,* http://www.control4.com/residential/ [accessed 15 February 2013].

Davidoff, S., M. Lee, C. Yiu, J. Zimmerman and A. Dey (2006), 'Principles of Smart Home Control', in P. Dourish and A. Friday (eds), *UbiComp 2006: Ubiquitous Computing* (Berlin and Heidelberg: Springer), vol. 4206, 19–34.

DECC (2009), *Smarter Grids: The Opportunity. 2050 Roadmap: Discussion Paper* (Department of Energy and Climate Change, London).

Dourish, P. and G. Bell (2011), *Divining a Digital Future* (Cambridge, MA: MIT Press).

Forty, A. (1986), *Objects of Desire: Design and Society 1750–1980* (London: Thames and Hudson).

Gann, D., J. Barlow and T. Venables (1999), *Digital Futures: Making Homes Smarter* (Coventry: Chartered Institute of Housing).

Hacking, I. (1982), 'Biopower and the Avalanch of Printed Numbers', *Humanities in Society* 5: 279–95.

Hamilton, B., C. Thomas, S. J. Park and J.-G. Choi (2012), 'The Customer Side of the Meter', in F. P. Sioshansi (ed.), *Smart Grid* (Boston: Academic Press), 397–418.

Hargreaves, T., M. Nye and J. Burgess (2010), 'Making Energy Visible: A qualitative field study of how householders interact with feedback from smart energy monitors', *Energy Policy*, 38: 6111–19.

Hargreaves, T., M. Nye and J. Burgess (2013), 'Keeping Energy Visible? Exploring how householders interact with feedback from smart energy monitors in the longer term', *Energy Policy* 52: 126–34.

Harper-Slaboszewicz, P., T. McGregor and S. Sunderhauf (2012), 'Customer View of Smart Grid – Set and Forget?', in F. P. Sioshansi (ed.), *Smart Grid* (Boston: Academic Press), 371–95.

Horrigan, B. (1986), 'The Home of Tomorrow, 1927–1945', in J. J. Corn (ed.), *Imagining Tomorrow: History, Technology and the American Future* (Cambridge, MA: MIT Press), 137–63.

IEA (2011), *Technology Roadmap: Smart Grids* (International Energy Agency (IEA) and the Organisation of Economic Co-operation and Development (OECD), Paris, France).

Jelsma, J. (2006), 'Designing "Moralized" Products: Theory and Practice', in P.-P. Verbeek and A. Slob (eds), *User Behavior and Technology Development: Shaping Sustainable Relations Between Consumers and Technologies* (The Netherlands: Springer), 221–31.

Koskela, T. and K. Väänänen-Vainio-Mattila (2004), 'Evolution Towards Smart Home Environments: Empirical Evaluation of Three User Interfaces', *Personal Ubiquitous Computing* 8 (3–4): 234–40.

Kuijer, L., A. de Jong and D. van Eijk (2013), 'Practices as a Unit of Design: An Exploration of Theoretical Guidelines in a Study on Bathing', *ACM Trans. Comput.–Hum. Interact.* 20 (4): 1–22.

Leshed, G. and P. Sengers (2011), '"I lie to myself that I have freedom in my own schedule": Productivity tools and experiences of busyness', paper presented to *Proceedings of the 2011 Annual Conference on Human Factors in Computing Systems*, Vancouver, BC, Canada.

Marres, N. (2012), *Material Participation: Technology, the Environment and Everyday Publics* (London: Palgrave Macmillan).

Meier, A., C. Aragon, B. Hurwitz, D. Mujumdar, D. Perry, T. Peffer and M. Pritoni (2010), 'How people actually use thermostats', paper presented to *2010 ACEEE Summer Study on Energy Efficiency in Buildings*, Pacific Grove, CA.

Morozov, E. (2013), *To Save Everything Click Here: Technology, Solutionism and the Urge to Fix Problems That Don't Exist* (London: Penguin).

Mozer, M. C. (2005), 'Lessons from an Adaptive Home', in D. J. Cook and S. K.

Das (eds), *Smart Environments: Technologies, Protocols and Applications* (New Jersey: John Wiley & Sons), 273–94.

Nicholls, L. and Y. Strengers (2015), *Changing Demand: Flexibility of Energy Practices in Households with Children. Final Report* (Centre for Urban Research, RMIT University for Consumer Advocacy Panel, Melbourne).

Nyborg, S. and I. Røpke (2011), 'Energy impacts of the smart home – conflicting visions', paper presented to *Energy Efficiency First: The foundation of a low-carbon society*, Stockholm.

OSTP (2012), 'New industry commitments to give 15 million households tools to shrink their energy bills' (Office of Science and Technology Policy (OSTP), Washington), http://www.whitehouse.gov/administration/eop/ostp/pressroom/03222012

Pierce, J., C. Fan, D. Lomas, G. Marcu and E. Paulos (2010), 'Some considerations of the (in)effectiveness of residential energy feedback systems', paper presented to *Designing Interactive Systems (DIS) 2010*, Aarhus, Denmark.

Pierce, J. and E. Paulos (2010), 'Materializing energy', paper presented to *Proceedings of the 8th ACM Conference on Designing Interactive Systems*, Aarhus, Denmark.

Pink, S. and K. Leder Mackley (2014), 'Flow and Intervention in Everyday Life: Situating Practice', in *Social Practices, Intervention and Sustainability: Beyond Behaviour Change*, Y. Strengers and C. J. Maller (eds) (London: Routledge).

Reckwitz, A. (2002), 'The Status of the "Material" in Theories of Culture. From "Social Structure" to "Artefacts"', *Journal for the Theory of Social Behaviour* 32 (2): 195–217.

Røpke, I. and T. H. Christensen (2012), 'Energy Impacts of ICT – Insights from an Everyday Life Perspective', *Telematics and Informatics*, 29 (4): 348–61.

Shove, E. (2003), *Comfort, Cleanliness and Convenience: The Social Organisation of Normality* (Oxford: Berg).

Shove, E. (2010), 'Beyond the ABC: Climate Change Policy and Theories of Social Change', *Environment and Planning A* 42: 1273–85.

Shove, E., M. Pantzar and M. Watson (2012), *The Dynamics of Social Practice: Everyday Life and How it Changes* (London: Sage).

Shove, E., M. Watson, M. Hand and J. Ingram (2007), *The Design of Everyday Life* (Oxford: Berg).

Silverstone, R., E. Hirsch and D. Morley (1992), 'Information and Communication Technologies and the Moral Economy of the Household', in *Consuming Technologies: Media and Information in Domestic Spaces*, R. Silverstone and E. Hirsch (eds) (London: Routledge), 15–31.

Southerton, D. (2003), '"Squeezing Time": Allocating Practices, Coordinating Networks and Scheduling Society', *Time & Society* 12 (1): 5–25.

Strengers, Y. (2013), *Smart Energy Technologies in Everyday Life: Smart Utopia?, Consumption and Public Life* (London: Palgrave Macmillan).

Strengers, Y. (2014), 'Smart Energy in Everyday Life: Are You Designing for Resource Man?', *Interactions* 21 (4): 24–31.

Strengers, Y., L. Nicholls and C. Maller (2014), 'Curious Energy Consumers: Humans and Nonhumans in Assemblages of Household Practice', *Journal of Consumer Culture* (online).

Toffler, A. (1980), *The Third Wave* (New York: Bantam).

Warde, A. (2005), 'Consumption and theories of practice', *Journal of Consumer Culture* 5 (2): 131–53.

Wilson, C., T. Hargreaves and R. Hauxwell-Baldwin (2014), 'Smart Homes and Their Users: A Systematic Analysis and Key Challenges', *Personal and Ubiquitious Computing* 19 (2): 463–76.

Woodruff, A., S. Augustin and B. Foucault (2007), 'Sabbath Day Home Automation: "It's like mixing technology and religion"', paper presented to *Proceedings of the SIGCHI Conference on Human Factors in Computing Systems*, San Jose, CA, USA.

Wyche, S. P., A. Taylor and J. Kaye (2007), 'Pottering: A design-oriented investigation', paper presented to *CHI '07 Extended Abstracts on Human Factors in Computing Systems*, San Jose, CA, USA.

Yang, R., M. W. Newman and J. Forlizzi (2014), 'Making Sustainability Sustainable: Challenges in the design of eco-interaction technologies', paper presented to *Proceedings of the SIGCHI Conference on Human Factors in Computing Systems*, Toronto, Ontario, Canada.

Zpryme (2011), *The New Energy Consumer* (Austin: Zpryme Smart Grid Insights).

Chapter 5

Abrahamse, W., L. Steg, C. Vlek and T. Rothengatter (2007), 'The Effect of Tailored Information, Goal Setting, and Tailored Feedback on Household Energy Use, Energy-related Behaviors, and Behavioral Antecedents', *Journal of Environmental Psychology* 27: 265–76.

Akama, Y. and A. Prendiville (2013), 'A Phenomenological View to Co-designing Services', *Swedish Design Research Journal* 1 (13): 29–40.

Anderson, B. (2009), 'Affective Atmospheres', *Emotion, Space and Society* 2: 77–81.

Bille, M. (2014), 'Lighting Up Cosy Atmospheres in Denmark', *Emotion, Space and Society*, http://dx.doi.org/10.1016/j.emospa.2013.12.008 [accessed 3 October 2015].

Bille, M. and T. Sørensen (2007), An Anthropology of Luminosity: The Agency of Light, *Journal of Material Culture* 12 (3): 263–84.

Bille, M., P. Bjerregaard and T. Flohr Sørensen (2015), 'Staging Atmospheres: Materiality, Culture, and the Texture of the In-between', *Emotion, Space and Society* 15: 31–8.

Bissell, D. (2010), 'Passenger Mobilities: Affective Atmospheres and the Sociality of Public Transport', *Environment and Planning D* 28: 270–89.

Böhme, G. (1993), 'Atmosphere as the Fundamental Concept of a New Aesthetics', *Thesis Eleven* 36: 113–26.

Böhme, G. (2013), 'The Art of the Stage Set as a Paradigm for an Aesthetics of Atmospheres', *Ambiances: International Journal of Sensory Environment, Architecture and Urban Space* (online) http://ambiances.revues.org/315 [accessed 3 October 2015].

Couldry, N. (2012), *Media, Society, World: Social Theory and Digital Media Practice* (Cambridge: Polity Press).

Couldry, N. and T. Markham (2008), 'Troubled Closeness or Satisfied Distance? Researching Media Consumption and Public Orientation', *Media, Culture and Society* 30 (1): 5–21.

Dourish, P. (2001), *Where The Action Is: The Foundations of Embodied Interaction* (Boston, MA: MIT Press).

Edensor, T. (2012), 'Illuminated Atmospheres: Anticipating and Reproducing the Flow of Affective Experience in Blackpool', *Environment and Planning D: Society and Space* 30: 1103–22.

Edensor, T. (2014), 'Producing Atmospheres at the Match: Fan Cultures, Commercialization and Mood Management in English Football', *Emotion, Space and Society* doi:10.1016/j.emospa.2013.12.010 [accessed 10 January 2014].

Gunn, W. and J. Donovan (2012), 'Design Anthropology: An Introduction', in W. Gunn and J. Donovan (eds), *Design and Anthropology* (Farnham: Ashgate).

Gunn, W. and J. Donovan (eds) (2012), *Design and Anthropology* (Farnham: Ashgate).

Gunn, W., T. Otto and R. C. Smith (eds) (2013), *Design Anthropology: Theory and Practice* (Oxford: Bloomsbury).

Harris, M. (2007), 'Introduction: Ways of Knowing', in *Ways of Knowing: New Approaches in the Anthropology of Experience and Learning*, M. Harris (ed.) (Oxford: Berghahn).

Ingold, T. (2000), *The Perception of the Environment* (London: Routledge).

Ingold, T. (2007), *Lines: A Brief History* (London: Routledge).

Ingold, T. (2008), 'Bindings Against Boundaries: Entanglements of Life in an Open World', *Environment and Planning A*, 40: 1796–810.

Ingold, T. (2011a), *Being Alive: Essays on Movement, Knowledge and Description* (Oxford: Routledge).

Ingold, T. (2011b), 'Reply to David Howes', *Social Anthropology* 19 (3): 323–7.

Ingold, T. (2012), 'Introduction: The Perception of the User–Producer', in W. Gunn and J. Donovan (eds), *Design and Anthropology* (Farnham: Ashgate).

Ingold, T. (2013), *Making* (Oxford: Routledge).

Ingold, T. and E. Hallam (2007), 'Creativity and Cultural Improvisation: An Introduction', in E. Hallam and T. Ingold (eds), *Creativity and Cultural Improvisation* (Oxford: Berg).

Leder Mackley, K. and S. Pink (2013), 'From Emplaced Knowing to Interdisciplinary Knowledge: Sensory Ethnography in Energy Research', *Senses and Society* 8 (3): 335–53.

Massey, D. (2005), *For Space* (London: Sage).

Miller, D. (1988), 'Appropriating the State on the Council Estate', *Man* 23: 353–72.

Miller, D. (ed.) (2001), *Home Possessions* (Oxford: Berg).

Moores, S. (2012), *Media, Place and Mobility* (Basingstoke: Palgrave Macmillan).

Otto, T. and C. Smith (2013), 'Design Anthropology: A Distinct Style of Knowing', in W. Gunn, T. Otto and R. C. Smith (eds), *Design Anthropology: Theory and Practice* (Oxford: Bloomsbury).

Pink, S. (2015), *Doing Sensory Ethnography* (London: Sage).

Pink, S. and K. Leder Mackley (2012), 'Video as a Route to Sensing Invisible

Energy', *Sociological Research Online,* http://www.socresonline.org.uk/17/1/3.
html [accessed 3 October 2015].

Pink, S. and K. Leder Mackley (2014), 'Reenactment Methodologies for Everyday
Life Research: Art Therapy Insights for Video Ethnography', *Visual Studies*
29 (2): 146–54.

Pink, S., K. Leder Mackley, V. Mitchell, C. Escobar-Tello, M. Hanratty, T. Bhamra
and R. Moroşanu (2013), 'Applying the Lens of Sensory Ethnography to
Sustainable HCI', ACM *Transactions on Computer–Human Interaction* 20
(4), article no. 25. http://dl.acm.org/citation.cfm?doid=2494261 [accessed 3
October 2015].

Pink, S. and K. Leder Mackley (forthcoming, published online first 2014),
'Moving, Making and Atmosphere: Routines of Home as Sites for Mundane
Improvisation', *Mobilities.*

Pink, S. and K. Leder Mackley (2015), 'Social Science, Design and Everyday
Life: Refiguring Showering through Anthropological Ethnography', *Journal of
Design Research*, 13(3): 278–92.

Shove, E. (2010), 'Beyond the ABC: Climate Change Policy and Theories of Social
Change', *Environment and Planning A* 42 (6): 1273–85.

Steg, L. and C. Vlek (2009), 'Encouraging Pro-environmental Behavior: An
Integrative Review and Research Agenda', *Journal of Environmental
Psychology* 29: 309–17.

Strengers, Y. (2013), *Smart Energy Technologies in Everyday Life: Smart Utopia?,
Consumption and Public Life* (London: Palgrave Macmillan).

Weiser, M. (1996), 'Ubiquitous Computing #1', Computer Science Lab, Xerox
Park, 1988, http://www.ubiq.com/weiser/UbiHome.html [accessed 23 March
2015].

Chapter 6

Akrich, M. (1992), 'The De-scription of Technical Objects', in W. E. Bijker and
J. Law (eds), *Shaping Technology/Building Society* (Cambridge, MA: MIT
Press), 205–24.

Austin, J. L. (1962), *How To Do Things with Words* (Oxford: Clarendon Press).

Barad, K. (2007), *Meeting the Universe Halfway* (Durham, NC: Duke University
Press).

Boehner, K., W. Gaver and A. Boucher (2012), 'Probes', in C. Lury and
N. Wakeford (eds), *Inventive Methods: The Happening of the Social* (London:
Routledge), 185–201.

Connolly, W. E. (2011), *A World of Becoming* (Durham, NC: Duke University Press).

DiSalvo, C. (2012), *Adversarial Design* (Cambridge, MA: MIT Press).

Dunne, A. (2005), *Hertzian Tales: Electronic Products, Aesthetic Experience, and
Critical Design* (Cambridge MA: MIT Press).

Dunne, A. and F. Raby (2001), *Design Noir: The Secret Life of Electronic Objects*
(London/Basel: August/Birkhauser).

Dunne, A. and F. Raby (2013), *Speculative Everything: Design, Fiction and Social
Dreaming* (Cambridge, MA: MIT Press).

Ehn, P. (2003), 'Participation in Interaction Design – Actors and Artefacts in

Interaction', paper presented at the International Symposium *Foundations of Interaction Design*, Interaction Design Institute, Ivrea, Italy, November 2003, http://projectsfinal.interactionivrea.org/2004-2005/SYMPOSIUM%202005/communication%20material/Participation%20in%20Interaction%20Design_Ehn.pdf [accessed 31 August 2013].

Fraser, M. (2010), 'Facts, Ethics and Event', in C. Bruun Jensen and K. Rödje (eds), *Deleuzian Intersections in Science, Technology and Anthropology* (New York: Berghahn), 57–82.

Gaver, W., A. Boucher, A. Law, S. Pennington, J. Bowers, J. Beaver, J. Humble, et al. (2008), 'Threshold Devices: Looking Out From the Home', *Proceedings of the 26th Annual SIGCHI Conference on Human Factors in Computing Systems, Florence, Italy* (New York: ACM Press), 1429–38.

Gaver, W., A. Boucher, A. Law, S. Pennington, J. Bowers, J. Beaver, J. Humble, T. Kerridge, N. Villar and A. Wilkie (2008), 'Anatomy of a Failure: How we knew when our design went wrong, and what we learned from it', *Proceedings of the SIGCHI Conference on Human Factors in Computing Systems*, Boston, MA, USA.

Gaver, W., P. Sengers, T. Kerridge, J. Kaye and J. Bowers (2007), 'Enhancing Ubiquitous Computing with User Interpretation: Field-testing the Home Health Horoscope', *Proceedings of CHI ACM 2007*, 537–46.

Geuss, R. (1981), *The Idea of a Critical Theory* (Cambridge: Cambridge University Press).

Haraway, D. (1991), *Simians, Cyborgs and Nature* (London: Free Association Books).

Haraway, D. (1997), *Modest_Witness@Second_Millennium.FemaleMan.Meets_OncoMouse: Feminism and Technoscience* (London: Routledge).

Hawkins, H. (2013), 'Geography and Art, an Expanding Field: Site, the Body and Practice', *Progress in Human Geography* 37 (1): 52–71.

Latour, B. (1992), 'Where are the Missing Masses? A Sociology of a Few Mundane Artifacts', in W. E. Bijker and J. Law (eds), *Shaping Technology/Building Society* (Cambridge, MA: MIT Press).

Latour, B. (2004), 'How to Talk About the Body? The Normative Dimension of Science Studies', *Body & Society* 10 (2–3): 205–29.

Latour, B. (2008), 'A cautious Prometheus? A few steps toward a philosophy of design (with special attention to Peter Sloterdijk)', paper presented at *Networks of Design Meeting of Design History Society*, Falmouth, Cornwall, (http://www.bruno-latour.fr/sites/default/files/112-DESIGN-CORNWALL-GB.pdf [accessed 21 September 2015].

Law, J. (2004), *After Method: Mess in Social Science Research* (London: Routledge).

Lupton, D. (2015), *Digital Sociology* (London: Routledge).

Lury, C. and N. Wakeford (eds) (2012), *Inventive Methods: The Happening of the Social* (London: Routledge).

Michael, M. (2002), 'Comprehension, Apprehension, and Prehension: Heterogeneity and the Public Understanding of Science', *Science, Technology and Human Values* 27 (3): 357–70.

Michael, M. (2012a), 'Anecdote', in C. Lury and N. Wakeford (eds), *Inventive Methods: The Happening of the Social* (London: Routledge), 25–35.

Michael, M. (2012b), '"What are we busy doing?": Engaging the Idiot', *Science, Technology and Human Values* 37 (5): 528–54.

Michael, M. and Gaver, W. (2009), 'Home Beyond Home: Dwelling with Threshold Devices', *Space and Culture* 12: 359–70.

Pink, S. (2012), *Situating Everyday Life: Practices and Places* (London: Sage).

Prins, B. (1995), 'The Ethics of Hybrid Subjects: Feminist Constructivism According to Donna Haraway', *Science, Technology and Human Values* 20: 352–67.

Stengers, I. (2005), 'The Cosmopolitical Proposal', in B. Latour and P. Webel (eds), *Making Things Public* (Cambridge, MA: MIT Press), 994–1003.

Stengers, I. (2010), *Cosmopolitics I* (Minneapolis: University of Minnesota Press).

Storni, C. (2012), 'Unpacking Design Practices: The Notion of Thing in the Making of Artifacts', *Science, Technology, and Human Values* 37 (1): 88–123.

Tonkinwise, C. (2014), 'How We Future: Review of Dunne and Raby – Speculative Everything', https://www.academia.edu/7710031/DRAFT_-_How_We_Future_Review_of_Dunne_and_Raby_Speculative_Everything [accessed 31 August 2014].

Whitehead, A. N. (1929), *Process and Reality* (Cambridge: Cambridge University Press).

Woolgar, S. (1991), 'Configuring the User: The Case of Usability Trials', in J. Law (ed.), *A Sociology of Monsters* (London: Routledge).

Chapter 7

Cavill, N., S. Kahlmeier and F. Racioppi (2006), 'Physical Activity and Health in Europe: Evidence for Action', *WHO Library Cataloguing in Publication Data* (World Health Organization), www.euro.who.int/document/e89490.pdf [accessed 25 February 2015].

Crabtree, A., T. Rodden and S. Benford (2005), 'Moving with the Times: IT Research and the Boundaries of CSCW', *Computer Supported Cooperative Work* 14 (3): 217–51.

Delden, R. van, A. Moreno, C. Ramos, G. Carrasco, D. Reidsma and R. Poppe (2014), 'Hang In There: A Novel Body-Centric Interactive Playground', in *Innovative and Creative Developments in Multimodal Interaction Systems* (Berlin and Heidelberg: Springer), 160–78.

Dourish, P. (2006), 'Implications for Design', *Proceedings of the SIGCHI Conference on Human Factors in Computing Systems – CHI '06*, 541–50.

Grudin, J. (1993), 'Interface', *ACM* 36 (4): 112–19.

Gunn, W. and J. Donovan (eds) (2012), *Design and Anthropology* (Surrey: Ashgate).

Halse, J. (2012), 'Ethnographies of the Possible', in W. Gunn and J. Donovan (eds), *Design and Anthropology* (Surrey: Ashgate).

Hodder, I. (2012), *Entangled: An Archaeology of the Relationships between Humans and Things* (Oxford: Wiley-Blackwell).

Hornecker, E. (2007), 'Sketches, Drawings, Diagrams, Physical Models, Prototypes, and Gesture as Representational Forms', *Gesture* (September): 2–3.

Ingold, T. (2011), *Being Alive: Essays on Movement, Knowledge and Description* (New York: Routledge).

Irani, L., J. Vertesi, P. Dourish, K. Philip, and R. E. Grinter (2010), 'Postcolonial Computing: A Lens on Design and Development', *Proceedings of the SIGCHI Conference on Human Factors in Computing Systems*, 1311–20.

Kilbourn, K. (2012), 'The Patient as Skilled Practitioner', in W. Gunn and J. Donovan (eds), *Design and Anthropology* (Surrey: Ashgate).

Kjaersgaard, M. G. (2012), '(Trans)forming Knowledge and Design Concepts in the Design Workshop', in W. Gunn and J. Donovan (eds), *Design and Anthropology* (Surrey: Ashgate).

Kuutti, K. (2001), 'Hunting for the Lost User: From Sources of Errors to Active Actors and Beyond', *Cultural Usability Seminar*, Helsinki: Media Lab. University of Art and Design.

Latour, B. (2005), *Reassembling the Social: An Introduction to Actor-Network Theory* (Oxford: Oxford University Press).

Mackenzie, A. (2003), 'These Things Called Systems: Collective Imaginings and Infrastructural Software', *Social Studies of Science* 33 (3): 365–87.

McCarthy J. and P. Wright (2004), *Technology as Experience* (Cambridge, MA: MIT Press).

Mueller, F., S. Agamanolis and R. Picard (2003), 'Exertion Interfaces: Sports Over a Distance for Social Bonding and Fun', *Proceedings of the SIGCHI Conference on Human Factors in Computing Systems – CHI '03* (New York: ACM), 561–8.

Rowe, A. (2014), 'Designing for Engagement in Mixed Reality Experiences That Combine Projection Mapping and Camera-based Interaction', *Digital Creativity* (October): 1–14.

Sanders, E. B., P. J. Stappers and O. P. Ave (2008), 'Co-creation and the New Landscapes of Design', *Co-design* 4 (1): 5–18.

Schatzki, T., K. Knorr-Cetina and E. von Savigny (2001), *The Practice Turn in Contemporary Theory* (London: Routledge).

Soler-Adillon, J. (2009), 'A Novel Approach to Interactive Playgrounds: The Interactive Slide Project', *Structure*: 131–9.

Stirling, A. (2008), '"Opening Up" and "Closing Down": Power, Participation, and Pluralism in the Social Appraisal of Technology', *Science, Technology and Human Values* 33 (2): 262–94.

Stringer, M., E. Harris and G. Fitzpatrick (2006), 'Exploring the Space of Near-future Design with Children', *Proceedings of the 4th Nordic Conference on Human–Computer Interaction – NordiCHI 2006* (New York: ACM Press).

Suchman, L. (2002), 'Practice-based Design of Information Systems: Notes from the Hyperdeveloped World', *The Information Society* 18 (2): 139–44.

Suchman, L. (2005), 'Affiliative Objects', *Organization* 12 (3): 379–99.

Suchman, L. (2011), 'Anthropological Relocations and the Limits of Design', *Annual Review of Anthropology* 40 (1): 1–18.

Thrift, N. (2008), *Non-representational Theory: Space, Politics, Affect* (London: Routledge).

Chapter 8

Antle, A. N. (2009), 'Embodied Child Computer Interaction: Why Embodiment Matters', *ACM Interactions* (March/April): 27–30.

Benford, S., C. Greenhalgh, G. Giannachi, B. Walker, J. Marshall and T. Rodden (2012), 'Uncomfortable Interactions', *Proceedings of the 2012 ACM Annual Conference on Human Factors in Computing Systems*, Austin, Texas, USA. 2005–14. doi:10.1145/2207676.2208347.

Björk, S. and J. Holopainen (2005), *Patterns in Game Design* (Charles River Media).

Bogost, I. (2006), 'Persuasive Games: Wii's Revolution is in the Past', http://www.seriousgamessource.com/features/feature_112806_wii_1.php [accessed 1 June 2013].

Bogost, I. (2007), 'Persuasive Games: The Missing Social Rituals of Exergames', http://seriousgamessource.com/features/feature_013107_exergaming_1.php [accessed 1 June 2013].

Borchers, J. O. (2001), 'A Pattern Approach to Interaction Design', *AI & Society* 15 (4): 359–76.

contributors, W. *Kinect Adventures!*, http://en.wikipedia.org/w/index.php?title=Kinect_Adventures!&oldid=577747109 [accessed 1 June 2014].

Dourish, P. (2001), *Where the Action Is: The Foundations of Embodied Interaction* (Cambridge, MA: MIT Press).

Fogtmann, M. H., J. Fritsch and K. J. Kortbek (2008), 'Kinesthetic Interaction – Revealing the Bodily Potential in Interaction Design', paper presented at *OZCHI '08: Conference of the Computer–Human Interaction Special Interest Group (CHISIG) of Australia on Computer-Human Interaction*, Cairns, Australia.

González, J. A. (1995), 'Autotopographies', in G. Brahm Jr. and M. Driscoll (eds), *Prosthetic Territories: Politics and Hypertechnologies* (Boulder, CO: Westview Press), 133–50.

Harrison, S., D. Tatar and P. Sengers (2007), 'The Three Paradigms of HCI', *alt.chi Session at the SIGCHI Conference on Human Factors in Computing Systems*, San Jose, California, USA.

Hornecker, E. and J. Buur (2006), 'Getting a Grip on Tangible Interaction: A Framework on Physical Space and Social Interaction', *Proceedings of the SIGCHI Conference on Human Factors in Computing Systems*, Montreal, Quebec, Canada, 437–46.

Huggard, A., A. De Mel, J. Garner, C. C. Toprak, A. D. Chatham and F. Mueller (2013a), 'Understanding a Socially Awkward Digital Play Journey', DiGRA.

Huggard, A., A. De Mel, J. Garner, C. C. Toprak, A. Chatham and F. Mueller (2013b), 'Musical Embrace: Exploring Social Awkwardness in Digital Games', *Proceedings of the 2013 ACM International Joint Conference on Pervasive and Ubiquitous Computing*, Zurich, Switzerland, 725–8 doi:10.1145/2493432.2493518.

Isbister, K. (2010), 'Enabling Social Play', in R. Bernhaupt (ed.), *Evaluating User Experience in Games: Concepts and Methods* (New York: Springer-Verlag), 11–22.

Khot, R. A., L. Hjorth and F. Mueller (2014), 'Understanding Physical Activity Through 3D Printed Material Artifacts', *Proceedings of the SIGCHI Conference on Human Factors in Computing Systems*, Toronto, Ontario, Canada, 3835–44. doi:10.1145/2556288.2557144.

Larssen, A., L. Loke, T. Robertson, J. Edwards and A. Sydney (2004), 'Understanding Movement as Input for Interaction – A Study of Two Eyetoy Games', *Proceedings of OzCHI '04*, Wollongong, Australia.

Lehrer, J. (2006) 'How the Nintendo Wii will get you emotionally invested in video games', *Seedmagazine.com – Brain & Behavior*, http://www.seedmagazine.com/news/2006/11/a_console_to_make_you_wiip.php [accessed 1 June 2012].

Loke, L., A. Larssen, T. Robertson and J. Edwards (2007), 'Understanding Movement for Interaction Design: Frameworks and Approaches', *Personal and Ubiquitous Computing* 11 (8: Special Issue Movement-Based Interaction): 691–701.

Marshall, J., D. Rowland, S. R. Egglestone, S. Benford, B. Walker and D. McAuley (2011), 'Breath Control of Amusement Rides', *Proceedings of the SIGCHI Conference on Human Factors in Computing Systems*, Vancouver, BC, Canada, 73–82. doi:10.1145/1978942.1978955.

Merleau-Ponty, M. (1945), *Phenomenology of Perception* (London: Routledge).

Moen, J. (2006), 'KinAesthetic Movement Interaction: Designing for the Pleasure of Motion', unpublished dissertation, Stockholm: KTH, Numerical Analysis and Computer Science.

Mueller, F., S. Agamanolis and R. Picard (2003), 'Exertion Interfaces: Sports Over a Distance for Social Bonding and Fun', paper presented at *SIGCHI Conference on Human Factors in Computing Systems*, Fort Lauderdale, Florida, USA. 561-568. doi:http://doi.acm.org/10.1145/642611.642709.

Mueller, F., S. Agamanolis, F. Vetere and M. R. Gibbs (2009), 'A Framework for Exertion Interactions over a Distance', *ACM SIGGRAPH*, 143–50.

Mueller, F., D. Edge, F. Vetere, M. R. Gibbs, S. Agamanolis, B. Bongers and J. G. Sheridan (2011), 'Designing Sports: A Framework for Exertion Games', *CHI '11: Proceedings of the SIGCHI Conference on Human Factors in Computing Systems*, Vancouver, Canada, 2651–60.

Mueller, F., M. Gibbs and F. Vetere (2008), 'Taxonomy of Exertion Games', *OzCHI '08: Proceedings of the 20th Australasian Conference on Computer–Human Interaction*, Cairns, Australia, 263–6.

Mueller, F., M. Gibbs and F. Vetere (2009), 'Design Influence on Social Play in Distributed Exertion Games', *CHI '09: Proceedings of the SIGCHI Conference on Human Factors in Computing Systems*, Boston, MA, USA, 1539–48.

Mueller, F., M. R. Gibbs, F. Vetere and D. Edge (2014), 'Supporting the Creative Game Design Process with Exertion Cards', *Proceedings of the SIGCHI Conference on Human Factors in Computing Systems*, Toronto, Ontario, Canada, 2211–20. doi:10.1145/2556288.2557272.

Mueller, F. and K. Isbister (2014), 'Movement-Based Game Guidelines', *Proceedings of the SIGCHI Conference on Human Factors in Computing Systems*, Toronto, Ontario, Canada, 2191–200. doi:10.1145/2556288.2557163.

Nintendo (n.d.), 'Wii Sports', retrieved from http://wii.nintendo.com/software_wii_sports.html [accessed 1 June 2012].

Rogers, Y. (2011), 'Interaction Design Gone Wild: Striving for Wild Theory', *interactions*, 18 (4): 58–62.

Salen, K. and E. Zimmerman (2003), *Rules of Play: Game Design Fundamentals* (Cambridge, MA: MIT Press).

Sheridan, J., A. Dix, S. Lock and A. Bayliss (2005), 'Understanding Interaction in Ubiquitous Guerrilla Performances in Playful Arenas', in *People and Computers XVIII – Design for Life*, S. Fincher, P. Markopoulos, D. Moore and R. Ruddle (eds) (London: Springer), 3–17. http://dx.doi.org/10.1007/1-84628-062-1_1. doi:10.1007/1-84628-062-1_1.

Zimmerman, J., J. Forlizzi and S. Evenson (2007), 'Research Through Design as a Method for Interaction Design Research in HCI', *Proceedings of the SIGCHI Conference on Human Factors in Computing Systems*, San Jose, California, USA, 493–502. doi:10.1145/1240624.1240704.

Chapter 9

Berlant, L. (1998), 'Intimacy: A Special Issue', *Critical Inquiry* 24 (2): 281–8.

Buchli, V. (2002), *The Material Culture Reader* (London: Berg).

Campbell, S. W. and Y. Park (2008), 'Social Implications of Mobile Telephony: The Rise of Personal Communication Society', *Sociology Compass* 2 (2): 371–87.

Clark, L. S. (2012), *The Parent App: Understanding Families in the Digital Age* (New York: Oxford University Press).

Clarke, A. (ed.) (2011), *Design Anthropology: Object Culture in the 21st Century* (New York: Springer).

Donner, J. (2007), 'The Rules of Beeping: Exchanging Messages Using Missed Calls on Mobile Phones in Sub-Saharan Africa', *Journal of Computer Mediated Communication* 13 (1): 1–22.

Drazin, A. (2012), 'Digital Anthropology in Design Anthropology', in H. Horst and D. Miller (eds), *Digital Anthropology* (London: Berg), 245–65.

Eglash, R. (2006), 'Technology as Material Culture', in C. Tilley, W. Keane, S. Kuechler, M.Rowlands and P. Spyer (eds), *Handbook of Material Culture* (London: Sage), 329–40.

Eglash, R. (1999), *African Fractals: Modern Computing and Indigenous Design* (New Brunswick, NJ: Rutgers University Press).

Fortunati, L. (2002), 'Italy: Stereotypes, True and False', in J. E. Katz and M. Aakhus (eds), *Perpetual Contact: Mobile Communications, Private Talk, Public Performance* (Cambridge: Cambridge University Press), 42–62.

Fortunati, L. (2002), 'The Mobile Phone: Towards New Categories and Social Relations', *Information, Communication & Society* 5 (4): 513–28.

Galloway, A., J. Brucker-Cohen, L. Gaye, E. Goodman and D. Hill (2004), 'Design for Hackability', in *Proceedings of the 5th Conference on Designing Interactive Systems: Processes, Practices, Methods, and Techniques*, ACM, 363–6.

Gell, A. (1998), *Art and Agency: An Anthropological Theory* (Oxford: Oxford University Press).

Goggin, G. and L. Hjorth (2009), *Mobile Technologies: From Telecommunications to Media*, vol. 20 (London: Taylor & Francis).

Gopinath, S. (2007), 'Ringtones, or the Auditory Logic of Globalization', *First Monday*, 10(12), http://firstmonday.org/htbin/cgiwrap/bin/ojs/index.php/fm/article/view/1295/1215 [accessed 14 July 2015].

Gregg. M. (2010), *Work's Intimacy* (Cambridge: Polity Press).

Hjorth, L. (2009), *Mobile Media in the Asia-Pacific: Gender and Art of Being Mobile* (Abingdon: Routledge).

Hjorth, L. (2011), 'Mobile Spectres of Intimacy: The Gendered Role of Mobile Technologies in Love – Past, Present and Future', in The Mobile Communication Research Series: Volume II, *Mobile Communication: Bringing Us Together or Tearing Us Apart?*, R. Ling and S. Campbell (eds) (Edison, NJ: Transaction Books), 37–60.

Hjorth, L. and S. Lim (2012), 'Mobile Intimacy in an Age of Affective Mobile Media', *Feminist Media Studies* 12 (4): 477–84.

Hjorth, L., S. Pink, K. Sharpe, and L. Williams (2016), *Screen Ecologies: Art, Media and the Environment in the Asia-Pacific region.* MIT Press.

Horst, H. (2006), 'The Blessings and Burdens of Communication: Cell Phones in Jamaican Transnational Social Fields', *Global Networks* 6 (2): 143–59.

Horst, H. (2009), 'Aesthetics of the Self: Digital Mediations', in D. Miller (ed.), *Anthropology and the Individual* (Oxford: Berg), 99–113.

Horst, H. (forthcoming), *Building Aspirations: Property and Personhood in Jamaica.*

Horst, H. A. (2004), 'A Pilgrimage Home: Tombs, Burial and Belonging in Jamaica', *Journal of Material Culture* 9 (1): 11–26.

Horst, H. A. (2008), 'Planning to Forget: Mobility and Violence in Urban Jamaica', *Social Anthropology* 16 (1): 51–62.

Horst, H. A. (2012), 'New Media Technologies in Everyday Life', in H. A. Horst and D. Miller (eds), *Digital Anthropology* (New York: Berg), 61–79.

Horst, H. A. (2014a), 'From Roots Culture to Sour Fruit: The Aesthetics of Mobile Branding Cultures in Jamaica', *Visual Studies,* 29 (2): 125–7.

Horst, H. A. (2014b), Calling My Name: Sound, Orality and the Cell Phone Contact List', in S. Gopinath and J. Stanyek (eds), *The Oxford Handbook of Mobile Media and Sound, Volume 1* (Oxford: Oxford University Press), 201–10.

Horst, H. A. and D. Miller (2005), 'From Kinship to Link-Up: Cell Phones and Social Networking in Jamaica', *Current Anthropology* 46 (5): 755–78.

Horst, H. A. and D. Miller (2006), *The Cell Phone: An Anthropology of Communication* (Oxford: Berg).

Horst, H. A. and D. Miller (eds) (2012), *Digital Anthropology* (London: Berg).

Horst, H. A. and E. Taylor (2014), 'The Role of Mobile Phones in the Mediation of Border Crossings: A Study of Haiti and the Dominican Republic', *The Australian Journal of Anthropology (TAJA)* 25 (2): 155–70.

Ito, M., D. Okabe and M. Matsuda (eds) (2005), *Personal, Portable, Pedestrian: Mobile Phones in Japanese Life* (Cambridge, MA: MIT Press).

Ito, M., D. Okabe and K. Anderson (2009), 'Portable Objects in Three Global Cities: The Personalization of Urban Places', in R. Ling and S. Campbell (eds), *The Mobile Communication Research Annual Volume 1: The Reconstruction of Space & Time Through Mobile Communication Practices* (New Brunswick, NJ: Transaction Books), 67–88.

Kopytoff, I. (1986), 'The Cultural Biography of Things: Commoditization as Process', in A. Appadurai (ed.), *The Social Life of Things: Commodities in Cultural Perspective* (Cambridge: Cambridge University Press), 64–91.

Lasen, A. (2010), 'Mobile Culture and Subjectivity: An Example of the Shared Agency Between People and Technology', in L. Fortunati, J. Vincent,

J. Gebhardt, A. Petrovcic and O. Vershinskaya (eds), *Interacting with Broadband Society* (Frankfurt: Peter Lang), 109–24.

Licoppe C. (2004), 'Connected Presence: The Emergence of a New Repertoire for Managing Social Relationships in a Changing Communications Technoscape', *Environment and Planning: Society and Space*, 22: 135–56.

Licoppe, C. (2011), 'What Does Answering the Phone Mean? A Sociology of the Phone Ring and Musical Ringtones', *Cultural Sociology* 5 (3): 367–84.

Ling, R. (2004), *The Mobile Connection: The Cell Phone's Impact on Society* (Amsterdam: Elsevier/Morgan Kaufmann).

Ling, R. S. (2008), *New Tech, New Ties: How Mobile Communication is Reshaping Social Cohesion* (Cambridge, MA: MIT Press).

Makovicky, N. (2010), '"Erotic Needlework": Vernacular Designs on the 21st Century Market', in A. Clarke (ed.), *Design Anthropology: Object Culture in the 21st Century* (New York: Springer), 155–68.

Miller, D. (2006), 'Introduction', in D. Miller (ed.), *Materiality* (Durham: Duke University Press).

Miller, D. (2013), *Stuff* (Cambridge: Polity Press).

Miller, D. and J. Sinanan (forthcoming), *Visualising Facebook*.

Miller, D. and H. Horst (2012), 'The Digital and the Human', in H. Horst and D. Miller (eds), *Digital Anthropology* (London: Berg), 3–38.

Myers, F. (2002), *The Empire of Things: Regimes of Value and Material Culture*, School of American Research Advanced Seminar Series (SAR Press).

Pertierra, R. (2006), *Transforming Technologies, Altered Selves: Mobile Phone and Internet Use in the Philippines* (Malate, Manila, Philippines: De La Salle University Press).

Rapoport, A. (1980), 'Vernacular Architecture and the Cultural Determinants of Form', in A. King (ed.), *Buildings and Society: Essays on the Social Development of the Built Environment* (London and Boston: Routledge & Kegan Paul), 293–305.

Rapoport, A. (1990), 'Defining Vernacular Design', in M. Turan (ed.), *Vernacular Architecture Paradigms of Environmental Response* (Avebary: Gower Publishing Company Limited).

Taylor, E. B. and H. A. Horst (2014), 'The Aesthetics of Mobile Money Platforms in Haiti', in G. Goggin and L. Hjorth (eds), *Mobile Media Companion* (London: Routledge), 462–71.

Wajcman, J., J. Brown and M. Bittman (2009), 'Intimate Connections: The Impact of the Mobile Phone on Work–Life Boundaries', in G. Goggin & L. Hjorth (eds), *Mobile Technologies*, (London and New York: Routledge), 9–22.

Wallis, C. (2013), *Technomobility in China: Young Migrant Women and Mobile Phones* (New York: New York University Press).

Wellman, B. (2001), 'Phsyical Place and Cyber Place: The Rise of Personalized Networking', *International Journal of Urban and Regional Research,* 25 (2): 225–52.

Were, G. (2010), *Lines That Connect: Rethinking Pattern and Mind in the Pacific* (Honolulu: University of Hawai'i Press).

Zelizer, V. (2007), *The Purchase of Intimacy* (Princeton, NJ: Princeton University Press).

Chapter 10

Allen, J. (2010), 'Depth-Charge in the Archive: The Documentation of Performance Revisited in the Digital Age', *Research in Dance Education* 11 (1): 61–70.

Assmann, A. (2008), 'Canon and Archive', in A. Erll and A. Nünning (eds), *Cultural Memory Studies: An International and Interdisciplinary Handbook* (Berlin and New York: Walter de Gruyter), 97–107.

Auslander, P. (2008), *Liveness: Performance in a Mediatized Culture* (New York: Routledge).

Barthes, R. (1981), *Camera Lucida: Reflections on Photography* (New York: Hill and Wang).

Barthes, R. (2011), *The Preparation of the Novel: Lecture Courses and Seminars at the College de France (1978–1979 and 1979–1980)* (New York: Columbia University Press).

Baston, K. (2014), 'Kim's Notes', http://archive.circusoz.com/sideshows/kim_notes/ [accessed 24 November 2014].

Burdick, A., J. Drucker, P. Lunenfeld, T. Presner and J. Schnapp (2012), *Digital Humanities* (Cambridge. MA: MIT Press).

Carlin, D. (2010), *Our Father Who Wasn't There* (Melbourne: Scribe Publications).

Carlin, D. (2011), 'The True History of the Circus', *Griffith REVIEW 33: Such Is Life* (Brisbane: Griffith University).

Carlin, D. (2014), 'A Digital Archive in the Circus: Between the Archive and the Repertoire', *Media International Australia, Incorporating Culture and Policy* 153: 98–106.

Carlin, D. (2015), 'Time and Narrative in the Digital Archive: On Account of a Circus', in D. Carlin and L. Vaughan (eds), *Performing Digital: Multiple Perspectives on a Living Archive* (London: Ashgate).

Carlin, D. and J. Mullett (2010), 'Performing Data: The Circus Oz Living Archive', in *eResearch Australasia 2010* (Gold Coast).

Carlin, D. and L. Vaughan (eds) (2015), *Performing Digital: Multiple Perspectives on a Living Archive* (London: Ashgate).

Deleuze, G. and F. Guattari (2004), *A Thousand Plateaux: Capitalism and Schizophrenia*, trans. B. Massumi (London: Continuum).

Derrida, J. (1996), *Archive Fever: a Freudian Impression* (Chicago: University of Chicago Press).

Eichhorn, K. (2008), 'Archival Genres: Gathering Texts and Reading Spaces', *Invisible Culture* 12: 1–10.

Ernst, W. (2013), *Digital Memory and the Archive* (Minneapolis: University of Minnesota Press).

Geismar, H. (2012), 'Museum + Digital = ?', in D. Miller and H. A. Horst (eds), *Digital Anthropology* (Oxford: Berg).

Featherstone, M. (2006), 'Archive', *Theory, Culture and Society* 23 (2–3): 591–6.

Horst, H. and D. Miller (2012), 'Normativity and Materiality: A View from Digital Anthropology', *Media International Australia*, incorporating *Culture and Policy*, 145: 103–11. http://search.informit.com.au/documentSummary;dn=992400290 951081;res=IELLCC ISSN: 1329-878X [accessed 6 December 2014].

Huvila, I. (2008), 'Participatory Archive: Towards Decentralised Curation, Radical

User Orientation, and Broader Contextualisation of Records Management', *Archival Science* 8 (1): 15–36.

Ingold, T. (2012a), 'Toward an Ecology of Materials', *Annual Review of Anthropology* 41: 427–42.

Ingold, T. (2012b), 'Introduction', in M. Janowski and T. Ingold (eds), *Imagining Landscapes: Past, Present and Future* (London: Ashgate).

Ingold, T. (2011), *Being Alive: Essays on Movement, Knowledge and Description* (Abingdon: Routledge).

Jenkins, H. (2006), *Convergence Culture: Where Old and New Media Collide* (New York: New York University Press).

Jenkins, H., S. Jenkins and J. Green (2013), *Spreadable Media: Creating Value and Meaning in a Networked Culture* (New York: New York University Press).

Lévy, P. and R. Bonomo (1999), *Collective Intelligence: Mankind's Emerging World in Cyberspace* (London: Perseus Publishing).

Miles, A. (2013), 'The Triumvirate', *vlog 4.0 [a blog about vlogs]*, http://vogmae.net.au/vlog/2013/06/the-triumvirate/ [accessed 27 February 2015].

O'Reilly, T. (2005), 'What Is Web 2.0', http://oreilly.com/web2/archive/what-is-web-20.html [accessed 15 December 2010].

Phelan, P. (2004), *Unmarked: The Politics of Performance* (London: Routledge).

Stanton, R. (2015), 'Designing in the Living Archive: Software and Representation', in D. Carlin and L. Vaughan (eds), *Performing Digital: Multiple Perspectives on a Living Archive* (Farnham: Ashgate).

Steedman, C. (1998), 'The Space of Memory: In an Archive', *History of the Human Sciences* 11 (4): 65–83.

Syke, L. B. (2014), 'Cranked Up Review: Circus Oz Sydney', *Crikey Daily Review*, crikey.com.au, http://dailyreview.crikey.com.au/cranked-up-review-circus-oz-sydney/2244 [accessed 27 November 2014].

Taylor, D. (2003), *The Archive and the Repertoire: Performing Cultural Memory in the Americas* (Duke University Press, Kindle Edition) [accessed 10 November 2013].

Varney, D. and R. Fensham (2000), 'More-and-Less-Than: Liveness, Video Recording, and the Future of Performance', *New Theatre Quarterly* 16 (1): 88–96.

Whitelaw, M. (2012), 'Towards Generous Interfaces for Archival Collections', *Comma* 2: 123–32.

Chapter 11

2GN (2014), *New Wi Fi sign erected* [online], Goulburn, Capital Radio Network, http://www.2gn.com.au/news/local/3251-new-wi-fi-sign-erected [accessed 21 November 2014].

Australian Library and Information Association (2013), *ALIA Internet Access in Public Libraries Survey* (Canberra: Australian Library and Information Association).

Anson, G. (2008), *Project Proposal: Free Goulburn Wireless Internet Access*, Orb Consulting for The Goulburn Group, Goulburn.

Callon, M. (2004), 'The Role of Hybrid Communities and Socio-Technical

Arrangements in the Participatory Design', *Journal of the Center for Information Studies* 5: 3–10.

Connolly, B. (2014), 'Gosford Council Gets Fibre NBN Over Power Poles', *CIO Magazine*, 27 May.

Constine, J. (2012), 'Cisco Aquires Enterprise Wi-Fi Startup Meraki for $1.2 Billion in Cash', *Techcrunch*, 18 November.

Dubber, A. (2014), 'Goulburn Free Wi-Fi Proves Popular', *Goulburn Post*, 13 June.

Dunbar-Hester, C. (2014), *Low Power to the People: Pirates, Protest, and Politics in FM Radio Activism* (Cambridge, MA: MIT Press).

Egyedi, T. and D. Mehos (eds) (2012), *Inverse Infrastructures: Disrupting Networks From Below* (Cheltenham: Edward Elgar).

Frangoudis, P., G. Polyzos and V. Kemerlis (2011), 'Wireless Community Networks: An Alternative Approach for Nomadic Broadband Network Access', *Communications Magazine, IEEE* 49 (5): 206–13.

Given, J. (2008), 'Australia's Broadband: How Big is the Problem?', *Media International Australia* 127 (May): 6–10.

Godwin, M. (1998), *Cyber Rights: Defending Free Speech in the Digital Age* (New York: Times Books).

Goulburn Post (1992), '$84 million bypass set to bring significant benefits to Goulburn', supplement to the *Goulburn Post and Highlands Post*: 2.

Goulburn Post (2010), 'Free WiFi set for CBD?', *Goulburn Post*, 7 June.

Gow, G. A. and R. Smith (2006), *Mobile and Wireless Communications: An Introduction* (Maidenhead: Open University Press).

Graham, S. and S. Marvin (2001), *Splintering Urbanism: Networked Infrastructures, Technological Mobilities and the Urban Condition* (London: Routledge).

Graham, S. and N. Thrift (2007), 'Out of Order: Understanding Repair and Maintenance', *Theory, Culture and Society* 25 (3): 1–25.

Harte, L. (2007), 'Australia's big icons on the move', *PM, ABC Radio National*, 23 May, http://www.abc.net.au/pm/content/2007/s1931360.htm

Horst, H. and D. Miller (eds) (2012), *Digital Anthropology* (London and New York: Berg).

ITU (International Telecommunications Union) (2014), *Facts and Figures* http://www.itu.int/en/ITU-D/Statistics/Documents/facts/ICTFactsFigures2014-e.pdf [accessed 24 November 2014].

Jungnickel, K. (2013), *DIY WiFi: Re-imagining Connectivity* (London: Palgrave Macmillan).

Jungnickel, K. and G. Bell (2009), 'Home Is Where the Hub Is? Wireless Infrastructures and the Nature of Domestic Culture in Australia', in M. Foth (ed.), *Handbook of Research on Urban Informatics: The Practice and Promise of the Real-time City* (Hershey, PA: Information Science Reference – IGI Global), 310–25.

Marino, M. (2005), 'Goulburn could run dry in eight months', *The Age*, 20 May, http://www.theage.com.au/news/Drought/Goulburn-could-run-dry-in-eight-months/2005/05/19/1116361673744.html

Massy, C. (2011), *Breaking the Sheep's Back: The Shocking True Story of the Decline and Fall of the Australian Wool Industry* (St Lucia: University of Queensland Press).

McShane, I., C. Wilson and D. Meredyth (2014), 'Broadband as Civic Infrastructure – The Australian Case', *Media International Australia* 151: 127–36.

Middleton, C. and A. Potter (2008), 'Is it good to share? A case study of FON and Meraki approaches to broadband provision', *International Telecommunications Society 17th Biennial Conference*, Montreal.

OECD (2014), *Broadband Portal* [online], http://www.oecd.org/sti/broadband/oecdbroadbandportal.htm.

Postill, J. (2011), *Localising the Internet – An Anthropological Account* (Oxford: Berghahn).

Poblet, M., H. Fünfgeld and I. McShane (2014), 'Telecommunications and Disaster Management. Participatory Approaches and Climate Change Adaption', *Australian Journal of Telecommunications and the Digital Economy* 2(4).

Sebo, T. (2013a), 'A High-tech Present', *Goulburn Post*, 5 March.

Sebo, T. (2013b), 'City's Tech Tourism', *Goulburn Post*, 3 September.

Star, S. and A. Strauss (1999), 'Layers of Silence, Arenas of Voice: The Ecology of Visible and Invisible Work', *Computer Supported Cooperative Work (CSCW)* 8 (1–2): 9–30.

Spigel, B. (2013), 'Bourdieuian Approaches to the Geography of Entrepreneurial Cultures', *Entrepreneurship and Regional Development* 25 (9–10): 804–18.

Strachan, J. (2014), 'Goulburn dangles childcare carrot in advertising campaign to lure Canberrans to the municipality', *The Age* [online edition 6 September] http://www.theage.com.au/it-pro/goulburn-dangles-childcare-carrot-in-advertising-campaign-to-lure-canberrans-to-the-municipality-20140906-104ozv.html

Telstra (2014), *Telstra T-Bundle BizEssentials®* [online] http://www.telstra.com.au/small-business/bundles/tbundle-bizessentials/index.htm [accessed 18 December 2014].

TGG (2014), *About TGG: Who are we?* [online], Goulburn, The Goulburn Group (TGG), http://www.goulburngroup.com.au/about_tgg.php [accessed 18 July 2014].

Van Oost, E., S. Verhaegh and N. Oudshoorn (2009)', 'From Innovation Community to Community Innovation: User-initiated Innovation in Wireless Leiden', *Science, Technology, and Human Values* 34 (2): 182–205.

Verhaegh, S. and E. van Oost (2012), 'Who Cares? The Maintenance of a Wi-Fi Community Infrastructure', in T. M. Egyedi and D. C. Mehos (eds), *Inverse Infrastructures: Disrupting Networks From Below* (Cheltenham: Edward Elgar), 141–60.

Index

The letter *f* after an entry denotes a figure